TGfU
Teaching Games for Understanding

By
Nicholas Stratigopoulos

Copyright © 2015 Nicholas Stratigopoulos

All rights reserved.

Table of Contents

INTRODUCTION 4

INVASION/TERRITORIAL 5

NET/WALL 45

PURSUIT/EVADE 86

STRIKING/FIELDING 127

TARGET/MISCELLANEOUS 168

ABOUT THE AUTHOR 208

Note:

Categories are arranged by grade level, then by alphabetical order.

Introduction

TGfU was developed to help physical and health education professionals incorporate fun in lessons aimed at keeping children active. TGfU combines technology, education, and fun to create an environment where children enjoy learning.

Whether you are a physical education teacher, camp counselor, activity specialist, animator or any other professional dedicated to keeping school-aged children active, TGfU is a must-have book to include in your curriculum.

KEY FEATURES

- Comprehensive Collection of Games

TGfU includes more than 200 games to keep children active! There is sure to be a favorite for everyone. Have a great game you want to share? Feel free to submit your own games to include in our database.

- Wide Variety of Skill Levels

The games available in TGfU are targeted for children in kindergarten to sixth grade; an age group that is very receptive to the TGfU model.

- Broad Categories of Games and Activities

The book includes 4 categories of games and activities that are based on the TGfU curriculum model: Invasion & Territorial, Net & Wall, Striking & Fielding, and Target. Pursuit & Evade category is also included as an additional game category that is popular among youth.

- TGfU Model

The Teaching Games for Understanding (TGfU) learning model is a game-based learning approach that was developed after considerable research for understanding how to provide game instructions that are educational and fun.

Interested in learning about TGfU or want to submit your own games to our database? Visit http://educationisphysical.com/apps/tgfu-games-pe/

Invasion/Territorial

Noodle Hockey

Recommended Grades:

- Kindergarten – Grade 4

Equipment:

Pinnies, hockey nets, pool noodles, wiffle balls, and brooms.

Tactical Problems:

Keeping possession, accurate passing and receiving, traveling, change of speed, change in direction, and transition.

Rules of Play:

1. Divide the students into two teams.
2. Game of hockey, but with pool noodles instead of hockey sticks!
3. Goalies are equipped with brooms.
4. As the game progresses, add in additional wiffle balls.

Safety:

Keep your head up to avoid collisions and watch out for butting heads when hunching over.

Variations/Progressions:

- Increase or decrease the size of the playing area.
- Reduce the number of players on the playing area at once.
- Add in multiple nets.

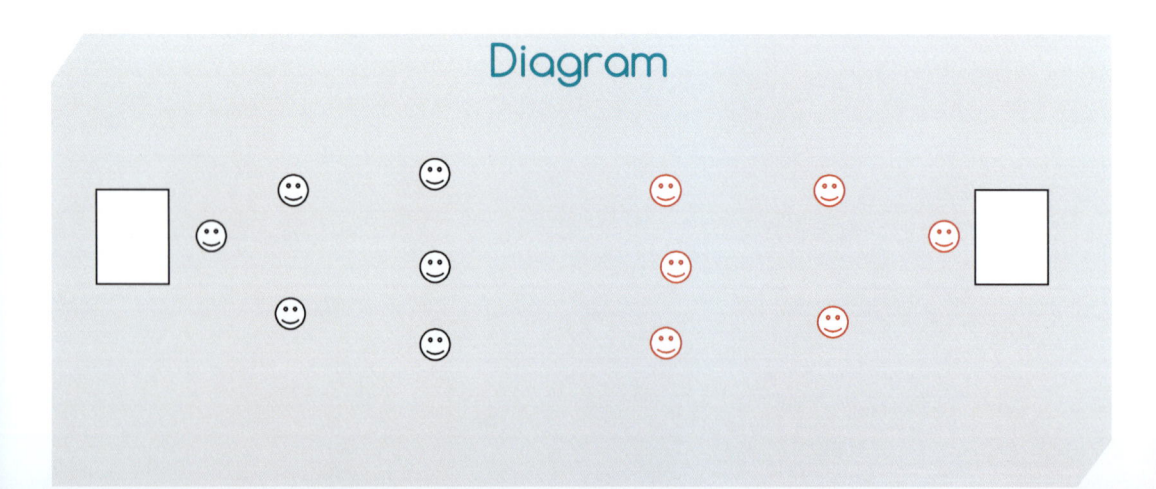

Diagram

Down The Lane

Recommended Grades:
Grades 1-6

Equipment:
Cones and soft foam balls.

Tactical Problems:
Accurate passing and receiving, footwork, and traveling.

Rules of Play:
1. Create teams of 8 – 10 with half lined up on one side and the other half lined up on the other.
2. In the middle, there will be two cones – the goal is for the players to make accurate passes within the distance between the two cones.
3. The first person in line passes it to the first player of the other line trying to get it through the cones.
4. After the pass is made, he/she will run to the back of the line.
5. The player who receives the ball only has two touches with the ball.
6. As the task progresses, decrease the distance between the two cones.
7. If a player does not get the pass through the cones, the entire line must run around the opposite line before returning in position.

Safety:
Ensure there is enough space between the players.

Variations/Progressions:
- Only allowed one touch with the ball.
- Vary the distance between the two lines.

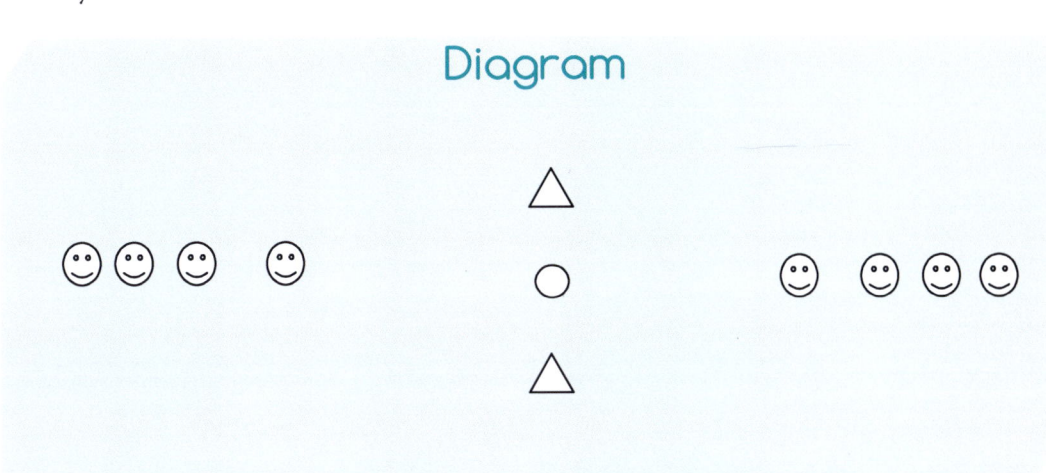

Diagram

Middle Defense

Recommended Grades:

Grades 1-6

Equipment:

Hoops, cones, and soft foam balls.

Tactical Problems:

Accurate passing and receiving, footwork, change of speed, and change in direction.

Rules of Play:

1. Divide students into groups of 6.
2. Within the groups, assign 4 attackers and 2 defenders.
3. Set up 3 cones inside a hula-hoop placed in the middle.
4. The attackers will have 2 foam balls.
5. The goal of the game is for the attackers to knock down the cones by kicking the balls past the defenders (who cannot enter the hula-hoop).
6. Switch roles when all the cones are knocked down.

Safety:

Keep your head up to avoid collisions and keep the balls low..

Variations/Progressions:

- Increase the number of targets by either adding cones or adding an entire new hula-hoop.
- Switch up kicking with throwing.
- Increase or decrease the distance to the target

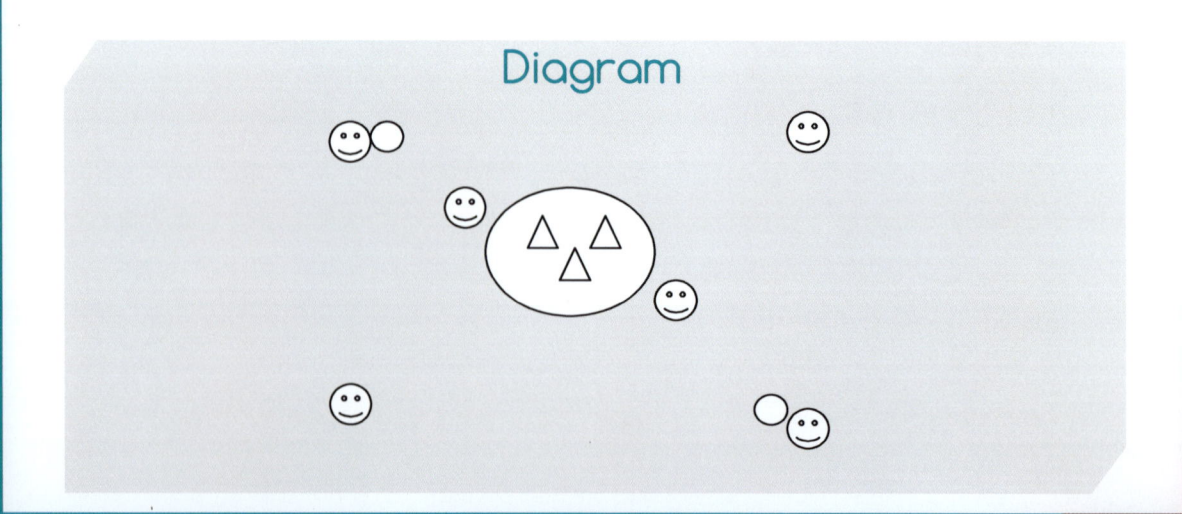

Diagram

5 Pass Possession

Recommended Grades:
Grades 3-4

Equipment:
Gator Ball and Pinnies.

Tactical Problems:
Keeping possession, accurate passing and receiving, creating space, communication, and change of direction.

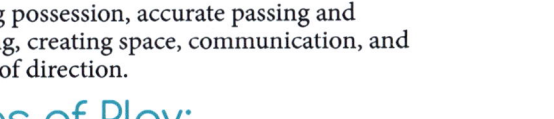

Rules of Play:
1. There are 2 teams in one court (using badminton boundaries) with 1 ball in play at all times.
2. The team with possession of the ball must make 5 consecutive passes without dropping the ball or having it intercepted to be awarded a point.
3. The last person who touches the ball before it hits the floor restarts the game with possession of the ball.
4. Warm defense is used; therefore there is no stripping of the ball from someone's hands whatsoever.

Safety:
Students should keep their heads up when running to avoid collisions amongst themselves.

Variations/Progressions:
- You cannot pass the ball back to the person who just passed it to you.
- If the ball hits the ground off you or one of your teammates, the other team starts with the bal
- You may also designate a zone where a teammate must be to receive a pass after having made 5 consecutive passes to score a point.

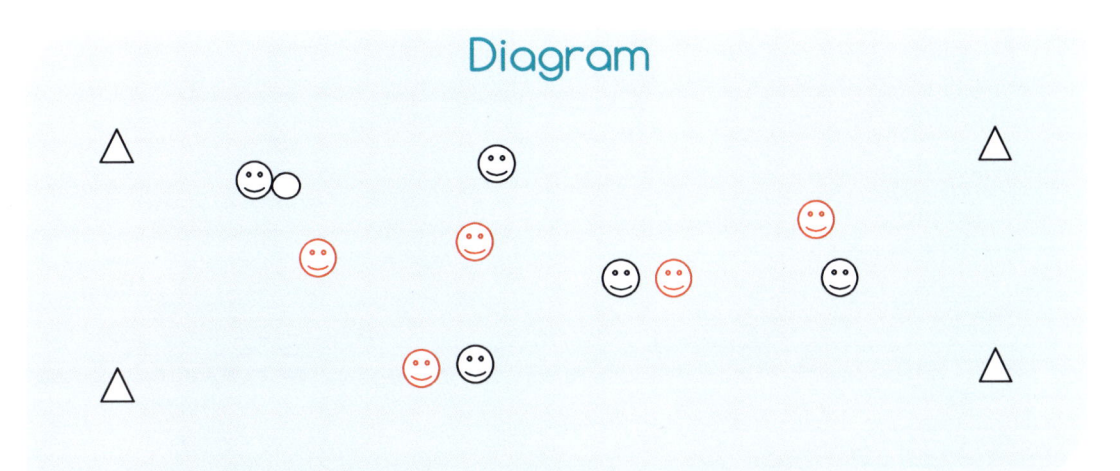

Diagram

Noodle Knockdown

Recommended Grades:

Grades 1-6

Equipment:

Pinnies, noodles, cones, and soft foam balls.

Tactical Problems:

Sending, receiving, travelling, change in direction, and change of speed.

Rules of Play:

1. There will be four teams, one in each corner.
2. Each team must defend their noodles.
3. The teams must knock the other teams noodle by throwing balls at them.
4. Teams cannot cross their zone.

Safety:

Keep your head up to avoid collisions and aim below the waist.

Variations/Progressions:

- Join two teams to make it a 2 V 2 game.

- Teams will be allowed to cross over to the opposing zones; however, they can be tagged and will be frozen until a teammate comes in the zone, grabs the person, and comes back to the team's respective zone (cannot be tagged while connected to frozen teammate.

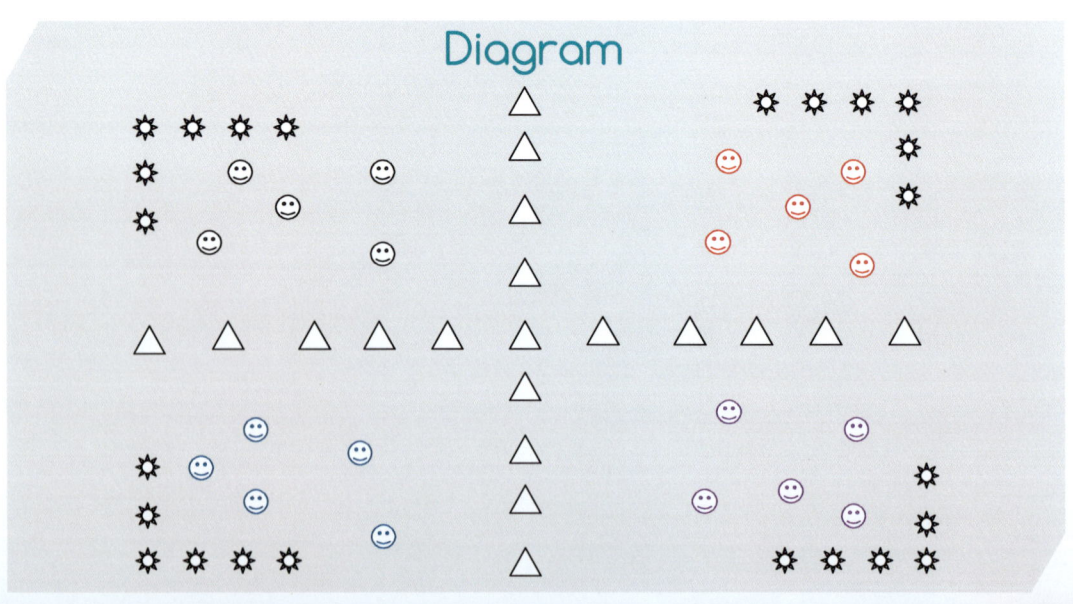

Diagram

Shuffle Ball

Recommended Grades:

Grades 3-4

Equipment:

Pinnies, benches, mats, and a gator skin ball.

Tactical Problems:

Sending, receiving, traveling, and change in direction.

Rules of Play:

1. At each end of the playing area, turn bench on its side and place mat in front of it.
2. Each team has 4-5 players; 1 of them will be the goal keeper.
3. The goal of the game is to score by throwing the ball at the opposition's bench.
4. If the ball lands behind the bench, the goal keeper starts with the ball.
5. All players must keep their bottom on the floor at all times.
6. Players move by shuffling along the floor.
7. Goal keepers may stand but cannot move off the mat.
8. Players must not move with the ball - they must pass the ball before moving into a new space or position.
9. Warm defense – no stripping of the ball.

Safety:

When shuffling, watch your hands so that they don't get stepped on.

Variations/Progressions:

- Minimum # of passes.
- Can only score after the centre-line.
- Introduce an additional bench – each team must defend two nets.

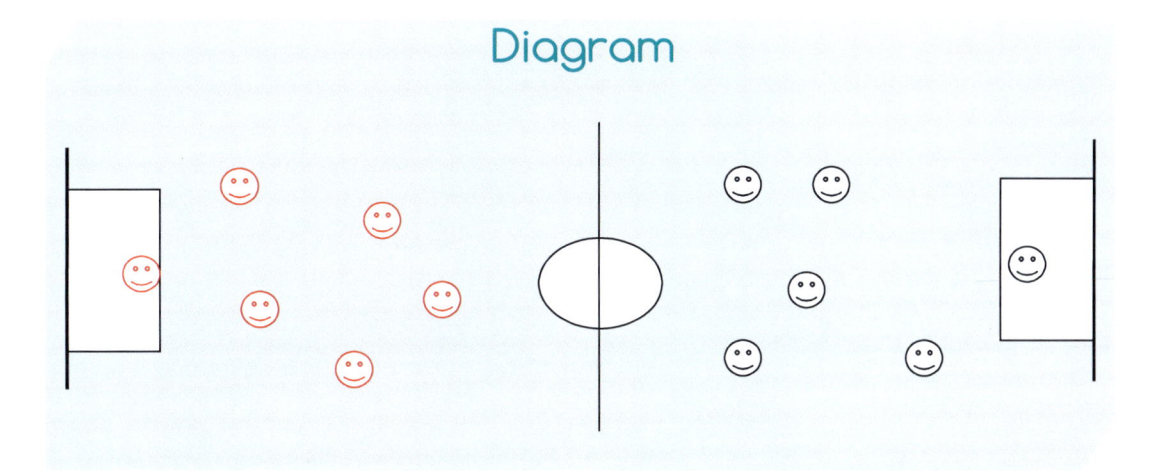

Diagram

21

Recommended Grades:
Grades 3-6

Equipment:
Basketball and a basketball net.

Tactical Problems:
Sending, traveling, change of speed, and change in direction.

Rules of Play:
1. Students will be divided into groups of 2 – 4.
2. The goal of the game is to be the first to score 21 points.
3. Shots are taken from the free-throw line (worth 2 points).
4. If player 1 misses the free-throw shot, player 2 has to pick up the rebound and shoot from wherever he/she recovers the ball (worth 1 point).
5. If player 2 misses as well, player 3 then chases the rebound and attempts to score for 1 point.
6. If following the rebound, the basket is made for 1 point, that same player then shoots from the free-throw line.

Safety:
Keep your distance from the shooting player.

Variations/Progressions:
- If the player is at 20 points, he/she must score 21 points exactly – he/she must purposely miss they're free-throw shot (2 points) and wait to pick up a rebound and score for 1 point.
- Increase or decrease the distance to the basket.

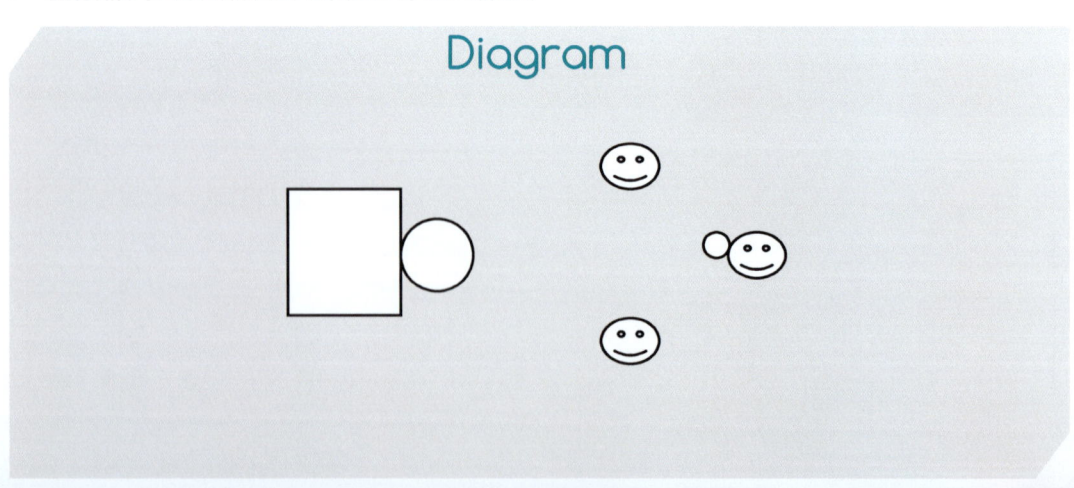

Diagram

50/50

Recommended Grades:

Grades 3-6

Equipment:

Soccer ball and soccer nets.

Tactical Problems:

Keeping possession, change of speed, change in direction, and intercepting the ball.

Rules of Play:

1. Students are divided into two teams, each of which will be assigned a number.
2. The teacher stands in the middle while the two teams line up next to their soccer net.
3. The teacher will call out a number and toss the ball in the middle.
4. The students from each team with the called-out number will attempt to gain possession of the 50/50 ball.
5. If the student wins the 50/50 ball, he/she must attempt to score on the net.
6. If the student loses the 50/50 ball, he/she must defend his/her goal in an attempt to regain possession.

Safety:

Keep your head up to avoid collisions and no slide tackling.

Variations/Progressions:

- Call out a double digit number (i.e. 14 – player #1 of team 1 and player #4 of team 2).
- Increase or decrease the size of the playing area.

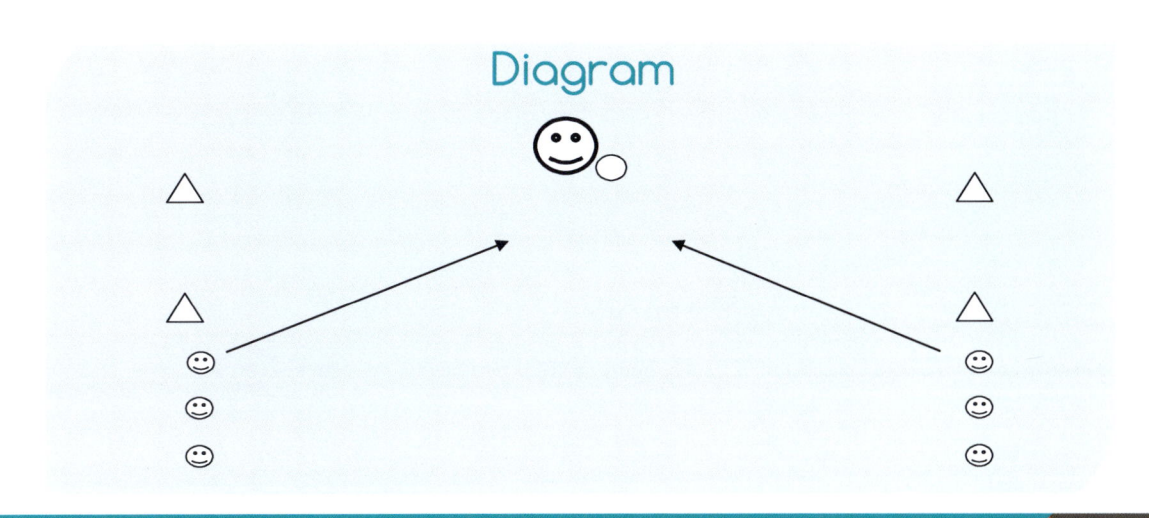

Diagram

Beanbag Invasion

Recommended Grades:

Grades 3-6

Equipment:

Beanbags and hula-hoops.

Tactical Problems:

Footwork, change of speed, change in direction, and communication.

Rules of Play:

1. Divide players in pairs or in groups of 3.
2. Set each group up with a hula-hoop and a certain number of beanbags to place inside the hula-hoop - Allow them to talk strategy for 30 seconds.
3. When the game begins, each team will try to simultaneously defend their own beanbags while trying to steal beanbags from the other teams.
4. Players do not have to move all at once, therefore, players can choose to defend and attack as they wish, but in order to succeed, a team strategy will surely have to take place.
5. The player defending the beanbag must stay outside the hula-hoop and cannot take any steps toward the player who is trying to steal a beanbag.
6. However, if the attacking player is touched by the defender, he/she is frozen and must wait for a teammate to grab onto his/her arm to free him/her.
7. Furthermore, a player can only take one beanbag at a time.
8. In the end, the winning team is the one to have collected the most beanbags.

Safety:

Watch out for butting heads when reaching and defending beanbags.

Variations/Progressions:

- Add or subtract the number of beanbags.
- Increase or decrease the playing area surface.
- Add a method to automatically unfreeze oneself by doing 10 jumping jacks or any other physical activity.

Diagram

Capture the Flag

Recommended Grades:

Grades 3-6

Equipment:

Hula-hoops, flags, cones and pinnies.

Tactical Problems:

Change of speed, change in direction, and transition from offense to defense (vice versa).

Rules of Play:

1. Students will be divided into two teams.
2. Each team will have a hula-hoop with flags at the corner of the playing area surrounded by cones (safe zone) where opposing students are safe as long as they stay within the cones.
3. Each team will also have a couple of hula-hoops designated as the jail.
4. Goal of the game is to capture the flags of the other team and bring them back to their hula-hoop.
5. Students can only be tagged once they cross over to the other team's half.
6. If tagged, they must stand in the jail.
7. To be freed, one of their players must get to them and grab hands, hook arms, or touch shoulders – they are now free to walk back to their end.
8. Players cannot safe a teammate and capture a flag at the same time.

Safety:

Keep your head up to avoid collisions.

Variations/Progressions:

- Introduce a time limit.
- Adjust playing size – decrease width and increase length or increase width and decrease length.

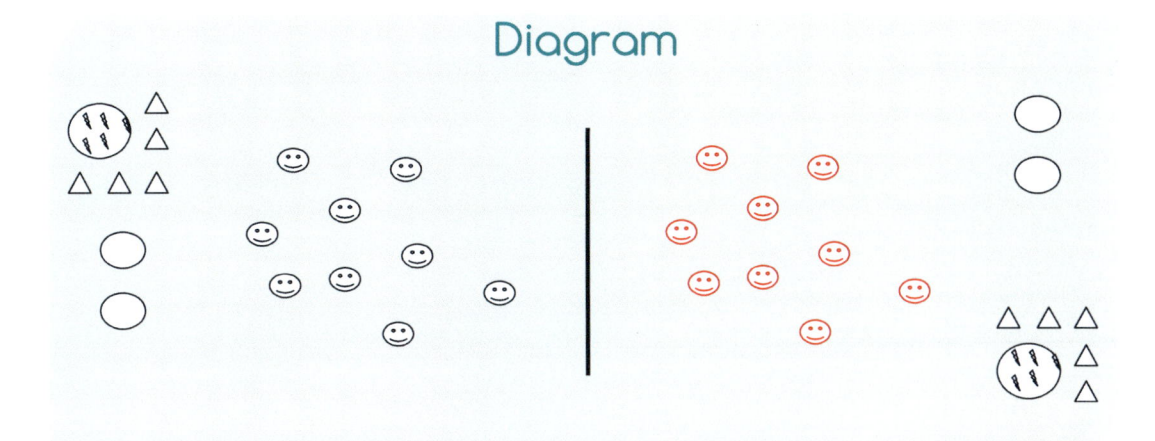

Diagram

End To End

Recommended Grades:

Grades 3-6

Equipment:

Pinnies, hula-hoops, cones, and soft foam balls.

Tactical Problems:

Keeping possession, accurate passing and receiving, change of speed, change in direction, and transition.

Rules of Play:

1. Divide students into two teams.
2. At each end, a cone with a ball on top of it will be placed inside a hula-hoop.
3. The game begins with a jumpball.
4. In order to move around the playing area, players must dribble with the ball, similar to basketball.
5. A team scores a point when a player knocks down the target.
6. If an attempt succeeds, the team that got scored on resets the target and starts with possession of the ball.
7. If an attempt fails, both teams battle for possession of the ball.

Safety:

Keep your head up to avoid collisions and don't aim too high.

Variations/Progressions:

- Cannot move with the ball or only allowed 3 steps with the ball before making a pass.
- Add more balls.
- Add more cone markers.

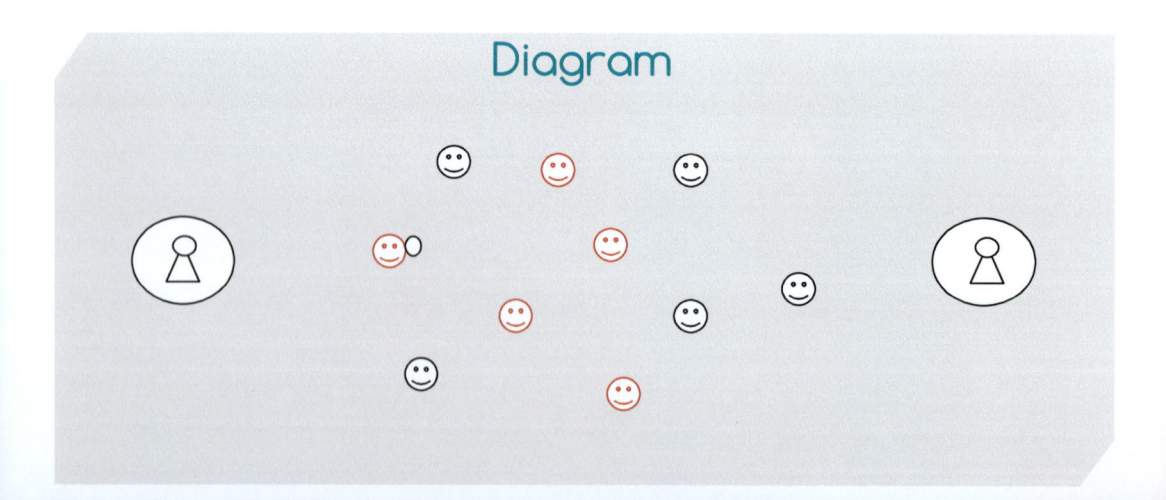

Diagram

Football Pairs

Recommended Grades:

Grades 3-6

Equipment:

Pinnies, football, and cones.

Tactical Problems:

Keeping possession, accurate passing and receiving, footwork, change of speed, and change in direction.

Rules of Play:

1. Divided students into teams of two – game will be 2 v 2.
2. The offensive team will choose a thrower and a receiver while the defending team will choose a player to defend the thrower while the other defends the receiver.
3. Before rushing the "quarterback", 5 steamboats must be said out loud.
4. The offensive team has 3 or 4 attempts to score a touchdown.
5. The receiver attempts to get open for a pass and may continue running with the ball until he/she is tagged, in which case the next pass attempt will be from that point.
6. If a pass is incomplete, the offensive team retains possession and must restart from where the pass was made.
7. Play until a certain time limit or score limit is reached.

Safety:

Keep your head up to avoid collisions and be aware of the ball at all times.

Variations/Progressions:

- Increase the number of players per team (i.e. 3v3, 4v4, etc.).
- Increase or decrease the size of the playing area.

Diagram

Four Corners

Recommended Grades:

Grades 3-6

Equipment:

Pinnies, hula-hoops, noodles, and soft foam balls.

Tactical Problems:

Keeping possession, accurate passing and receiving, traveling, change of speed, and change in direction.

Rules of Play:

1. Divided students into four groups and place one in each corner.
2. In their respective corner, they will have a hula-hoop and the students must strategically place 3 – 5 (or more) noodles in it.
3. Each team will start with 2 soft foam balls, but once the game begins, any team can pick up any ball.
4. The goal of the game is to knock over the other teams' noodles.
5. There is no moving allowed with the ball – only passes can be made to advance to a corner.
6. If a team's noodles are all knocked over, the team must perform a physical activity (i.e. 10 push-ups, jumping jacks, etc.) before resetting them and getting back into the game..

Safety:

Keep your head up to avoid collisions and aim low with the balls.

Variations/Progressions:

- Allow a certain number of steps with the ball.
- Increase or decrease the size of the playing area.
- Add more hoops and noodles.

Diagram

Grinches & Elves

Recommended Grades:

Grades 3-6

Equipment:

Pinnies, hula-hoops, beanbags, and soft foam balls.

Tactical Problems:

Dodging, travelling, change of speed, change in direction, and communication..

Rules of Play:

1. Two teams will spread out on each side of the gymnasium.
2. The goal of each team is to enter the other team's territory and steal a bean bag to return it to their end.
3. If they are hit by a ball when they enter the other team's zone, they are frozen.
4. To be unfrozen, a teammate has to grab the person by the arm and bring him/her back in their team's zone.

Safety:

Keep your head up to avoid collisions and aim below the waist.

Variations/Progressions:

- Increase or reduce the size of the playing area.
- Increase the number of balls.
- Allow or restrict movement with the ball

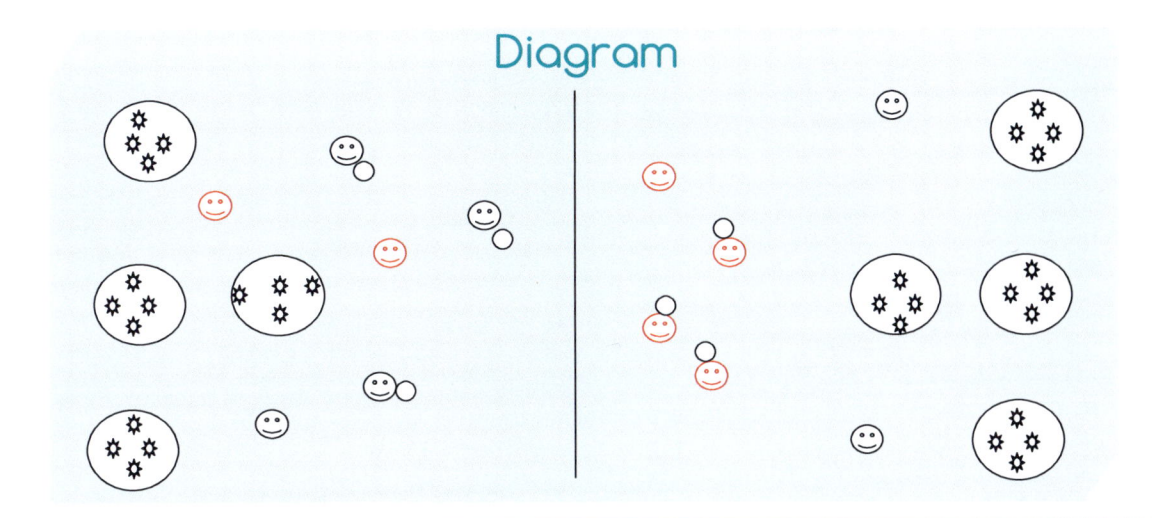

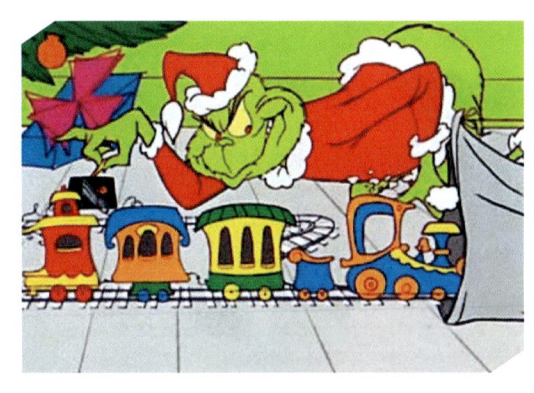

Diagram

Knock off

Recommended Grades:
Grades 3-6

Equipment:
Basketballs.

Tactical Problems:
Dodging, change of speed, change in direction, maintain possession, and intercept ball.

Rules of Play:
1. Students will spread out around the gymnasium, each with a basketball.
2. The goal of the game is to dribble around and maintain possession while trying to knock off the other players' basketball beyond the basketball boundary lines.
3. If this happens, that player is eliminated and must stand on the side; however, he/she could still knock off someone's ball if they come near him/her.
4. As time goes on, reduce the playing area.
5. Progressions: half-court, inside the 3-point arc, and inside the key.

Safety:
Keep your head up to avoid collisions and be aware of the balls at all times so you don't trip over them.

Variations/Progressions:
- Create your own boundary limits.
- Two balls for each student (i.e. two lives before getting eliminated).

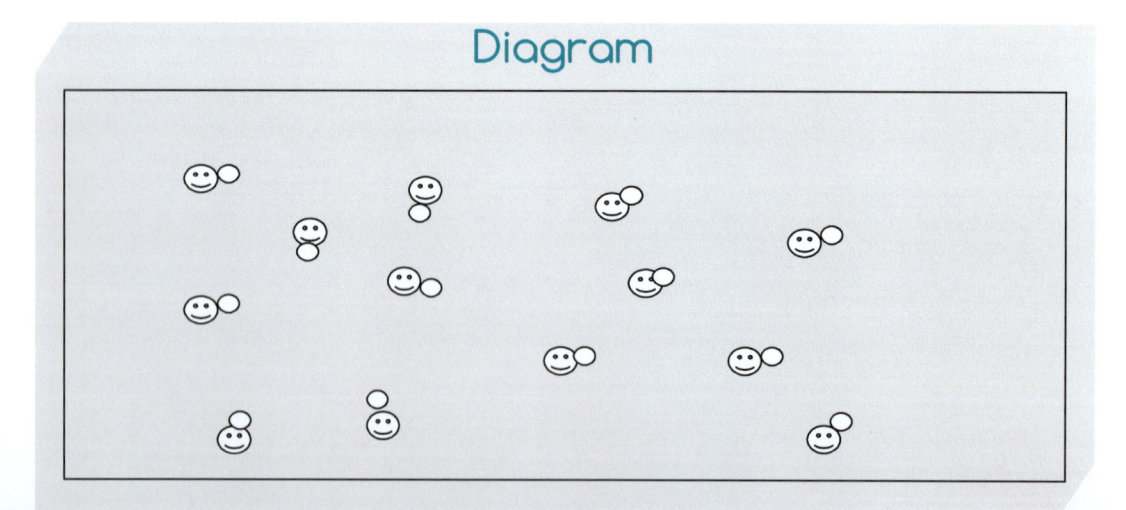

Diagram

Knockout

Recommended Grades:

Grades 3-6

Equipment:

Basketball net and two basketballs.

Tactical Problems:

Sending, accurate passing and receiving, change of speed, change in direction, and footwork.

Rules of Play:

1. The first player in line begins the game by taking an initial shot.
2. As soon as the first player has taken the initial shot, the second player may step up to the line and take his or her shot.
3. If a player's initial shot does not go in, he or she may rebound the basketball and attempt to make a basket from any location (most often, a layup would be attempted because it is an easier shot to make than a standard jump shot)
4. However, if the player behind him/her makes his/her basket before the initial player scores on their rebound, he/she is eliminated.
5. Once a player makes a basket, he or she must pass the ball to the next person at the front of the line and then go to the end of the line.
6. The person at the front of the line may take his or her shot immediately upon receiving a ball.

Safety:

Keep your head up to avoid collisions and be alert when anticipating the pass from your teammate.

Variations/Progressions:

- Give more than one life to every player on the team so that they have a second chance if they get knocked out the first time.

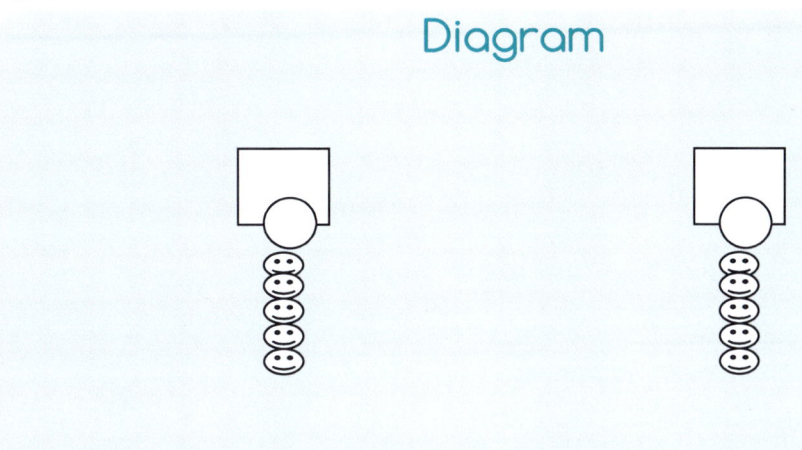

Diagram

Off the Wall

Recommended Grades:

Grades 3-6

Equipment:

Pinnies, hockey nets, and soft foam balls.

Tactical Problems:

Keeping possession, accurate passing and receiving, change of speed, change in direction, and transition.

Rules of Play:

1. Students will be divided into two teams (or could be further divided into smaller groups depending on the equipment available).
2. The hockey nets will be set up for each team upside down so that the opening is facing the wall.
3. Students must try to score a goal by banking it off the wall.
4. Players can take three steps with the ball.
5. Players must make three passes prior to attempting to score on net.
6. Play until a certain time limit or score limit is reached.

Safety:

Keep your head up to avoid collisions and play warm defense (no stripping of the ball).

Variations/Progressions:

- Adjust the number of players on each team.
- Increase or decrease the size of the playing area.
- Use four nets instead of two – create more areas to score.

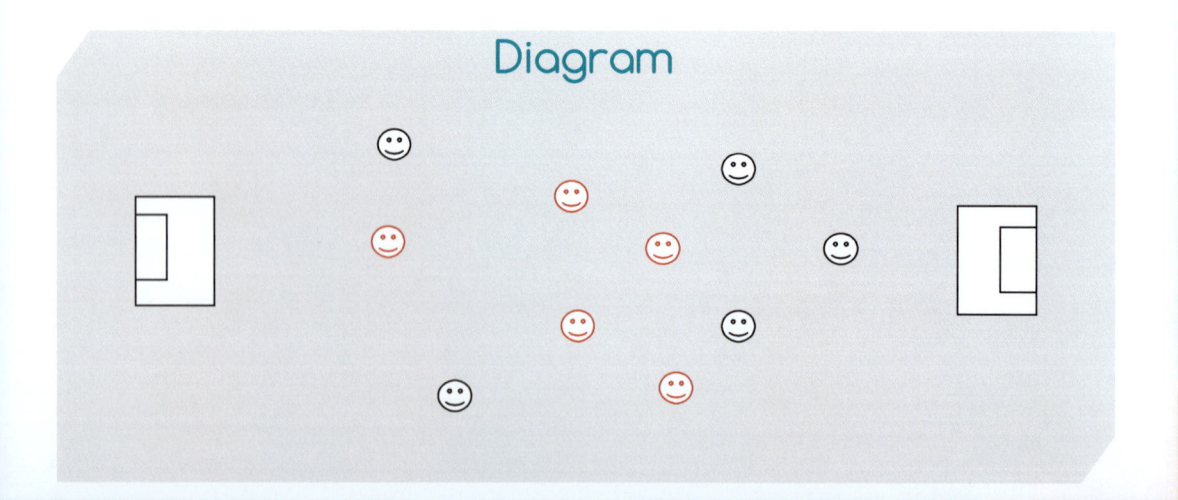

Diagram

Other Side

Recommended Grades:
Grades 3-6

Equipment:
Pinnies and cones, the latter to designate safety zones and playing area.

Tactical Problems:
Traveling, dodging, footwork, change of speed, shuffle, and change in direction.

Rules of Play:
1. When the game starts, players from one team must make their way to the opposing safety zones without getting touched by the opposing team's players.
2. If you get touched while in the offensive zone, you are frozen.
3. You can only be freed if your teammate grabs your arm and brings you back to the defensive zone.
4. While they are attached to the player's arm, they cannot be frozen as they are on base.
5. If you reach the safety zone, you may come back to save a teammate, but you must return to the defensive zone.
6. A time limit is usually instated.
7. The winner is the team with the more people in the safety zone or the first team to get all their members in the safety zone.

Safety:
Watch out for collisions when running.

Variations/Progressions:
- Adjust the playing field by making it wider and shorter or thinner and longer.

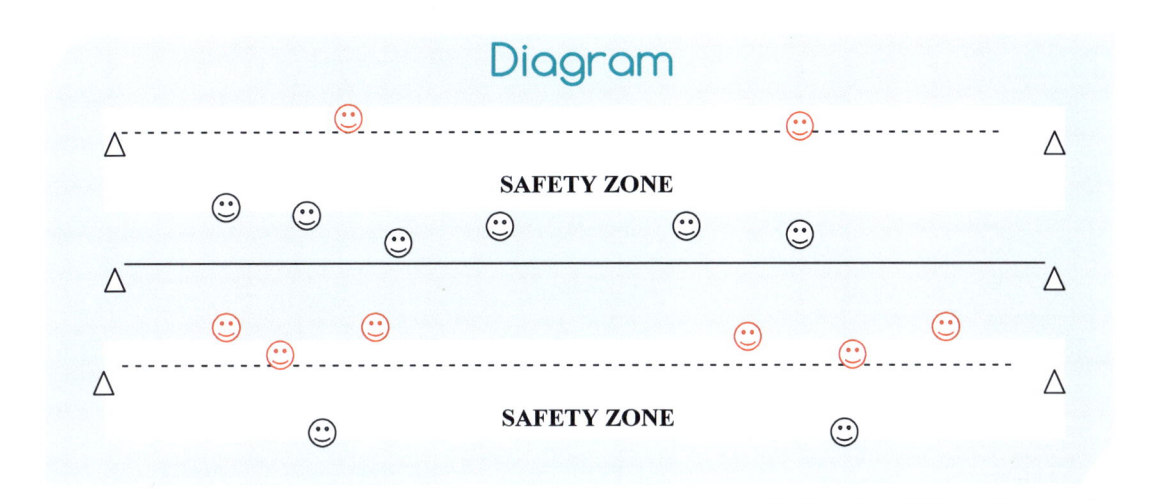

Diagram

SAFETY ZONE

SAFETY ZONE

Quarter Soccer

Recommended Grades:

Grades 3-6

Equipment:

Pinnies, soccer balls and soccer nets (or cones).

Tactical Problems:

Accurate passing and receiving, footwork, keeping possession, traveling, change of speed, and change in direction.

Rules of Play:

1. Students will be divided into four teams.
2. There will be one net for each team.
3. Start with one ball and introduce more as time goes on.
4. When a goal is scored, the goalie of that team must switch with another player.
5. Play until a certain time limit or score limit is reached.

Safety:

Keep your head up to avoid collisions and be aware of all the balls in play at all times.

Variations/Progressions:

- Increase or decrease the size of the playing area.
- Force students to use their non-dominant foot only.

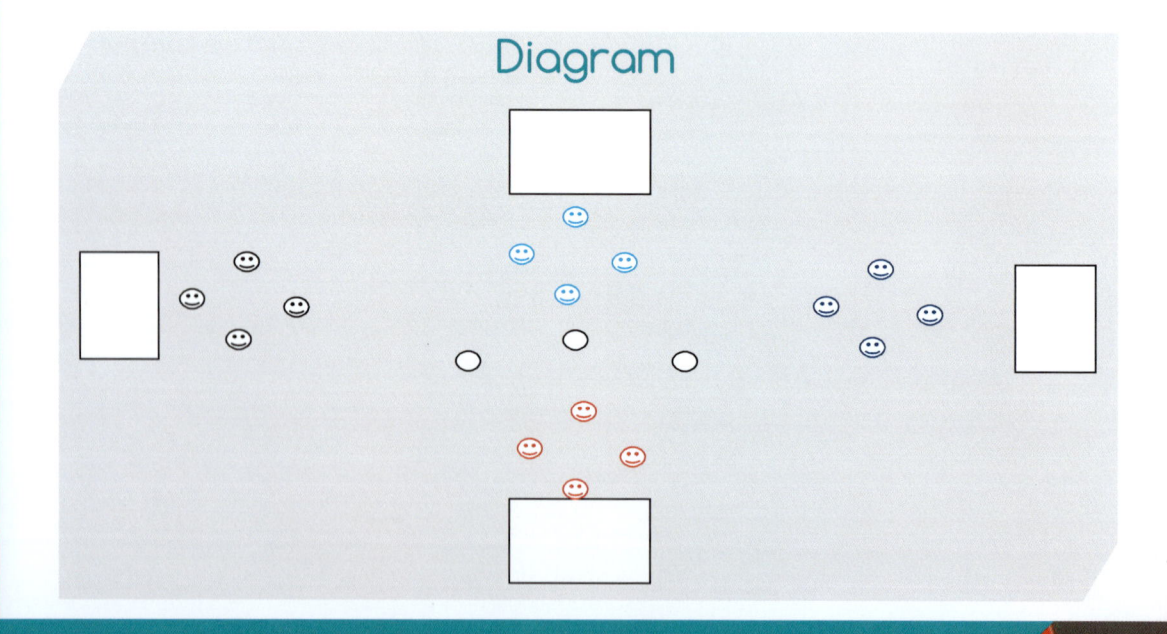

Diagram

Soccer Away

Recommended Grades:

Grades 3-6

Equipment:

Pinnies, nets and multiple soccer balls.

Tactical Problems:

Sending, receiving, maintain possession, and defending players in the area.

Rules of Play:

1. Start off a regular soccer game or a soccer game with modified rules.
2. There will only be one kick-off (initial kick-off) the entire game.
3. If a goalie makes a save or if a team gets scored on, that team will simply put the ball back into play.
4. As time progresses, introduce an additional soccer ball.
5. As more time goes by, introduce another as you see fit.

Safety:

Keep your head up and be aware of the balls in play.

Variations/Progressions:

- Modify the number of soccer balls introduced into play.
- Type of nets used.
- Increase or reduce the size of the playing area.

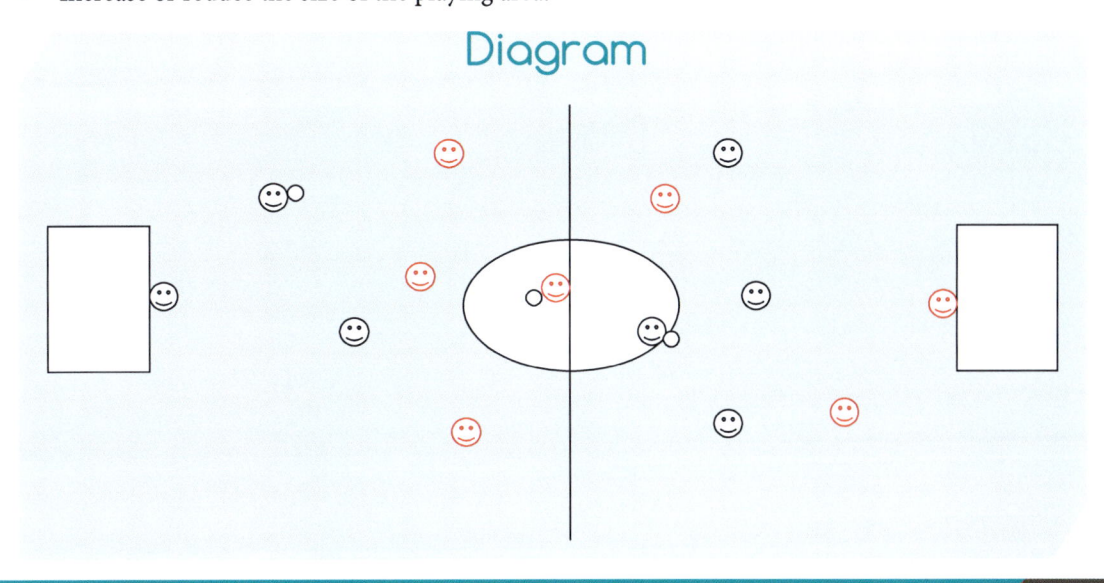

Diagram

Treasure

Recommended Grades:
Grades 3-6

Equipment:
Pinnies, hula-hoops, and bean bags.

Tactical Problems:
Traveling, change of speed, and running in different directions.

Rules of Play:
1. Introduce a time limit.
2. There is no tagging.
3. There will be four teams, each with a hula-hoop and a set number of bean bags.
4. On "Go", students from one team will steal bean bags from any of the other three teams.
5. Each student is only allowed to steal one bean bag at a time and must return this bean bag to their proper hula-hoop before stealing another.
6. Team with the most bean bags at the end of the time limit wins..

Safety:
Keep your head up to avoid collisions with others and no throwing of bean bags will be permitted.

Variations/Progressions:
- Introduce tagging.
- Form coalitions (i.e. 2 V 2 games).

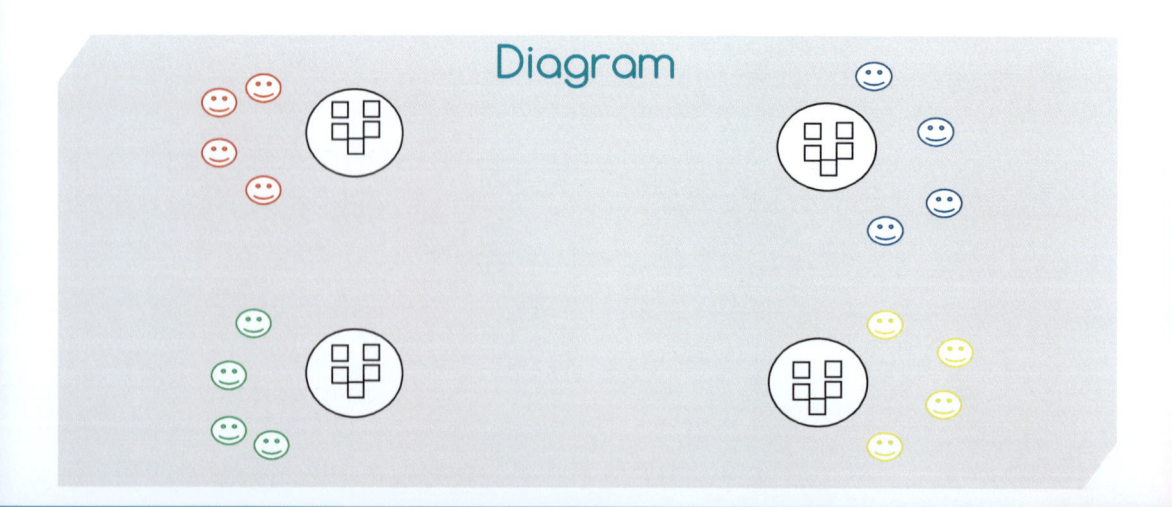

Diagram

Star Wars

Recommended Grades:

Grades 3-6

Equipment:

Hula-hoops, noodles, hockey nets (upside down so that the top of the net is facing the playing area), pinnies, gator skin balls.

Tactical Problems:

Traveling, sending, receiving, passing, dodging, and change in direction

Rules of Play:

1. Teams are made as the noodles are placed inside the hula-hoops while the hockey nets are a foot or two away from the wall.
2. The first objective is to knock down the opposition's noodles with the ball.
3. Once this is done, the second and final objective is to throw the ball into the net by bouncing it off the wall to destroy the generator and win.
4. Players are allowed entering the opposition's zone.
5. However, if you get touched by the opponents, you are frozen and must rely on a teammate to unfreeze you by grabbing your hand/arm.

Safety:

Avoid collisions when running around and be aware of the ball(s) in play.

Variations/Progressions:

- Add more balls.
- Increase or decrease the number of noodles.
- Bring noodles closer to the center line or further from it.

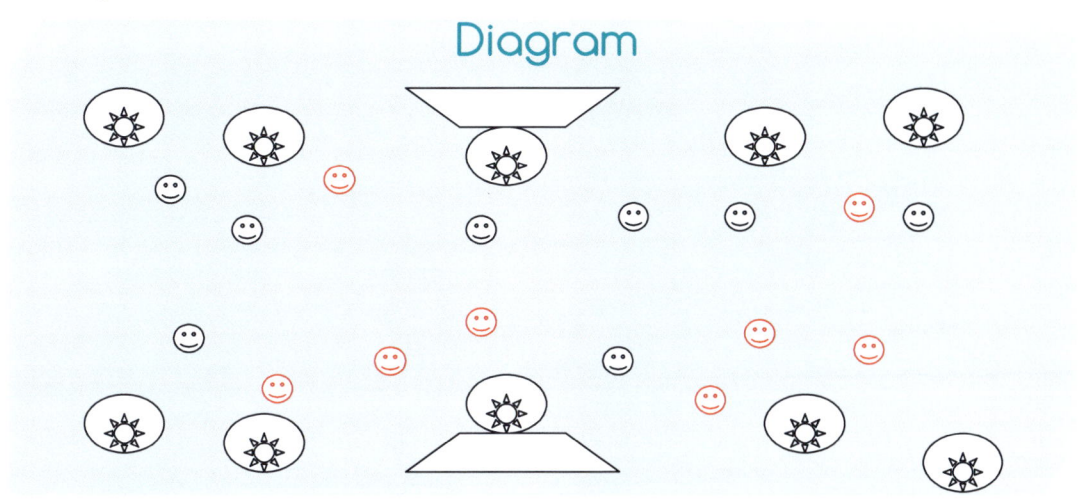

Diagram

VS Foul Line

Recommended Grades:

Grades 3-6

Equipment:

Baskets and basketballs.

Tactical Problems:

Sending, accurate passing and receiving, change of speed, change in direction, and footwork.

Rules of Play:

1. 2 lines (2 teams) on each foul line for each basket.
2. On the teacher's signal, both teams take a foul shot and continue in a race to be the team with the most points at the end of the elapsed time.
3. Each person in the line takes two shots regardless if they make the foul shot or not.
4. The foul shot is worth 2 points.
5. On the rebound, the player may take a shot or dribble and lay it up to the basket for 1 point.
6. He/She then passes the ball to the next person in lies and goes to the back of the line.

Safety:

Keep your head up to avoid collisions and be alert when anticipating the pass from your teammate.

Variations/Progressions:

- A team may take the rebound back to the foul line and go for 2 points instead of 1 for a maximum of 4 points (initial foul shot + rebound off the foul line).
- Increase or decrease the distance to the basket.
- Introduce both a time limit and a point limit

Diagram

360 Hockey

Recommended Grades:

Grades 5-6

Equipment:

Pinnies, hockey sticks, protective gear, and cones as hockey nets.

Tactical Problems:

Keeping possession, accurate passing and receiving, change of speed, change in direction, and transition.

Rules of Play:

1. Separate students into four teams.
2. One team defends the North/South goals (passing); the other team defends the East/West (stick handling) goals.
3. To score on the North/South goals, the offensive team must complete a pass through the cones and the ball must be stopped within 2 feet of the cones.
4. To score on the East/West goals, the offensive team must stick handle the ball through the cones and stop the ball within 1 foot of the cones.
5. Play until a time limit or score limit is reached.

Safety:

Keep your head up to avoid collisions and keep your stick below your waist.

Variations/Progressions:

- Give each team one North/South goal and one East/West goal to defend.
- Increase or decrease the size of the playing area.
- Can be adapted to different sports.

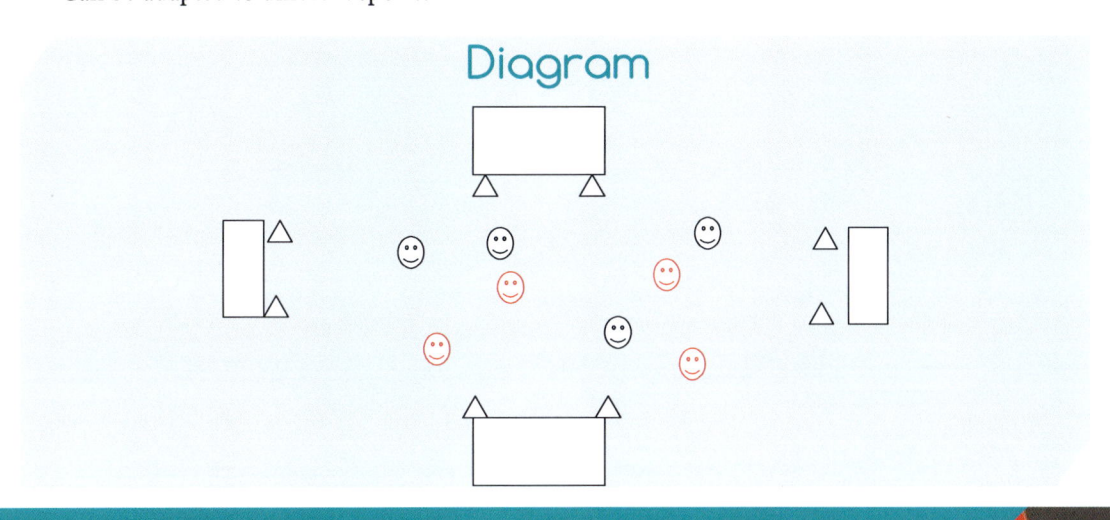

Diagram

Around the World

Recommended Grades:

Grades 5-6

Equipment:

Basketball net and a basketball.

Tactical Problems:

Accurate shooting and footwork.

Rules of Play:

1. Minimum of 2 players in each group under one basket.
2. Goal of the game is to be the first to make it "around the world".
3. There will be 6 – 9 spots chosen by the instructor in which students have to shoot from in order to make it around the world.
4. If the first player moves up to the first spot and makes the basket, he/she will move to spot #2.
5. If at any point a player misses his/her shot, he/she has the choice to stay or gamble.
6. If he/she chooses to gamble and makes the shot, he/she moves to the next spot.
7. If he/she misses the gamble, they have to start back at the beginning.

Safety:

Ensure students have space from other groups.

Variations/Progressions:

- Change the number of spots.
- Change the location of the spots.
- Play with no gamble.

Diagram

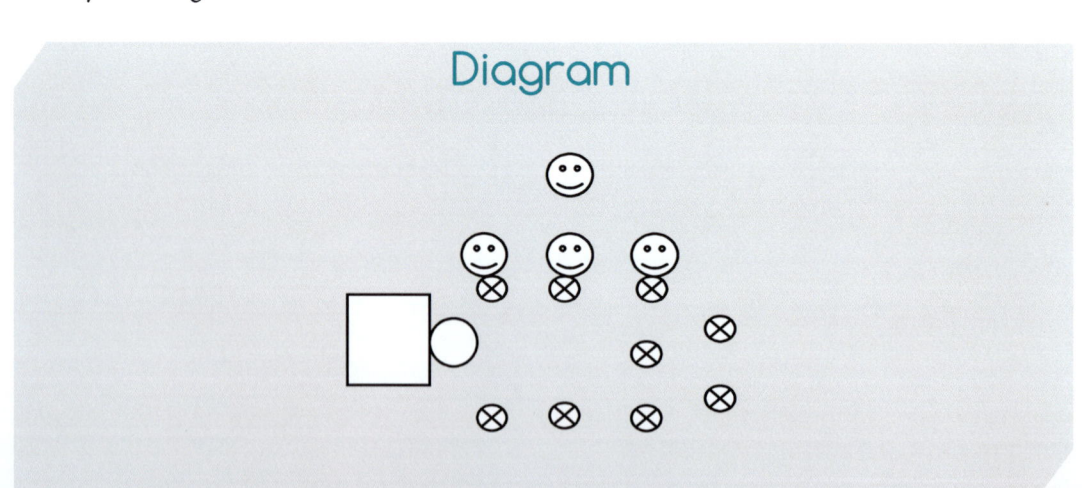

Basketball Threes

Recommended Grades:

Grades 5-6

Equipment:

Pinnies, basketball, and basketball nets.

Tactical Problems:

Keeping possession, accurate passing and receiving, traveling, change of speed, change in direction, intercepting the ball, and transition.

Rules of Play:

1. Students will be divided into teams of 5.
2. There will be three teams on each court – teams #1 & #2 will start on opposite baskets while team #3 will start with the ball at center court.
3. Team #3 will move down towards team #1 and play against them in an attempt to score.
4. If team #3 scores, they take the ball down towards team #2 and once more, attempt to score.
5. If team #3 doesn't score on its attempt to score on team #1, team #3 will stay put while team #1 dribbles towards team #2 in an attempt to score.
6. Keep track of the score – team with the most points at the end of the time limit wins.

Safety:

Keep your head up to avoid collisions and be aware of the ball at all times.

Variations/Progressions:

- Increase or decrease the size of the playing area.
- Disallow dribbling – could only make passes.

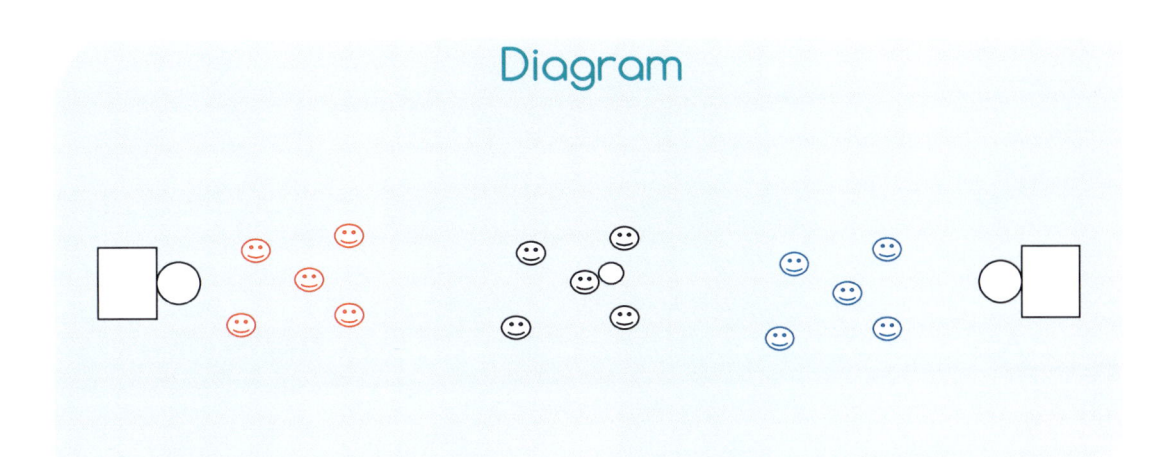

Diagram

Flickerball

Recommended Grades:

Grades 5-6

Equipment:

Pinnies, basketball nets and a rugby ball.

Tactical Problems:

Sending, accurate passing and receiving, change of speed, change in direction, and keeping possession.

Rules of Play:

1. Full court basketball with two teams.
2. Game is started with a jump-ball like in basketball instead it is played with a rugby ball.
3. Person with the rugby can only make 3 steps with the ball before passing or shooting.
4. There are no boundary lines.
5. Rugby must go through basketball net to score 1 point.
6. There is no out of bounds.
7. The ball may not touch the ground.
8. If the ball touches the ground, the team that DID NOT last touch it gains possession of it.

Safety:

Keep your head up to avoid collisions and be aware of the ball at all times.

Variations/Progressions:

- Introduce boundary lines.
- Introduce a certain number of passes that needs to be made in general if there is not enough passing going on in the gymnasium.
- Set up multiple games using half the court.

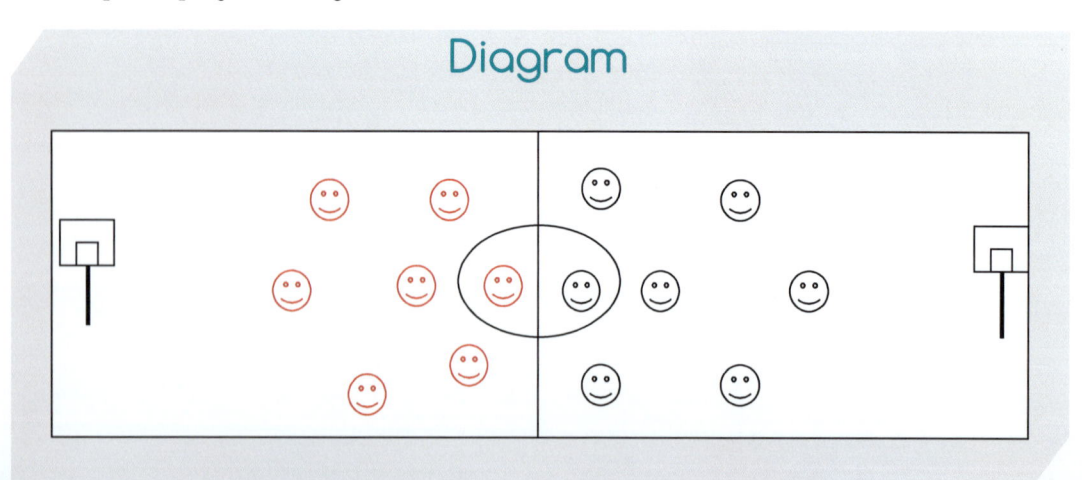

Diagram

Ghost Soccer

Recommended Grades:

Grades 5-6

Equipment:

Blindfolds, pinnies, noodles, and soft gator skin balls.

Tactical Problems:

Keeping possession, hitting targets, and strong communication.

Rules of Play:

1. Players are attached by their arms as the player without the blindfold guides the player that is blindfolded through verbal cues and movement.
2. Once the game starts, the player who is not blind is constantly moving the player with a blindfold and giving instructions on where to move, when to kick, and where the balls are located.
3. All this interaction goes on as one team is trying to knock down the other team's noodles.
4. Halfway through the game, the players switch roles as the other player wears the blindfold.

Safety:

Guider must keep his or her head up at all times and be careful that students are not kicking other students.

Variations/Progressions:

- Add or reduce the number of balls in play.
- Introduce a hockey net that can only be scored on after the noodles are knocked down

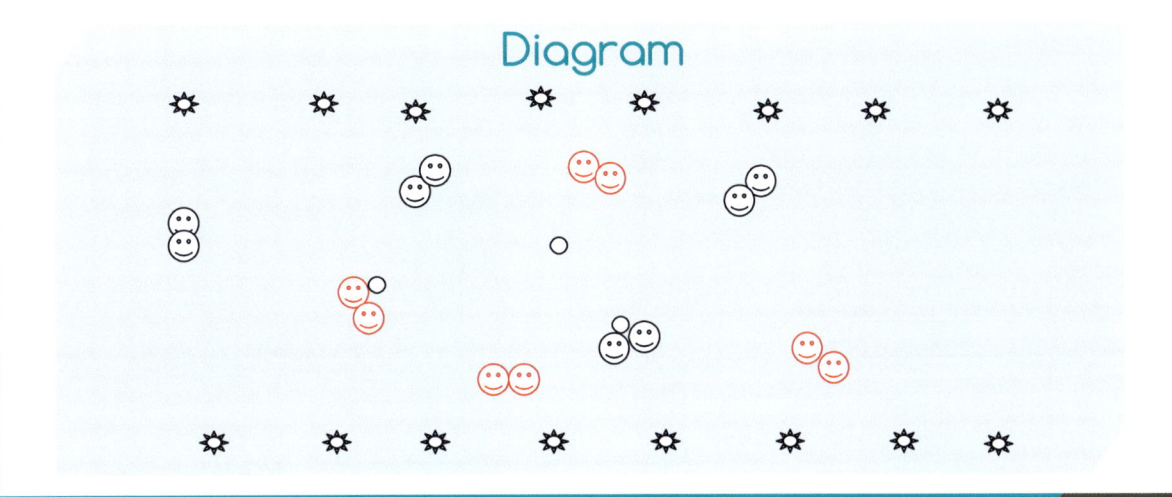

Diagram

Horse

Recommended Grades:
Grades 5-6

Equipment:
Basketball.

Tactical Problems:
Accurate shooting and footwork.

Rules of Play:

1. Minimum of 2 players in each group with one basket.
2. Decide who shoots first.
3. Goal of the game is to NOT spell out "H-O-R-S-E".
4. First player in line decides where on the court he/she wants to shoot the ball.
5. If the player makes the shot, the 2nd player in line must now duplicate this shot; if not, he/she gets the letter "H" (this goes all the way to "E" for HORSE).
6. If the player makes the shot and the 2nd player makes his/hers, he/she does not gain a letter and the first player in line must take a set shot once more anywhere on the court.
7. If the player misses the shot and the 2nd player makes his/hers, the first player does not gain a letter, but instead, the 2nd player is now responsible for making the set shot.
8. Winner is the student who hasn't spelled out the word HORSE.

Safety:
Ensure that each group has their proper basket.

Variations/Progressions:
- Introduce a time limit.
- Give players a 2nd chance on the same shot

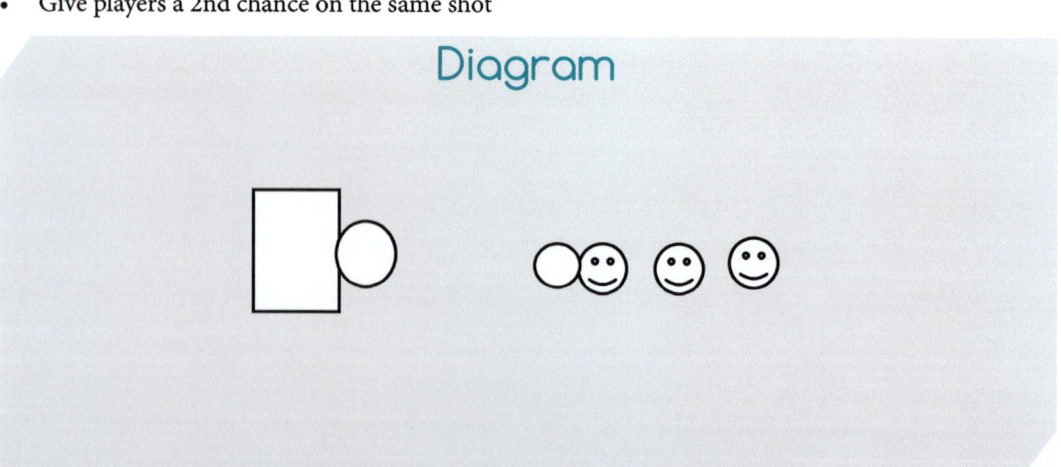

Diagram

Jailbreak

Recommended Grades:
Grades 5-6

Equipment:
Pinnies and cones, the latter to designate the jail, safety zones, and playing area.

Tactical Problems:
Traveling, dodging, footwork, change of speed, shuffle, and change in direction

Rules of Play:

1. When the game starts, players from one team must make their way to the opposing safety zones without getting touched by the opposing team's players.
2. If you get touched while in the offensive zone, you are sent to jail.
3. You can only be freed if your teammate manages to pass by the "guards" and run through the jail while shouting "JAILBREAK!"
4. However, once freed from the jail, both the teammate and the players that have just been freed could be touched again if they are not quick enough to escape.
5. If you reach the safety zone, you may come back to save a teammate, but you must return to the defensive zone.
6. A time limit is usually instated.
7. The winner is the team with the more people in the safety zone or the first team to get all their members in the safety zone.

Safety:
Watch out for collisions when running

Variations/Progressions:
- Adjust the playing field by making it wider and shorter or thinner and longer.
- Assigning a maximum number of "guards" protecting the jail.

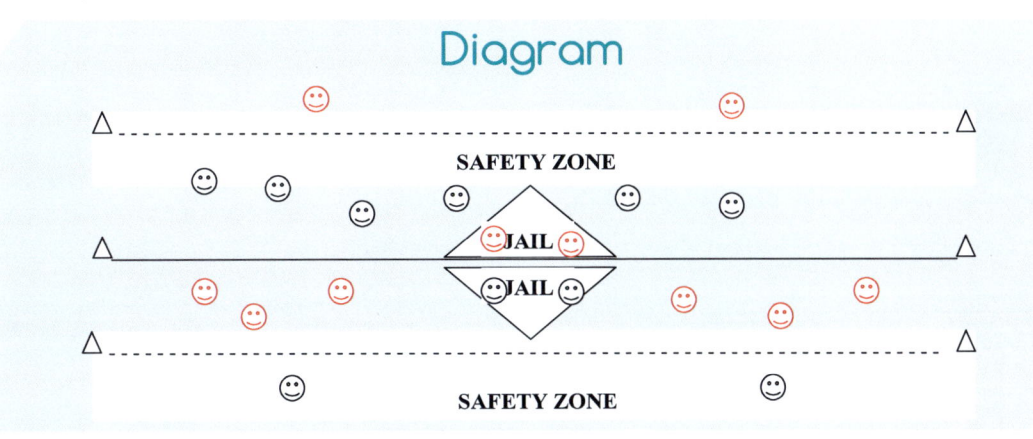

Diagram

Kick It Up

Recommended Grades:

Grades 5-6

Equipment:

Pinnies, beachballs and mats.

Tactical Problems:

Sending, receiving, traveling, keeping possession, change of speed, and change in direction.

Rules of Play:

1. Students will be divided into two teams.
2. Players can cross sides – they do not have to remain on their own side of the court.
3. There will be one mat on each end of the court set up in a manner in which there is a hole where the beachball must land in.
4. Students cannot use their arms or hands; in essence, it's like soccer with feet being the many point of contact.
5. Defending is allowed.
6. One point is scored for each time a beachball lands in the mat's entrance.
7. Play until a time limit or score limit is reached.

Safety:

Keep your head up to avoid collisions and do not keep the ball too hard.

Variations/Progressions:

- Change the type of ball used.
- Change the type of nets used.
- Increase or decrease the size of the playing area.
- Further divided the teams into four

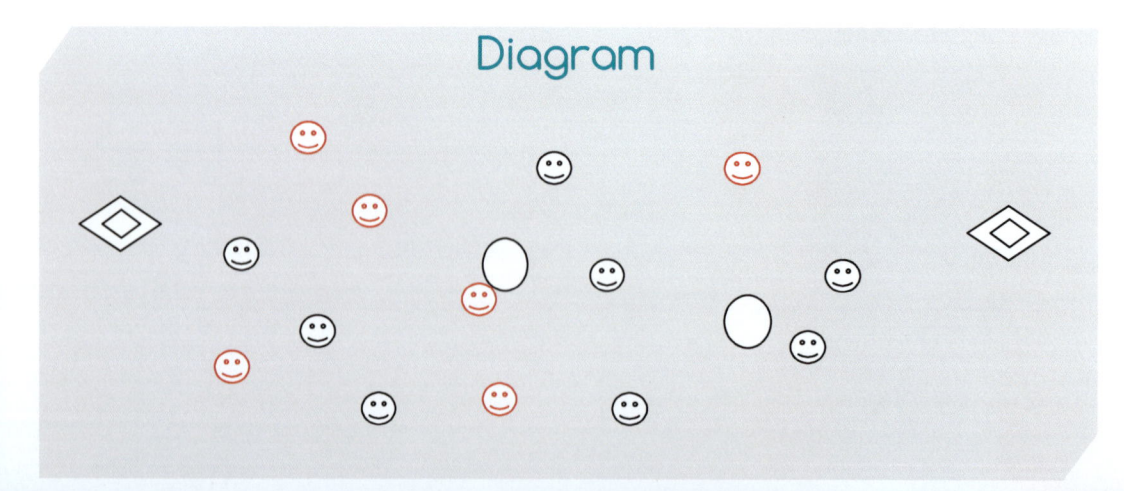

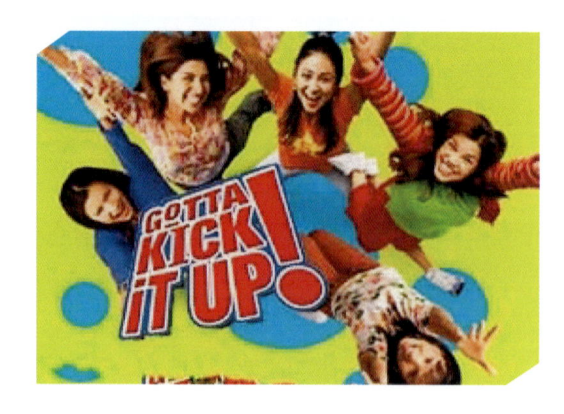

Diagram

Modified Lacrosse

Recommended Grades:

Grades 5-6

Equipment:

Pinnies, lacrosse sticks, balls, protective eyegear, and cones for nets.

Tactical Problems:

Keeping possession, accurate passing and receiving, change of speed, change in direction, and transition.

Rules of Play:

1. Class will be divided into four teams with two games going on at once on two different areas of the court.
2. Teams will comprise 5 players with no goalies.
3. To score, you must roll the ball between the stick placed on the cones.
4. Players must complete 3 passes before scoring.
5. There is no movement allowed with the ball.
6. Allowed 3 seconds with the ball.
7. Introduce more balls as the game goes along.

Safety:

Keep your head up to avoid collisions, be aware of the balls at all times, and be careful with the lacrosse sticks.

Variations/Progressions:

- Allow movement.
- Increase or decrease the size of the playing area.
- Vary the minimum number of passes required before scoring.

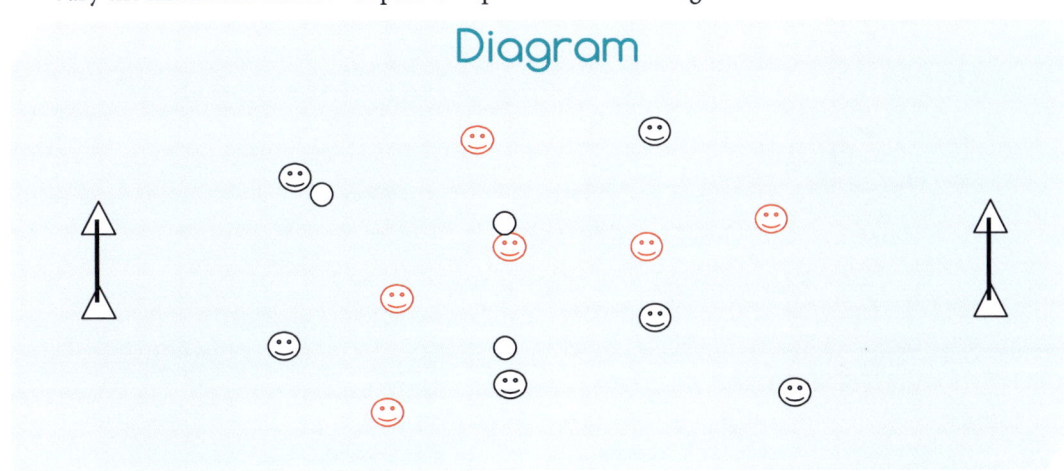

Diagram

Prairie Dog Pickoff

Recommended Grades:

Grades 5-6

Equipment:

Hula-hoops, gator skin balls, and noodles.

Tactical Problems:

Attacking and defending a goal, communication, sending ball to specified area, and moving from offense to defense and vice versa.

Rules of Play:

1. Every student takes a hoop and a noodle.
2. Players disperse anywhere in the playing area, put their hoop on the ground with the noodle in it standing upright in the middle of the hoop.
3. A ball is introduced, which can be used by students to throw at another student's prairie dog.
4. Students cannot move with the ball, they may only pivot.
5. When a student's prairie dog (noodle) is knocked over, he/she will pick up his hoop and noodle and will join the person who knocked his noodle over.
6. This is done by placing the hoop right beside the other player's hoop - they now become a team..

Safety:

Keep the ball low and keep their heads up when moving around.

Variations/Progressions:

- Allow a certain number of steps.
- Add more balls.
- Time limit with ball.

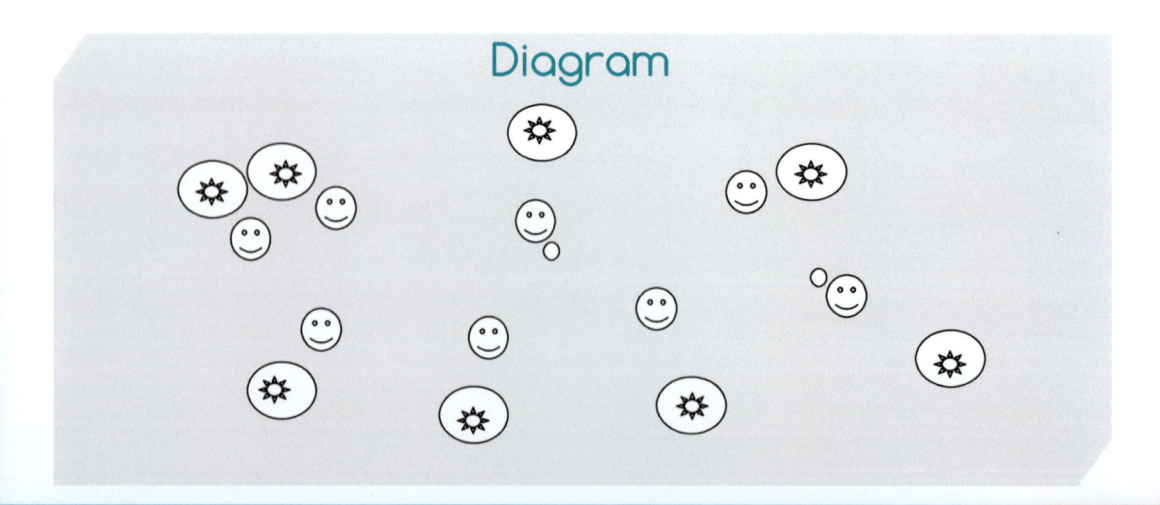

Diagram

Sidelines

Recommended Grades:

Grades 5-6

Equipment:

Pinnies, soccer ball and soccer nets.

Tactical Problems:

Keeping possession, accurate passing and receiving, change of speed, change in direction, and transition.

Rules of Play:

1. Set up a game of 6v6 in a small grid with small goals.
2. A player from each team must stand on the sidelines.
3. The players on the sidelines are not in-play and thus, they cannot be stripped of the ball.
4. They are allowed to move along the sidelines.
5. When they receive a pass from their teammate, they are not allowed to move and must pass the ball back into play.
6. Teams must complete a pass to the sidelines before scoring on the goal.
7. Rotate sideline players.

Safety:

Keep your head up to avoid collisions and be careful with the slide tackling.

Variations/Progressions:

- Allow the players on the sidelines to fight for the possession of the ball.
- Increase or decrease the size of the playing area.
- Add more players to the sidelines.
- Increase the minimum number of passes that needs to be made before scoring

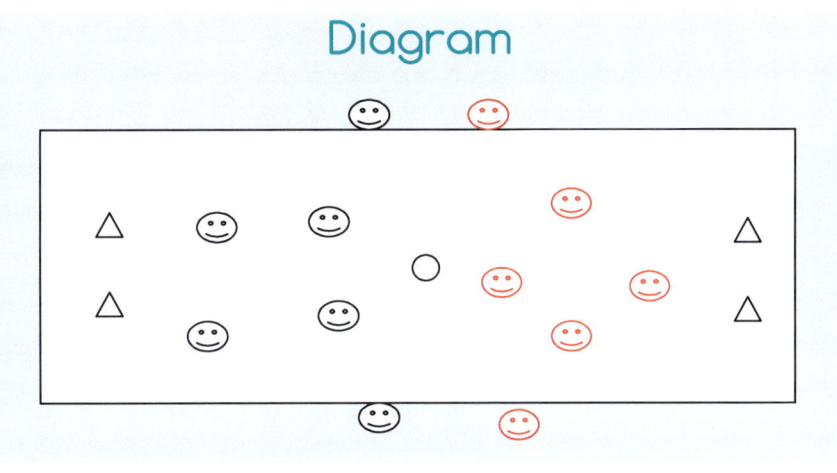

Diagram

Speedball

Recommended Grades:

Grades 5-6

Equipment:

Noodles, hockey nets (bottom part of the net up), and basketball nets must be set up on the playing area.

Tactical Problems:

Maintaining possession, sending and receiving the ball, attacking a goal, change of speed, change in direction, and creating space

Rules of Play:

1. Number of balls in play will vary, most likely by starting with one ball and adding a couple more as the game progresses.
2. Players are only allowed to use their feet unless the ball's last touch isn't off the floor, which would allow the player to catch it with his/her hands.
3. While having hands on ball, the players can only pivot.
4. There are 3 nets: noodles, hockey net, and basketball net.
5. Knocking down the noodles by using your feet awards 1 point.
6. Scoring in the hockey net by throwing the ball behind the 3-point line awards 2 points.
7. Lastly, scoring in the basketball net when shooting the ball in the key awards 3 points.

Safety:

Avoid collisions when running around, no body contact allowed, no kicking of the ball beyond knee level.

Variations/Progressions:

- Adding or decreasing number of balls.
- Allowing a certain number of steps with ball before releasing it.
- Restrict time allowed with possession of ball in hands.

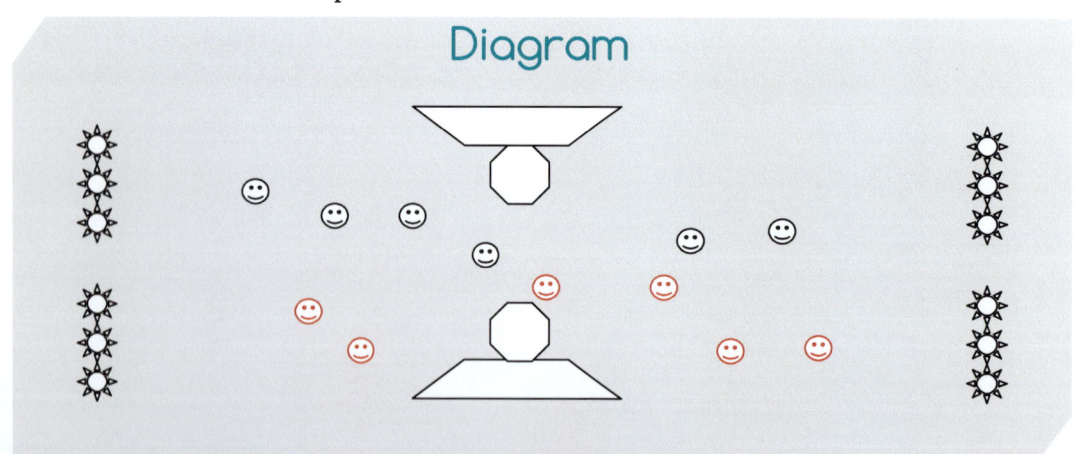

Diagram

Tchoukball

Recommended Grades:

Grades 5-6

Equipment:

Tchoukball, rebounders, pinnies, and cones.

Tactical Problems:

Accurate passing and receiving and closing down distribution options.

Rules of Play:

1. A rebounder is placed on each side of the playing area with cones creating a circular perimeter that students are forbidden to step into.
2. To score, each team attempts throw the ball on the rebounder so that the other team will not be able to catch it before it touches the ground.
3. Both teams can use either rebounder when trying to score.
4. If the ball is caught, there must be a minimum of one pass and maximum of 3 before shooting on the rebounder.
5. The person with the ball is not allowed to move.
6. Teams are not allowed to interfere with the other team's game play, whether it be blocking the ball, incepting, or defending a player.
7. The only thing that a team can do to prevent the other from scoring is to catch the ball before it touches the ground after it has hit the rebounder.

Safety:

Keep your head up to avoid getting struck by the ball or colliding with others.

Variations/Progressions:

- Allow 3 steps to the ball carrier.

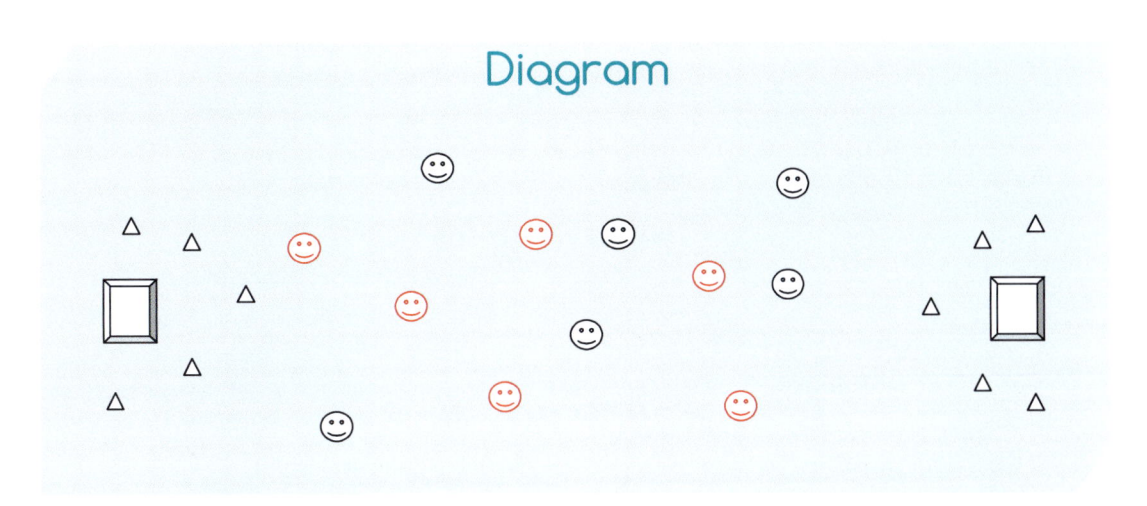

Diagram

Tennis Recovery

Recommended Grades:

Grades 5-6

Equipment:

Pinnies, cones to designate safety zones and playing area, and tennis balls.

Tactical Problems:

Traveling, dodging, footwork, change of speed, shuffle, and change in direction.

Rules of Play:

1. When the game starts, players from one team must make their way to the opposing safety zones and bring back the tennis balls to their own safety zone all while not getting touched by the opposing team's players.
2. If you get touched while in the offensive zone, you are frozen and must return the tennis ball.
3. You can only be freed if your teammate grabs your arm and brings you back to the defensive zone.
4. While they are attached to the player's arm, they cannot be frozen as they are on base.
5. If you reach the safety zone, you may come back to save a teammate, but you must return to the defensive zone without a tennis ball in your hands.
6. A time limit is usually instated.
7. The winner is the team with the most tennis balls in their safety zone or the team that has accumulated all of the tennis balls.

Safety:

Watch out for collisions when running.

Variations/Progressions:

- Adjust the playing field by making it wider and shorter or thinner and longer.
- Adding or subtracting number of tennis balls.
- Add or limit the amount of tennis balls you are allowed to grab at once.

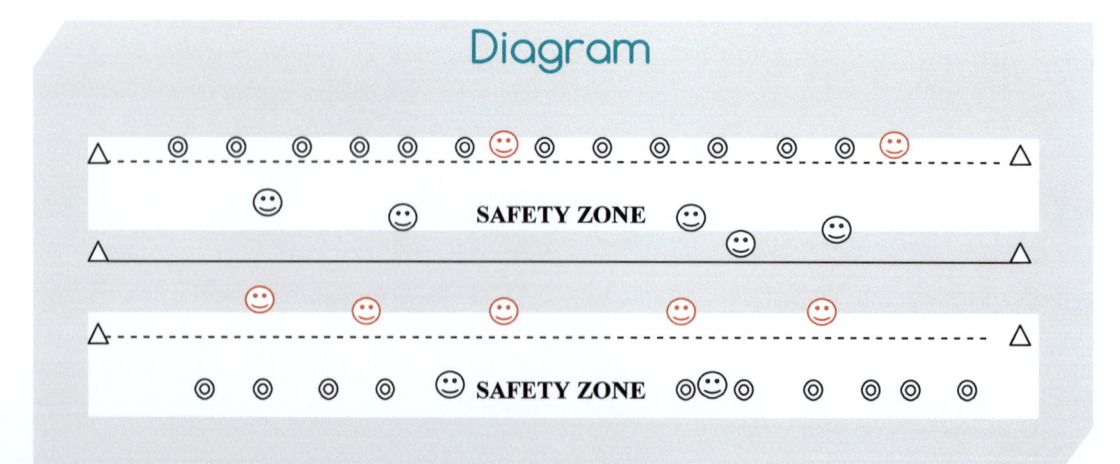

Diagram

Zig Zag Lacrosse

Recommended Grades:

Grades 5-6

Equipment:

Lacrosse sticks, balls, and cones.

Tactical Problems:

Keeping possession, accurate passing and receiving, and footwork.

Rules of Play:

1. Divide students into teams of 4 – 8.
2. A zig zag relay course will be set up for each team with one student standing next to each cone.
3. Students must roll the ball to the next player on their team.
4. That player must scoop up the ball before rolling it to the next player.
5. Students must get the ball across and back the course twice.
6. First team to do so wins.

Safety:

Be aware of the ball at all times and wear protective eyegear.

Variations/Progressions:

- Vary the distance between the cones.
- Pass the ball in the air to the next cone.
- Alternate between rolling and passing the ball

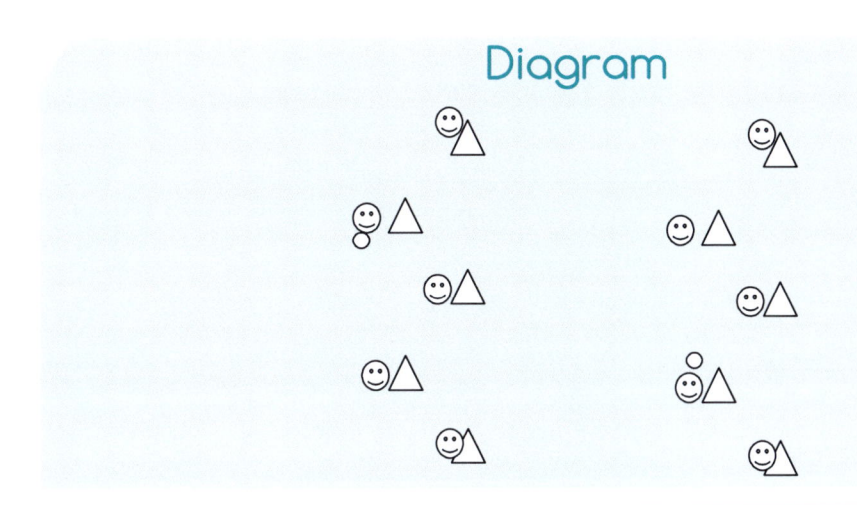

Diagram

Zone Soccer

Recommended Grades:

Grades 5-6

Equipment:

Soccer balls or soft foam balls, cones, and noodles.

Tactical Problems:

Keeping possession, sending, receiving, traveling, accurate passing and receiving, and footwork.

Rules of Play:

1. The playing area will be divided in three zones for each team.
2. The goal of the game is to be the first team to knock over the other team's noodles.
3. There will be two offensive zones where students will attempt to knock down the opposing team's noodles.
4. There will be two passing zones where students will receive the ball from the defensive zone and pass it to the offensive zone.
5. There will be two defensive zones where students will try to protect their noodles.
6. Only the defenders can use their hands for blocking.

Safety:

Keep your head up to avoid collisions and keep your eyes on the balls in play.

Variations/Progressions:

- Join zones together so that opposing team's "share" zones (i.e. defensive zone with offensive zone, passing zone with passing zone, and offensive zone with defensive zone).
- Increase the number of noodles.
- Increase the number of balls.
- Increase or decrease the size of the playing area.

Diagram

Net/Wall

Keep It Up

Recommended Grades:

Grades K-2

Equipment:

Balloons or gator skin balls.

Tactical Problems:

Moving to volley the ball, anticipating, and change in direction.

Rules of Play:

1. There is one balloon/gator skin ball in play per group.
2. The same player may not hit the balloon/gator skin ball twice as it must be passed to another teammate.
3. When the balloon/gator skin ball hits the floor, the count stops and the process must be restarted.

Safety:

Call for the ball/balloon to avoid collisions among students.

Variations/Progressions:

- Hitting the ball with different parts of the body.
- Adding more balloons/gator skin balls.
- Change the type of ball used.
- Decrease or increase the number of players in one group

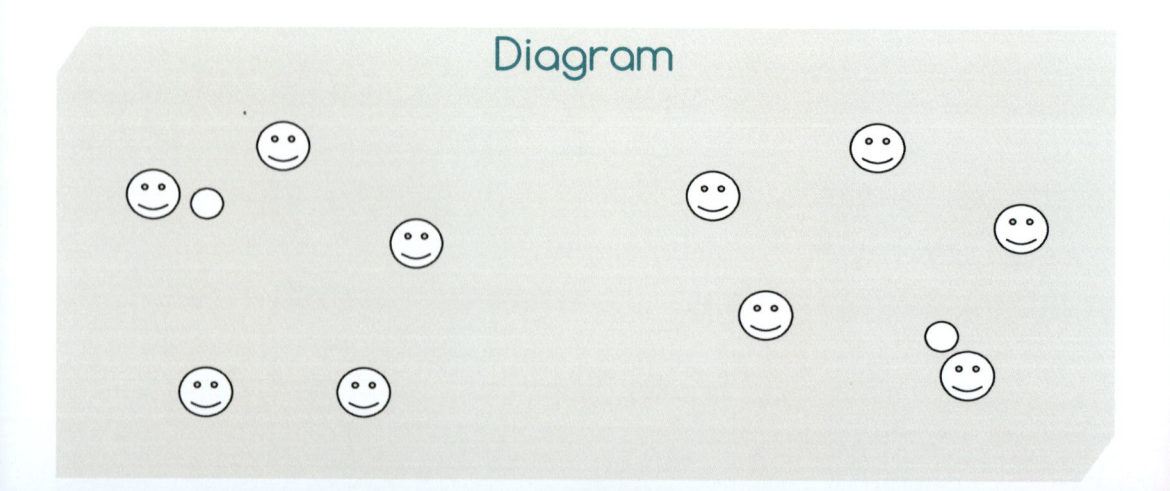

Diagram

One Bounce

Recommended Grades:

Grades 1-6

Equipment:

Bouncing ball.

Tactical Problems:

Catching on bounce, hitting with a specific force, placing the ball farthest away from player(s), and anticipation.

Rules of Play:

1. Divide students into groups of 2 or 4 (1 V 1 or 2 V 2 games).
2. Define the boundaries of the playing area and a dividing line between the two players or teams.
3. The goal of the game is to accumulate the most points by landing the ball on the opponent's side of the court.
4. Players must first bounce the ball on their own side before crossing the line.
5. The opposing player must catch the ball before it bounces on his/her side.
6. Players must bounce the ball back immediately from where they caught it.

Safety:

Ensure proper spacing among groups.

Variations/Progressions:

- Make the game cooperative in nature.
- Use cones to create a neutral zone in which the ball may not land in.
- Add a net.

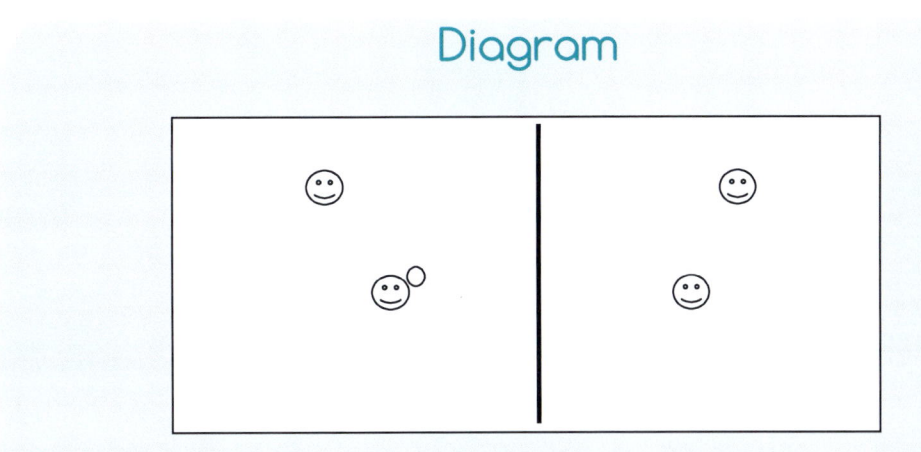

Diagram

Line Game

Recommended Grades:
Grades 3-4

Equipment:
Cones and volleyballs.

Tactical Problems:
Catching on bounce and volley, placing ball farthest away from player, anticipating, returning object and keeping it in bounds, placing ball close to boundary lines.

Rules of Play:
1. Each pair will have a volleyball.
2. There will be many 1 V 1 games going on at the same time all within similar boundaries using the same line on the court (center line).
3. The rules consist of the volleyball having to: bounce once on own side of the line, must go through cones, it cannot bounce on own side when receiving the ball, and the bounce must be done higher than the hip.
4. A point is scored when the opponent is unable to catch the ball and lands in the opponent's side of the line, if the player fails to pass the ball through the cones/bounce it once on their own side of the line, or shoots the ball out of bounds.

Safety:
Be aware of the other games going on around you.

Variations/Progressions:
- Designate a zone that the ball cannot touch rather than having just a line.
- Allowing an additional bounce, but removing the possibility of catching the ball.
- Change the type of ball used

Diagram

4 Corners

Recommended Grades:

Grades 3 – 6

Equipment:

Timers, badminton rackets, and cones.

Tactical Problems:

Change in direction and footwork.

Rules of Play:

1. Divide students into pairs.
2. This game can be played with or without badminton rackets.
3. Each pair will have their own square playing area with 5 cones – one on each corner and one in the middle.
4. One player starts in the middle cone in the ready position.
5. He/she will have to touch each of the 4 cones – each time he/she touches one of the cones, he/she must return to the middle cone before going for another.
6. Players must always be facing forward.
7. Partner will keep track of the time it takes to complete the task.

Safety:

Ensure there is sufficient space between groups.

Variations/Progressions:

- Using a badminton racket, the partner tosses a birdie to be hit each time the player reaches one of the 4 cones.
- Use one side of the badminton court.
- Use half of one side of the badminton court.
- Partner points at which corner for the player to shuffle to.

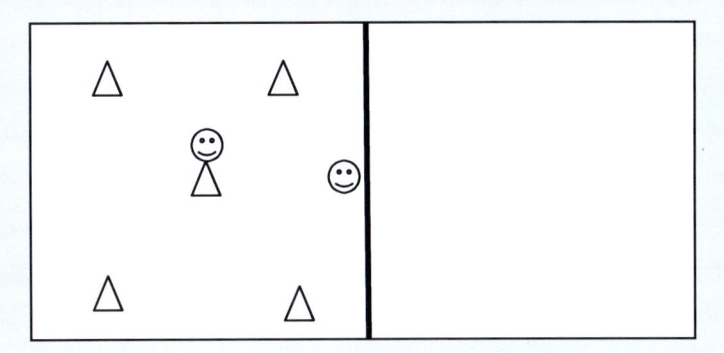

Diagram

Ball of Fire

Recommended Grades:
Grades 3-6

Equipment:
Volleyballs.

Tactical Problems:
Sending, receiving, balance, footwork, and hitting with a specific force.

Rules of Play:
1. Stand in a circle, at least five feet from any other player.
2. The ball is volleyed, using the set pass, to any other player on the circle.
3. This person MAY catch the ball and then volley to another player or volley it right away.
4. As the ball is being volleyed and caught, the instructor blows a whistle. The player who is in possession of the ball must sit down in the center of the circle while the others continue to volley, until one person remains.
5. Players in the middle of the circle may interact with the ball if it comes to them.

Safety:
Keep your distance from your group and keep your eye on the ball.

Variations/Progressions:
- Instead of volleying, use bumping.
- Introduce more than one "fire" ball in play to speed things up.
- For younger players, use beach balls, rubber balls, etc.

Diagram

Ballnis

Recommended Grades:

Grades 3-6

Equipment:

Cones and soft foam balls.

Tactical Problems:

Serving and receiving serve, hitting the ball in relation to the body, hitting with a specific force, placing ball close to boundary lines.

Rules of Play:

1. Students will play 1 V 1 cooperative games in a designated area marked by the cones.
2. The game begins with a "serve".
3. One player starts with the ball, bounces it once on his/her own side of the playing area, and then strikes it with an open palm towards the opponent's side of the court.
4. The receiving player will then attempt to return the bouncing ball by striking it in the same fashion towards the other player's court.
5. Count how many hits can be made within the 2 players without having to start over.

Safety:

Ensure students are not striking the ball with excessive force.

Variations/Progressions:

- Allow overhand hitting.
- Turn it into a competitive game.
- Create 2 V 2 games.
- Use different balls.

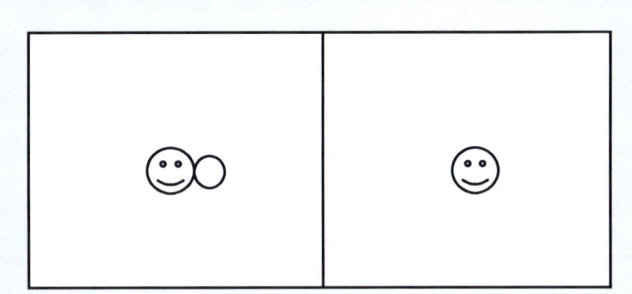

Diagram

Balls Away

Recommended Grades:
Grades 3-6

Equipment:
Volleyball nets and beach balls.

Tactical Problems:
Throwing, catching, hitting the ball in relation to the body, and hitting with a specific force.

Rules of Play:
1. Students will be divided into 2 equal teams on both sides of the volleyball court.
2. Each player will have a beach ball.
3. On the teacher's signal, the students will hit or throw their balls over to the other team's side of the court.
4. When a ball crosses the net, students can hit it directly back over to the net or pick a ball up and throw it over.
5. After a certain time limit is reached, the teacher will end the game and the winning team will be the one with the least amount of beach balls on their side of the court.

Safety:
Be aware of all the beach balls in play.

Variations/Progressions:
- Add more beach balls as the game goes on.
- Balls have to be kicked over.

Diagram

Birdie Down

Recommended Grades:

Grades 3-6

Equipment:

Badminton nets and birdies.

Tactical Problems:

Footwork, throwing, catching, placing the birdie farthest away from player(s), and anticipation.

Rules of Play:

1. Divide students into pairs.
2. Each pair will occupy one half of a badminton court with 1 shuttle in hand.
3. The goal of the game is to score points by having both birdies touching the floor of the opponent's side of the court at the same time.
4. Thus, this means throwing the 2nd birdie and landing it on the floor before the opponent has time to pick up the 1st.
5. Players must throw immediately from the spot where they caught the birdie.
6. Hitting the net or throwing the birdie out of bounds results in a point for the other player.
7. Play until a certain time limit or score limit is reached.

Safety:

Adequate distance between pairs.

Variations/Progressions:

- 4 birdies per player placed on the floor where players can only pick up one at a time – player with the least amount of birdies on their side after the time limit expires wins.
- 2 V 2 games – score a point

Diagram

Blanket Volley

Recommended Grades:

Grades 3-6

Equipment:

Volleyball nets, volleyballs, and blankets.

Tactical Problems:

Serving and receiving serve, throwing, catching, placing ball farthest away from player(s), hitting the ball with a specific force, and anticipation.

Rules of Play:

1. Students will be divided into teams of 4.
2. Each team will receive a blanket – each player will hold one of the 4 corners.
3. One team will start with the volleyball placed in the middle of the blanket and will serve it towards the other team.
4. The receiving team must catch the volleyball with the blanket and toss the ball back to the serving team with only the use of the blanket.
5. Play until a certain time limit or score limit is reached.

Safety:

Be careful that students don't trip and fall and communicate amongst each other in order to move in the same direction.

Variations/Progressions:

- Use a beach ball.
- Lower the net.
- Increase or decrease the size of the playing area.

Diagram

Foot Volley

Recommended Grades:

Grades 3-6

Equipment:

Volleyball or badminton nets and beach balls.

Tactical Problems:

Hitting the ball in relation to the body, hitting the ball with a specific force, balance, and returning object and keeping it in bounds.

Rules of Play:

1. Students will be divided into teams of 6.
2. Played on either a volleyball or badminton playing area, 2 teams of 6 will begin in a volleyball formation.
3. Players must stay in the crab position during the game and must hit the ball in such a position.
4. Three hits with feet or knees are allowed in order to get the ball over the net.
5. One bounce is allowed.
6. Rotation is the same as in volleyball.
7. Play until a certain time or score limit is reached.

Safety:

Make sure students do not step on one another's hands.

Variations/Progressions:

- No bounce permitted.
- Decrease the number of players per court.
- Allow the head to be used.

Diagram

Human Net

Recommended Grades:

Grades 3-6

Equipment:

Cones and volleyball or soft foam ball.

Tactical Problems:

Serving and receiving serve, hitting with a specific force, placing ball farthest away from player(s), and anticipation.

Rules of Play:

1. Divide students into pairs.
2. On each playing surface, there will be 3 teams.
3. One team will quite literally form the net with their arms outstretched upwards while the other 2 teams take their respective sides.
4. The first team will serve the ball (underhand only) towards the second team's side of the court.
5. A player from the second team must catch the ball, pass to his/her partner, and he/she will have to serve it over to the other side (underhand only).
6. Points are scored when the ball lands on the opposition's side of the court.
7. The net players must always stand on the centre line and attempt to block the serve.
8. Teams are rotated after 5 points or if the net team blocks a serve.

Safety:

Ensure that there is sufficient space between games.

Variations/Progressions:

- Increase the number of players on each team.
- Increase or decrease the size of the playing area.
- Enforce bumping/volleying skills

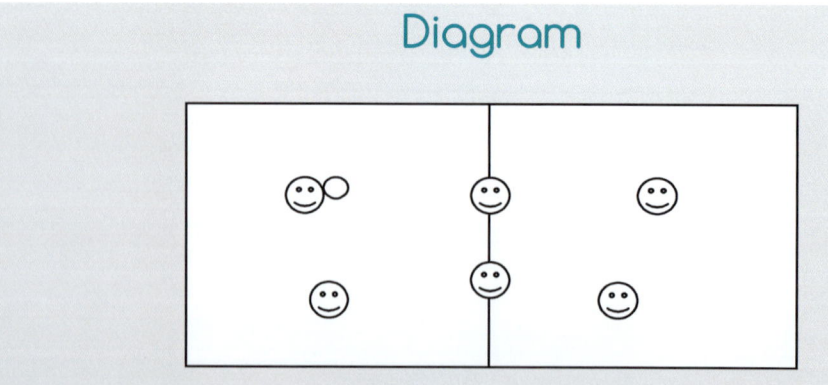

Diagram

Net Movement

Recommended Grades:

Grades 3-6

Equipment:

Beanbags and polyspots.

Tactical Problems:

Footwork, throwing and catching, placing ball farthest away from player, and anticipation.

Rules of Play:

1. Students are divided into pairs.
2. Each pair will have a beanbag and 4 polyspots positioned in a diamond formation.
3. One player with the beanbag will stand at the top of the diamond while the catcher will stand on the bottom of the diamond.
4. The tosser has to throw the beanbag underhand and attempts to make it land on 1 of the 2 polyspots on the sides of the diamond.
5. If the tosser hits the spot, he/she will get 1 point.
6. If the catcher makes 3 consecutive catches, he/she will get 1 point.

Safety:

Ensure there is enough space between pairs.

Variations/Progressions:

- Increase or decrease the size of the diamond to help the tosser or catcher accordingly.
- Add a 3rd target polyspot.

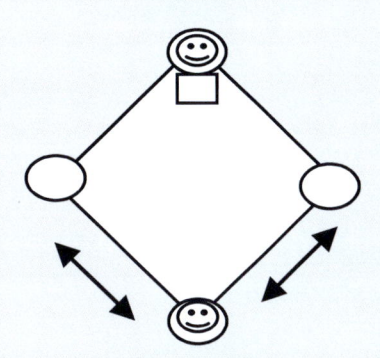

Diagram

Pickle This

Recommended Grades:

Grades 3-6

Equipment:

Cones, paddles, and wiffle balls.

Tactical Problems:

Hitting the ball in relation to the body, hitting with a specific force, placing ball farthest away from player(s), placing ball close to boundary lines, and anticipation.

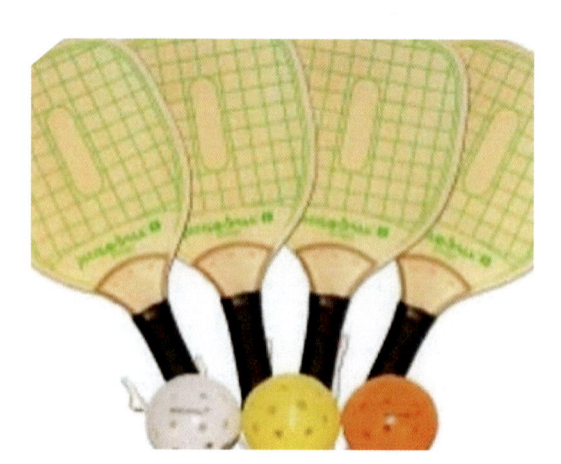

Rules of Play:

1. Games will be comprised of 1 V 1 matchups.
2. Using four cones, design a long and narrow court – additionally, create a net zone in the middle where the ball may not bounce (or use a low net).
3. Players will each have a paddle.
4. Goal of the game is to hit the wiffle ball on the opposition's side of the court so that the opponent cannot return it before it bounces twice.
5. Alternate serves (underhand) and play until a certain time limit or score limit is reached.

Safety:

Ensure students don't try to continuously "smash" the ball and encourage accuracy.

Variations/Progressions:

- Only allow one bounce.
- Change the equipment used.
- Increase the number of players.
- Use a short and wide court

Diagram

"Plus One"

Recommended Grades:
Grades 3-6

Equipment:
Volleyball net and volleyballs.

Tactical Problems:
Serving and receiving serve, hitting the ball in relation to the body, hitting the ball with a specific force, and positioning on court.

Rules of Play:
1. A player serves the ball over the net.
2. The receiving team must now play the ball twice before they may return the ball.
3. The serving team must now play the ball three times before they are allowed to return the ball over the net.
4. Play continues as each team forces the other side to "plus one" the previous achievement.
5. Players may not play the ball twice in succession.

Safety:
Keep your head up to avoid collisions and be aware of the ball.

Variations/Progressions:
- Allow students to catch the ball before volleying/bumping it back to one of your teammates.
- Allow the ball to bounce once between passes

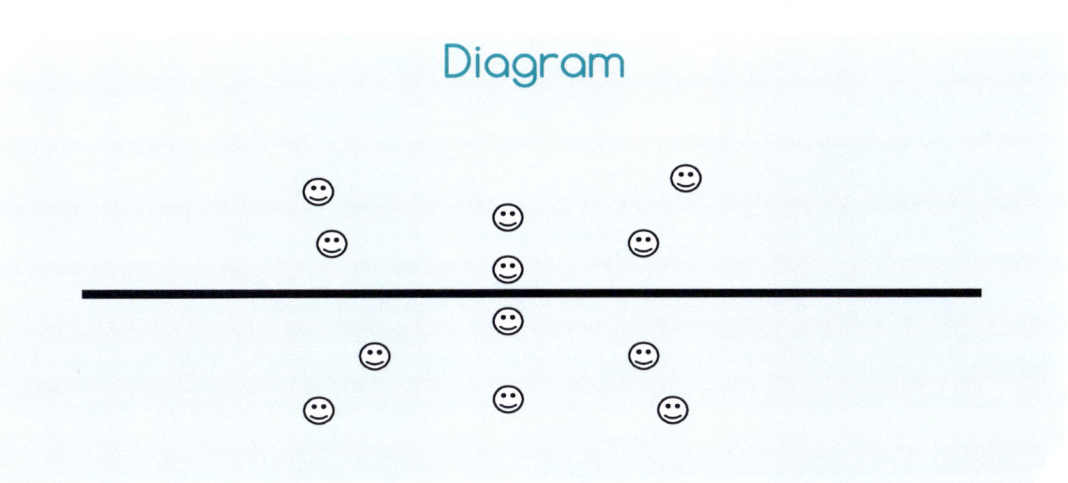

Diagram

Squish

Recommended Grades:

Grades 3-6

Equipment:

Cones and volleyballs.

Tactical Problems:

Shooting for angles, placing ball farthest away from player, placing ball close to boundary lines, anticipating, and returning object/keeping it in bounds.

Rules of Play:

1. Each pair will have a ball.
2. Both players will find a space near a wall where they will mark out a square area directly in front of the wall with a line that divides the square into two sides.
3. One player stands on each side of the court.
4. The players will use their hands to propel the ball to the wall in order to make it bounce back to the opposition's side of the square.
5. The ball must be returned before the 2nd bounce and must once again hit the wall and into the designated area or else a point is awarded to the other player.

Safety:

Be alert of the other groups around you and always be aware of the ball.

Variations/Progressions:

- Change the type of ball used.
- Create 2 V 2 games in which teammates switch alternatively.
- Make the square wider rather than longer to encourage shooting for angles rather than power.

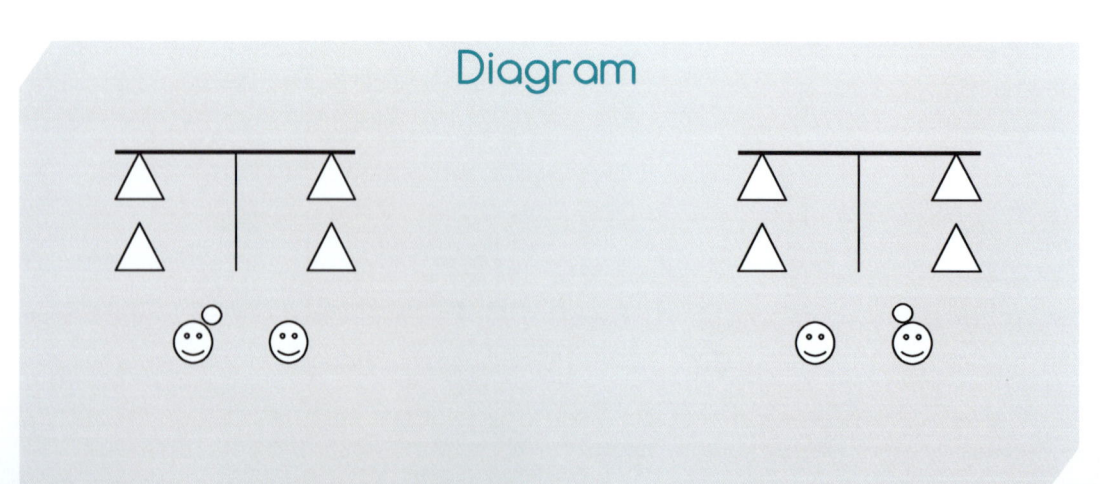

Diagram

4 Cone Grid, 1 Open Spot

Recommended Grades:

Grades 5-6

Equipment:

Cones and volleyballs.

Tactical Problems:

Catching on bounce and volley, hitting the ball in relation to the body, placing ball close to boundary lines, anticipating, and returning object/keeping it in bounds.

Rules of Play:

1. Each group of 3 will have a volleyball.
2. Each player will take a spot next to one of the 4 cones, leaving one cone vacant.
3. Players must then bump or set the ball towards that vacant cone where a receiving player must move towards the open cone to receive it.
4. The volleyball is allowed to bounce once.
5. This game forces players to continually move, pass, and receive.
6. Preferably, for everyone to receive equal playing time and avoiding collisions, a pattern should be established so that each player knows who's expected to be the player to move to the vacant cone to receive the ball.

Safety:

Keep your head up to avoid collisions and keep your eyes on the ball.

Variations/Progressions:

- Add a 5th cone so that there are 2 open spots for the 3 players.
- No bounces allowed.
- Calling out names of the person they are sending it to.

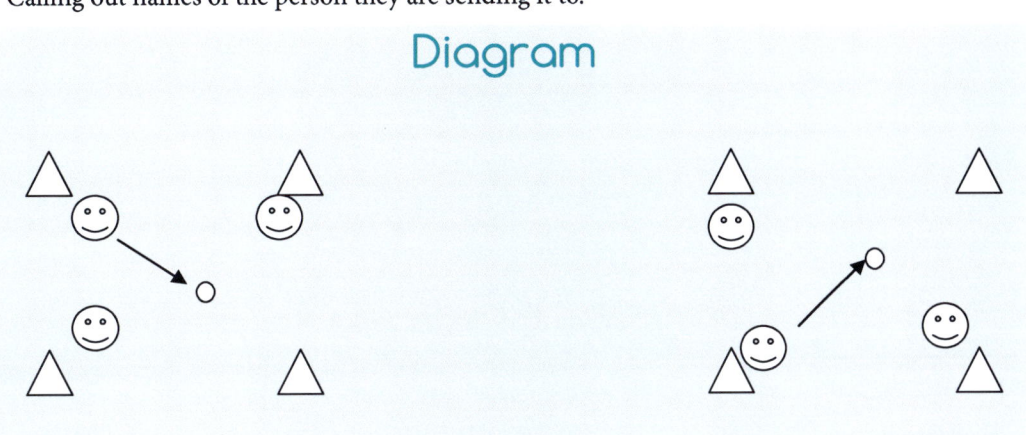

Diagram

Badminton 4s

Recommended Grades:

Grades 5-6

Equipment:

Badminton nets, birdies, and rackets.

Tactical Problems:

Serving and receiving serve, hitting the birdie in relation to the body, hitting the birdie with a specific force, placing ball furthest from player(s), and anticipation.

Rules of Play:

1. Divide students into pairs.
2. Set up badminton nets so that there are 4 courts – 2 players in each quarter.
3. Designate numbers 1 (head), 2, 3, and 4 to each quarter of the court.
4. #1 serves first to any of the other 3 courts.
5. If a team misses a shot, they will move to the #4 spot and everyone else will rotate accordingly.
6. Play continues until a certain time limit is reached.

Safety:

Ensure students are alert at all times.

Variations/Progressions:

- Add a 2nd birdie.
- Teams earn points when the others miss their shot.

Diagram

Castle Game

Recommended Grades:

Grades 5-6

Equipment:

Cones and volleyballs

Tactical Problems:

Hitting with specific force, placing ball close to boundary lines, and anticipate where opponent(s) will return object.

Rules of Play:

1. Each pair will have a volleyball.
2. There will be many 1 V 1 games going on at the same time all within similar boundaries placing the cone in the center of an imaginary circle.
3. Players will take turns bumping and setting the ball while attempting to hit the target before their opponent does.
4. The rules are that the ball must be bumped/set high in the air so that the ball will bounce off the floor and above head height and the ball may only bounce once before being contacted again by the opponent.
5. A point is scored when the ball hits the cone placed in the center.

Safety:

Be aware of the ball at all times and be careful of others pairs around you.

Variations/Progressions:

- Introduce 2 V 2 games.
- Force players to alternate between bumping and setting.

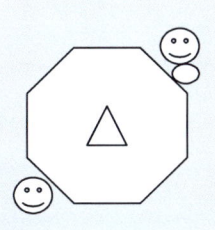

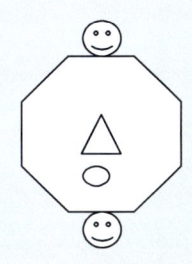

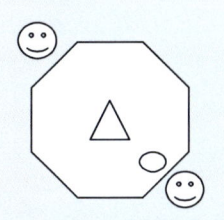

Diagram

Champ

Recommended Grades:

Grades 5-6

Equipment:

Badminton nets, badminton rackets, and birdies.

Tactical Problems:

Serving and returning serve, hitting the birdie in relation to the body, hitting with a specific force, placing ball farthest away from player(s), and anticipation.

Rules of Play:

1. Divide students into small groups.
2. One player will be designated as the "Champ" and will begin serving while one player on the other side of the court will be the challenger (more challengers will be lined up off court).
3. After the service, a rally will begin using the singles boundary lines of badminton.
4. If the Champ wins, he/she stays as the Champ and the challenger goes to the back of the line.
5. If the challenger wins, he/she becomes the new Champ and the former Champ goes to the back of the challenger line.
6. Each time a Champ wins a rally, he/she gains a point.
7. Whoever has the most points at the end of the time limit wins the game.

Safety:

Ensure that the students from the challenger's line keep a safe distance from the action.

Variations/Progressions:

- Play doubles.
- Create a maximum # of hits that either the Champ or the challenger can perform before eliminating the opposing player.

Diagram

Come In

Recommended Grades:

Grades 5-6

Equipment:

Tennis net and tennis rackets.

Tactical Problems:

Serving and returning serve, hitting the ball in relation to the body, hitting with a specific force, and placing the ball farthest from player(s).

Rules of Play:

1. Divide students into pairs – 1 V 1 games.
2. Player 1 will begin the game by either serving or simply starting a rally with a simple hit from behind the baseline.
3. Player 2 will return the serve and the rally shall commence.
4. Player 2 has the opportunity to call out "Come in" at any time he/she desires.
5. When "Come in" is called, player 1 must run to the net and play the next ball before returning to the baseline.
6. Player 2 can only call this once during a rally.
7. Swap roles for each point.

Safety:

Ensure balls are not being hit too hard and be aware of loose balls.

Variations/Progressions:

- Allow for the "Come in" shout to be called more than once in a rally.
- Give both players the opportunity to call "Come in".
- No lobs allowed.

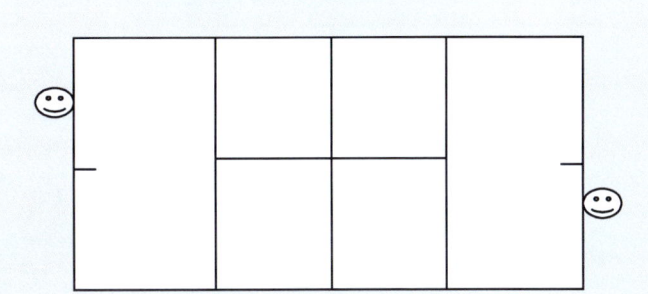

Diagram

Frisminton

Recommended Grades:

Grades 5-6

Equipment:

Frisbees and badminton nets.

Tactical Problems:

Throwing, catching, placing frisbee farthest away from player(s), and anticipation.

Rules of Play:

1. Divide students into pairs.
2. Each badminton court will contain a badminton net and comprise of doubles games (2 V 2).
3. The goal of the game is to send the frisbee over the net so that it drops on the opponents' side of the court.
4. Serves are done from behind the baseline.
5. Play until a certain time limit or score limit is reached..

Safety:

Ensure that everyone is alert of the frisbees in play and no one launches a frisbee with no sense of direction.

Variations/Progressions:

- Add or reduce the number of players on each side.
- Reduce the playing area.
- Remove the net.
- Allow 3 passes amongst teammates before launching it over.

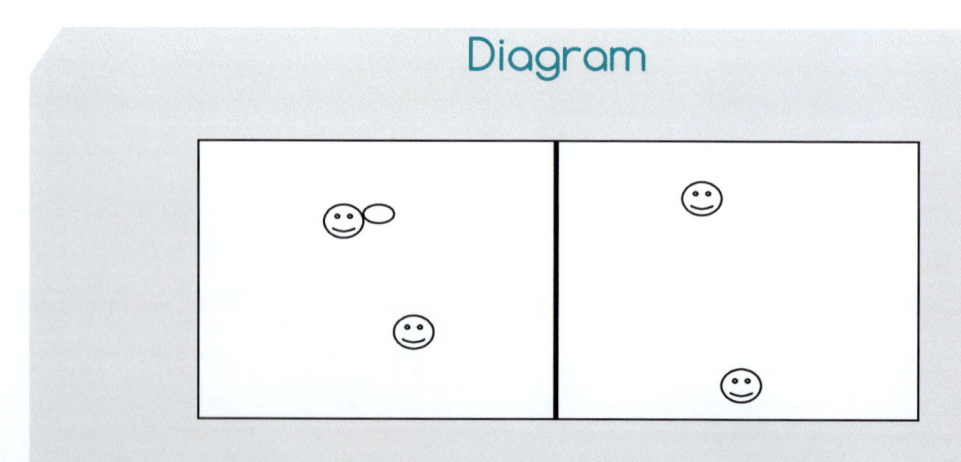

Diagram

Go Badminton

Recommended Grades:
Grades 5-6

Equipment:
Badminton nets, racquets, and birdies.

Tactical Problems:
Maintaining a rally, anticipating, placing birdie farthest away from player and close to boundary lines, and footwork.

Rules of Play:
1. Set up a doubles game in each court (four per court).
2. Extra players will be on the sides/outside of the playing area working on different skills.
3. On the instructors signal (usually every two minutes), students will rotate one spot clockwise.
4. Continue this rotation for as long as desired.

Safety:
Keep your head up to avoid receiving the birdie in the face and to avoid collisions with your doubles partner.

Variations/Progressions:
- Vary the time between rotations.
- Vary the skills that the outside students should be working on

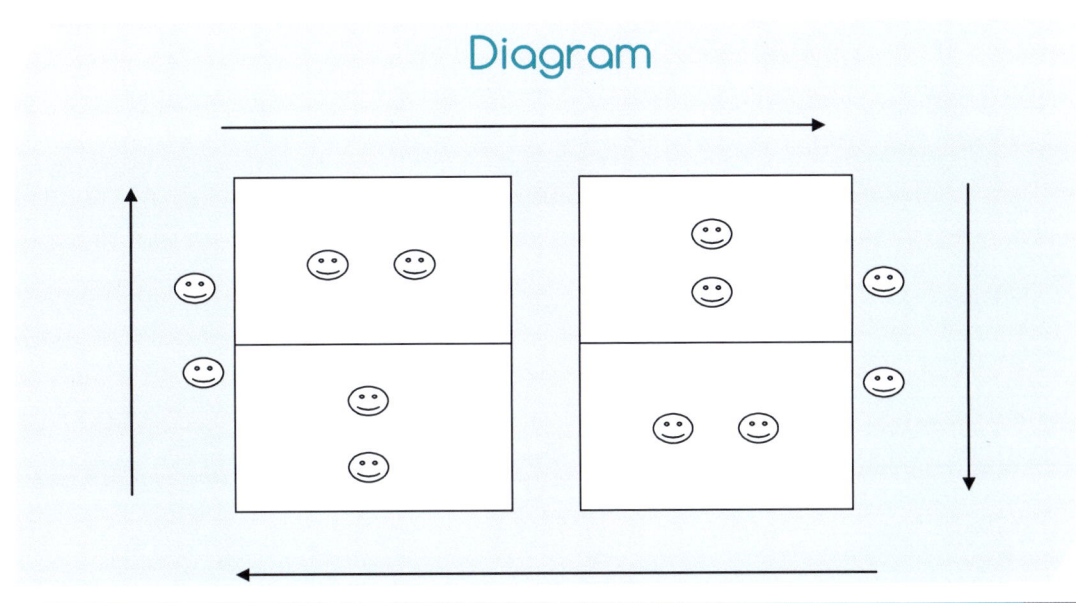

Diagram

Here Birdie

Recommended Grades:

Grades 5-6

Equipment:

Badminton rackets, birdies, and hula-hoops

Tactical Problems:

Hitting a birdie in relation to the body, hitting with a specific force, footwork, placing birdie farthest away from player, and anticipation.

Rules of Play:

1. Students will be divided into pairs.
2. One player will have 3 birdies and the other will have the racket.
3. The player with the racket will stand between 2 hula-hoops placed on both sides of him/her.
4. Player with the birdies will stand just a few feet away.
5. The tosser (underarm throw) will attempt to land the birdie inside either of the 2 hula-hoops.
6. The receiver will attempt to defend the hula-hoops by returning the toss and the birdie to the tosser.
7. Receiver has 3 lives – play for a short time limit (60 – 120 seconds).

Safety:

Provide adequate spacing between pairings.

Variations/Progressions:

- Increase the distance between the hula-hoops and the base position.
- Use polyspots instead to make it more difficult on the tosser.
- Receiver must "hold" the birdie on the racket before returning it to the tosser (i.e. birdie has to stay on top of the racket).

Diagram

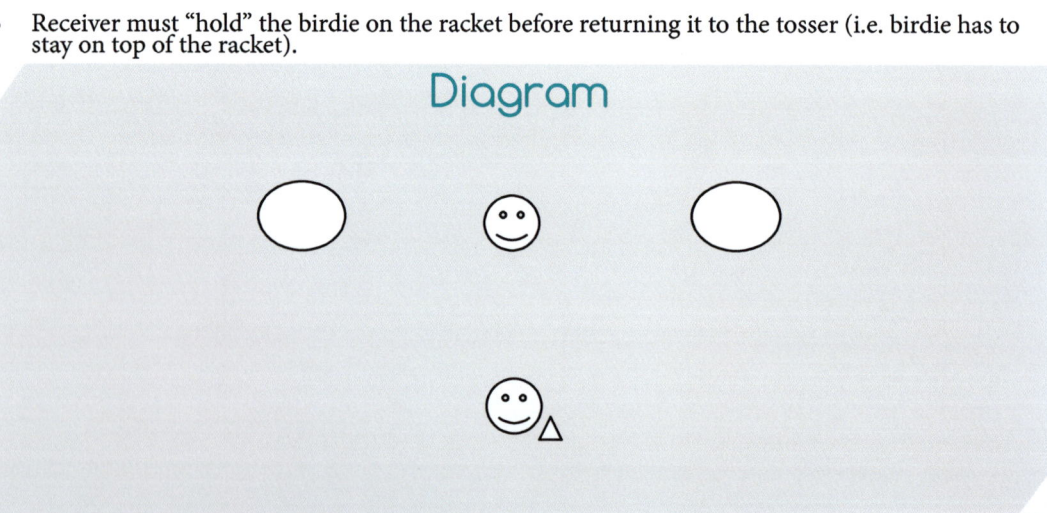

Hot Potato

Recommended Grades:

Grades 5-6

Equipment:

Volleyballs and volleyball net.

Tactical Problems:

Hitting the ball in relation to the body, hitting with a specific force, and moving to volley position at the net.

Rules of Play:

1. Divide students into pairs.
2. Playing area will consist of half the volleyball court per pair and in front of the 3 meter line.
3. Students will have to pass the ball using the overheard pass (volley) to their counterpart.
4. When the teacher calls out "Freeze!" or whistles, the point is given to the player if the ball is on the other side of the court.
5. Play until a certain time limit is reached.

Safety:

Ensure that students are aware of any loose balls on the playing area.

Variations/Progressions:

- Combine courts – 2 V 2 situation.
- Increase or decrease the length of the playing area

Diagram

In The Hoop

Recommended Grades:

Grades 5-6

Equipment:

Volleyballs and hula-hoops.

Tactical Problems:

Footwork, hitting the ball in relation to the body, hitting with a specific force, and anticipation.

Rules of Play:

1. Divide students into groups of 3.
2. Each group will have a hula-hoop positioned in the middle of all 3 of the players.
3. Each student takes a turn at landing the ball inside of the hoop (volley or bump).
4. Only one bounce is allowed – the bounce inside the hula-hoop.
5. Cooperative game – count the number of consecutive hits.

Safety:

Ensure that there is enough space between groups.

Variations/Progressions:

- Turn it competitive – students have to call out another student's name in the group when the initial player hits the ball and the called out player has to be able to keep the ball in play.

- Use cones to designate the "One Bounce" area

Diagram

Kick Over

Recommended Grades:

Grades 5-6

Equipment:

Badminton nets and soft foam balls.

Tactical Problems:

Serving and receiving serve, footwork, hitting with a specific force, catching, placing ball farthest away from player(s), and anticipation.

Rules of Play:

1. Divide students into groups of 3 onto a badminton court with a badminton net – 2 versus 1 games.
2. The sole player starts the game by sending the ball over the net with his/her feet.
3. The team of two must first receive the ball and then set up the other teammate, who must immediately kick the ball over the net.
4. The team of two is awarded a point if the sent ball bounces on the court within the boundaries of the court.
5. The lone player gains a point in one of the two ways: 1) He/she catches the ball before it lands on his/her side of the court, 2) The team of two fails to send the ball over the net within the boundaries of the court.

Safety:

Ensure students do not kick the ball for power and aim for accuracy.

Variations/Progressions:

- Bump and set with hands instead of feet.
- Add more players on each side of the court.
- Eliminate the net

Diagram

King's Court

Recommended Grades:
Grades 5-6

Equipment:
Volleyball and a volleyball net.

Tactical Problems:
Serving and receiving serve, balance, hitting the ball in relation to the body, placing ball furthest from the player, and anticipation.

Rules of Play:
1. Set up the court so that there are two teams facing one another with the other team(s) sitting on the side or practicing their volleyball skills.
2. Play up to 7, 11, 21 or set a time limit of 5 minutes.
3. The winner stays on the court while the losing team heads off the court.
4. The team on the side replaces them and they start a new a game.
5. Winning team always stays on the court while losing team substitutes out.

Safety:
Keep your head up to avoid collisions and call for the ball.

Variations/Progressions:
- Introduce a limit – after a certain number of consecutive wins, even the winning team must come off.
- Modify the number of touches permitted.

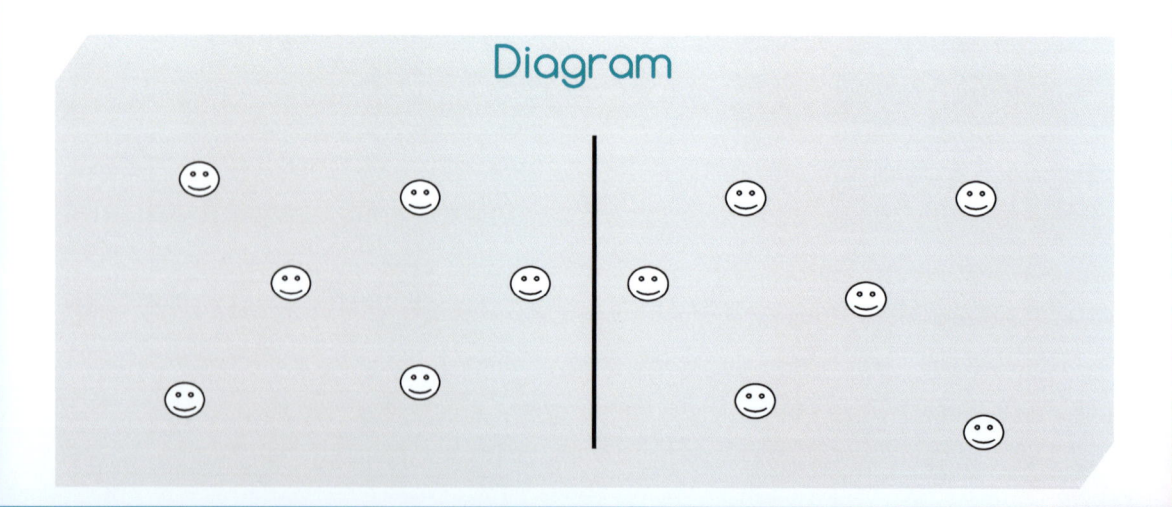

Diagram

Landing

Recommended Grades:

Grades 5-6

Equipment:

Hula-hoops or polyspots, badminton nets, birdies, and badminton rackets.

Tactical Problems:

Footwork, hitting the birdie in relation to the body, hitting the birdie with a specific force, returning object and keeping it in bounds, and anticipation.

Rules of Play:

1. Students are divided into pairs.
2. One player will be one side of the badminton court with 3 hula-hoop (left, middle, and right) while holding birdies in one hand.
3. The other player will have a racket on the other side of the court.
4. Players holding the birdie have to move towards one of their hoops before tossing the birdie over the net.
5. The hitter attempts to return the birdie and land it on the opponent's end of the court – more specifically, into the hula-hoops.
6. The thrower attempts to catch the birdie.
7. 1 point awarded to the thrower for landing a birdie on the opponent's side of the court, 1 point awarded to the hitter for returning the birdie and landing it on the opponent's side of the court, and 3 points for landing it in the hoop.

Safety:

Adequate spacing between pairs.

Variations/Progressions:

- Landing the birdie in a hula-hoop is an automatic victory.
- Increase or decrease the number of hoops in play.
- Use polyspots instead.

Diagram

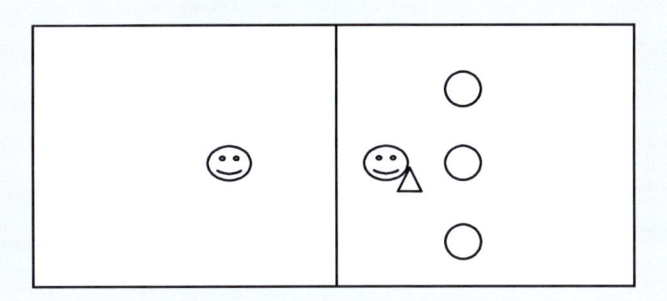

Life of 5

Recommended Grades:

Grades 5-6

Equipment:

Badminton nets, badminton rackets, and birdies.

Tactical Problems:

Serving and receiving serve, hitting the birdie in relation to the body, hitting with a specific force, placing ball farthest away from player(s), and anticipation.

Rules of Play:

1. Divide students into small groups.
2. On each court, select either a student or the teacher to be the leader of the activity.
3. On one side of the court, there will be the leader and on the other side, the line of players.
4. The leader begins with a shot and the first player in line is expected to return it.
5. If he/she fails to return it, he/she loses 1 of his/her 5 lives.
6. If he/she returns it, he/she goes to the back of the line.
7. If he/she returns it and the leader is unable to return it, he/she earns an extra life.
8. The leader does not simply serve a shot for each player – he/she will start the game with a serve, but continue to rally the birdie, so quick changes to the back of the line need to be made.
9. Winner is the one who is the last one standing.

Safety:

Ensure that the line is a reasonable distance away from the action.

Variations/Progressions:

- Reduce the number of lives.
- Play using half the court.

Diagram

Line or Square

Recommended Grades:

Grades 5-6

Equipment:

Volleyballs and polyspots.

Tactical Problems:

Serving and receiving serve, hitting the ball in relation to the body, hitting with a specific force, returning object and keeping it in bounds, and anticipation.

Rules of Play:

1. Students will play 1 V 1 games with a partner.
2. Each pair will create a "square" with 4 polyspots – 1 in each corner.
3. One student will stand on the imaginary line between 2 polyspots and the other student will mirror the same thing.
4. One player begins by tossing the ball towards one of the opponent's polyspots.
5. Players will attempt to return the ball with a bump or volley.
6. Ball must stay in bounds of the 4 polyspots.
7. 1 point is awarded if the opponent is unable to return the ball within the square and 4 points are awarded if a ball lands on one of the opponent's polyspots.

Safety:

Ensure there is enough space between pairs of students.

Variations/Progressions:

- Increase or decrease the size of the playing area.
- Add more polyspots to defend and attack.
- 4 players per square – introduce more polyspots.

Diagram

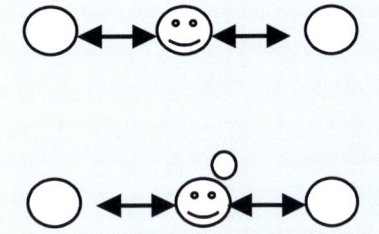

Modified Badminton

Recommended Grades:

Grades 5-6

Equipment:

Badminton nets, badminton rackets, and birdies.

Tactical Problems:

Serving and receiving serve, hitting the birdie in relation to the body, hitting with a specific force, and placing birdie close to boundary lines.

Rules of Play:

1. Divide students into pairs – 1 V 1 games.
2. Regular singles game of badminton, but with an exception to the rules.
3. To score a point, players must either hit a clear that lands in the back tramline or a drop shot that lands before the service line.
4. If a shot lands anywhere in the midcourt area, it is a point for the opposing player.
5. Play until 21 points or until a certain time limit is reached.

Safety:

Spacing between groups.

Variations/Progressions:

- Play doubles, but using the side tramlines instead of the back tramline.
- Play using half the court.

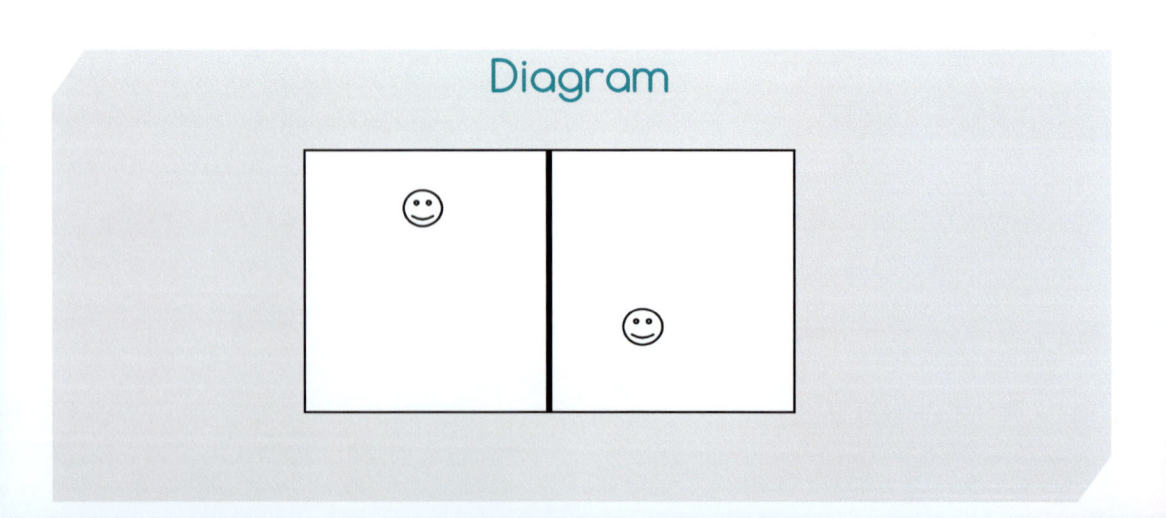

Diagram

Move It

Recommended Grades:

Grades 5-6

Equipment:

Volleyball nets and volleyballs.

Tactical Problems:

Serving and receiving serve, hitting the ball in relation to the body, hitting with a specific force, placing ball farthest away from player(s), and returning object and keeping it in bounds.

Rules of Play:

1. Divide students into 2 teams of 6.
2. One team will set up in a regular back and front volleyball formation while the other will set up in a straight line on the other end of the court.
3. The team in the straight line will start as they are the serving team.
4. The other team must return the serve – if they are unsuccessful, serving team earns a point and that same person serves again.
5. If the other team does return the serve, no point is scored and the serving player goes in back of the service line.
6. Game continues until each person has served 2 – 3 times.
7. Teams switch roles.
8. Winning team is the one with the most points after each team has served once.

Safety:

Keep an eye for loose balls.

Variations/Progressions:

- Have 2 serves at once.

- Receiving team earns a point for using 3 hits to return the ball. ncrease or decrease the number of noodles.

Diagram

Blind Parachute Volleyball

Recommended Grades:

Grades 5-6

Equipment:

Soft ball (beach ball or gator skin ball), volleyball net, and parachute.

Tactical Problems:

Serving and receiving serve, hitting with specific force, anticipating, and returning object/keeping it in bounds.

Rules of Play:

1. Set up a volleyball net with a large parachute covering most of the net so that the two teams cannot see each other on the opposite side of the court.
2. Start the game with a serve, either by striking the ball or throwing it.
3. Teams are allowed to catch the ball or hit the ball in while in the air.
4. Before the ball can go over the net, teams must make 3 passes to each other.
5. Players are not allowed to take steps with the ball.
6. After each point, players must rotate their position on the court.
7. A point is scored if: a team fails to hit the volleyball over the net after 3 passes, the ball is dropped, or the ball lands out of bounds.

Safety:

Use a soft ball to avoid any injuries from unexpected volleys hitting a student's face. If possible, call out for the ball to avoid collisions with teammates.

Variations/Progressions:

- Remove the ability to catch the ball.
- Allow one bounce.

Diagram

Serve!

Recommended Grades:

Grades 5-6

Equipment:

Volleyball net and volleyballs.

Tactical Problems:

Sending, receiving, hitting with a specific force, and ball placement.

Rules of Play:

1. Class will be divided into 2 teams.
2. One team will start on the service line with the volleyballs.
3. All at once, students must serve to the other side of the court and attempt to make the volleyball land within the boundary lines.
4. It is the responsibility of the student across from the server on the other team to be honest and call whether the ball is in or out.
5. The opposing team will get together and add up the opposing team's points (good serve = 1 point).
6. Repeat for the opposing team.
7. Play a certain number of rounds or until a point limit.

Safety:

Remain attentive as there will be many volleyballs travelling at the same time and make sure to have enough space from teammate to teammate on the service line.

Variations/Progressions:

- Start closer than the service line.
- Switch between underhand and overhand.
- Force students to perform a short or long serve

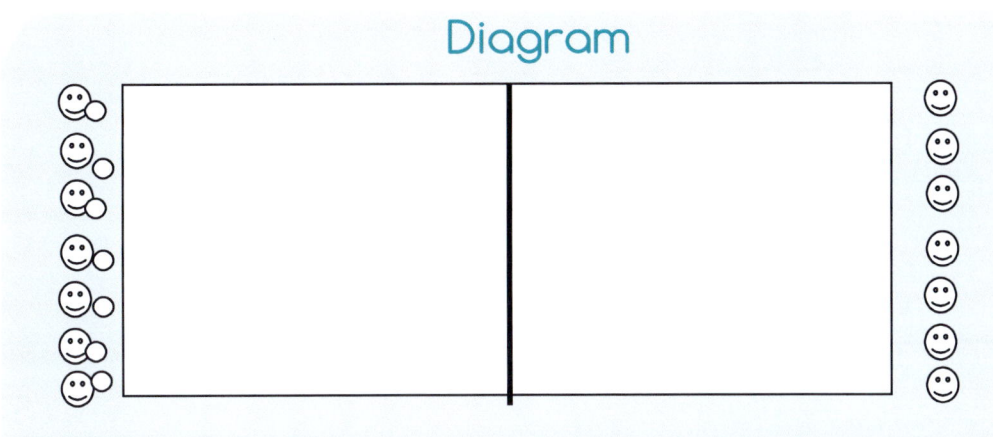

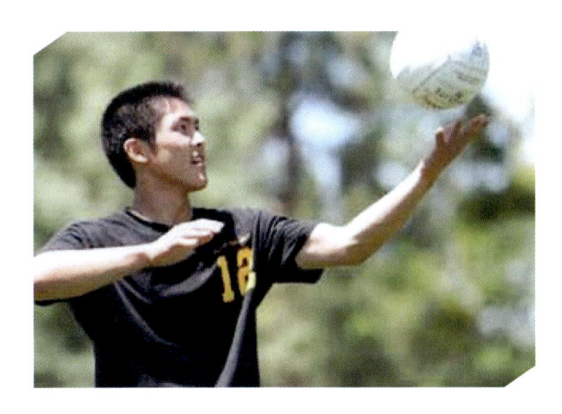

Diagram

Setter Concentration

Recommended Grades:

Grades 5-6

Equipment:

Volleyball net and volleyballs.

Tactical Problems:

Balance, footwork, hitting the ball in relation to the body, and hitting with a specific force.

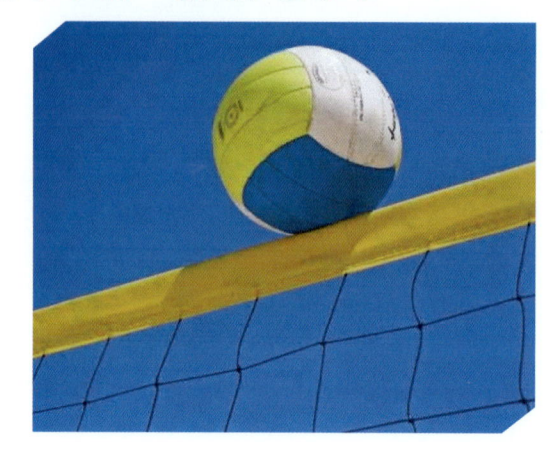

Rules of Play:

1. 5 V 5 cooperative game with one setter for both teams.
2. Focus on the setter & getting him the ball on first contact.
3. On the third contact, the hitters will not spike the ball, but tip the ball in a high motion to give time to the setter to change courts and get prepared.

Safety:

Keep your head up to avoid collisions and keep your eyes on the ball.

Variations/Progressions:

- Each game will have 2-4 setters waiting on the side. After each point, a new setter comes in for the team that is serving. Change either after every setter has gone or after 3-4 minutes.

- Move from 5 V 5 cooperative game to regular 6 V 6 volleyball; however, with the focus still on getting the ball to the setter upon first contact

Diagram

Swap Badminton

Recommended Grades:
Grades 5-6

Equipment:
Badminton nets, badminton rackets, and birdies.

Tactical Problems:
Serving and receiving serve, hitting the birdie in relation to the body, hitting with a specific force, placing ball farthest away from player(s), and anticipation.

Rules of Play:
1. Divide students into teams of 4.
2. On 1 badminton court, there will be a 4 V 4 game – in essence, one player in each quarter of their respective side of the court.
3. Play begins normally with a service followed by a rally.
4. The player who misses the shot or is unable to return the birdie will have to stand off on the side of the court.
5. The team that lost the player begins play with a serve.
6. If the team that lost a player the last round wins the following round, that player comes back into play AND the other team loses a player.
7. Goal of the game is to force all the opposing team members off the court by winning enough consecutive rallies.

Safety:
With that many players on one side of the court, it is important that everyone is in control of their rackets and call for the birdie.

Variations/Progressions:
- Add 2 courts together to make it an 8 V 8 situation.
- Introduce a time limit.

Diagram

Under Bounce

Recommended Grades:
Grades 5-6

Equipment:
Volleyballs and badminton nets.

Tactical Problems:
Catching on bounce, hitting the ball in relation to the body, hitting with a specific force, placing ball farthest away from player(s), and anticipation.

Rules of Play:
1. Students will play 2 V 2 games.
2. Game starts with either a serve over the net or a bounce under the net.
3. After the initial serve, the ball can only cross onto the opponent's side of the court by bouncing it under the net.
4. There must be 2 passes prior to bouncing it to the opponent's end of the court.
5. Scoring occurs when the opponent is unable to return the ball.
6. Ball must be released from shoulder height.
7. 1st and 2nd hits must be either a bump or a volley – 3rd touch will involve catching the ball and bouncing it under the net.

Safety:
Ensure that all players are aware of the balls in play so that no one trips over any loose balls.

Variations/Progressions:
- Modify the requirements of the 1st, 2nd, and 3rd touch.
- Change the type of ball used.

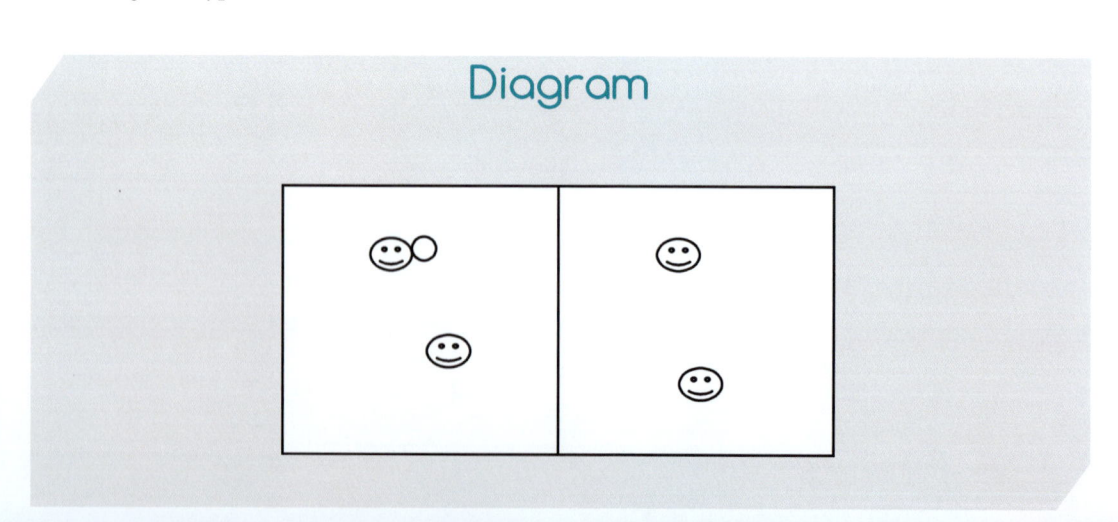

Diagram

Under The Net

Recommended Grades:

Grades 5-6

Equipment:

Volleyballs and badminton nets..

Tactical Problems:

Hitting the ball in relation to the body, hitting with a specific force, returning object and keeping it in bounds, and anticipation.

Rules of Play:

1. Students will play 2 V 2 games on a badminton court (doubles play).
2. One player will start by serving from the end line by knocking the ball to the opponent's court on the net.
3. The ball can only go under the net.
4. Maximum of 3 touches with the ball.
5. First contact with the ball can only be made once the ball has crossed the attack boxes.
6. Point is scored when ball crosses the opponent's end line.

Safety:

Students should be aware of all balls from other courts in order not to be tripped up by one.

Variations/Progressions:

- 3 V 3 games.
- Use a different ball.
- Shorten the court.

Diagram

Volley Baseball

Recommended Grades:

Grades 5-6

Equipment:

Volleyball nets and volleyballs.

Tactical Problems:

Serving and receiving serve, hitting the ball in relation to the body, hitting the ball with a specific force, and returning object and keeping it in bounds.

Rules of Play:

1. Students will be divided into teams of 4 on each court.
2. The goal of the game is to score points by eluding defenders and thus having the most points after a certain time limit.
3. The pitcher initiates play with an underhand pass to the batter, who must then set the ball over the net into open space.
4. The fielders must successfully pass the ball 3 times consecutively in order to get the batter out.
5. Rotate order after each out.

Safety:

Be aware of loose balls.

Variations/Progressions:

- Give each batter up to 3 outs.
- Increase or decrease the number of fielders on a team.
- Allow the player to perform an overhand serve as opposed to a set.

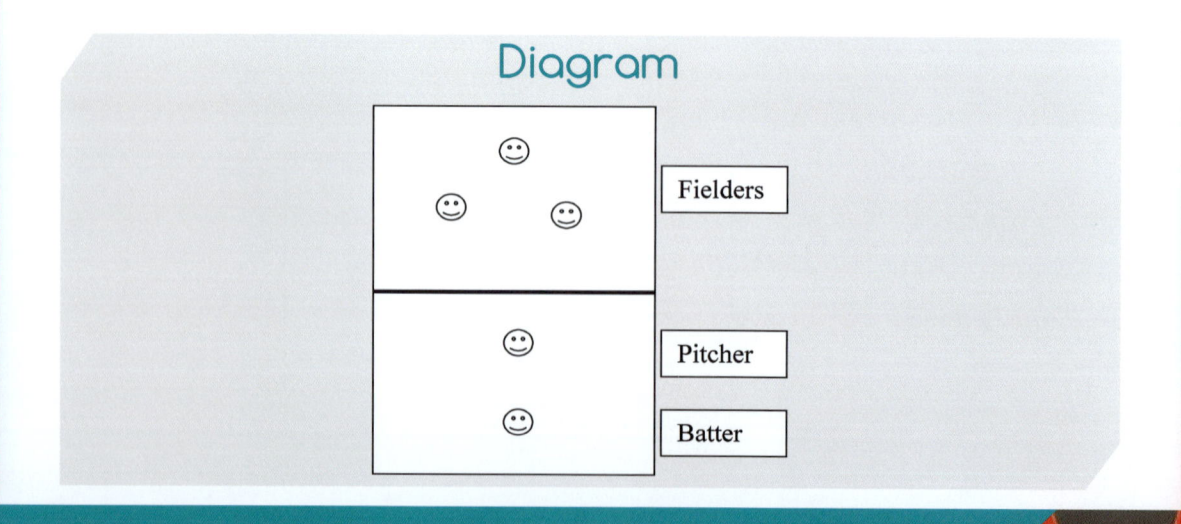

Diagram

Volley Basket

Recommended Grades:

Grades 5-6

Equipment:

Basketball nets and volleyballs.

Tactical Problems:

Volley, bump, hitting with a specific force, and hitting the ball in relation to the body.

Rules of Play:

1. Group of 5 – 6 students will be lined up one behind the other on the foul line facing a basketball net.
2. One student will have the volleyball in their hands next to the basketball net (baseline).
3. The student on the baseline will pass the ball to the first student in the line who will then volley or bump the ball accordingly in an attempt to get it into the basket.
4. Whether a basket is made or not, the student in the front of the line recuperates the rebound and keeps the process going as the student from the baseline runs to the back of the line.
5. One point for each basket made.

Safety:

Keep your eyes on the ball and provide enough spacing between each student.

Variations/Progressions:

- Permit only volleying.
- Permit only bumping.
- Increase or decrease distance from the basket.

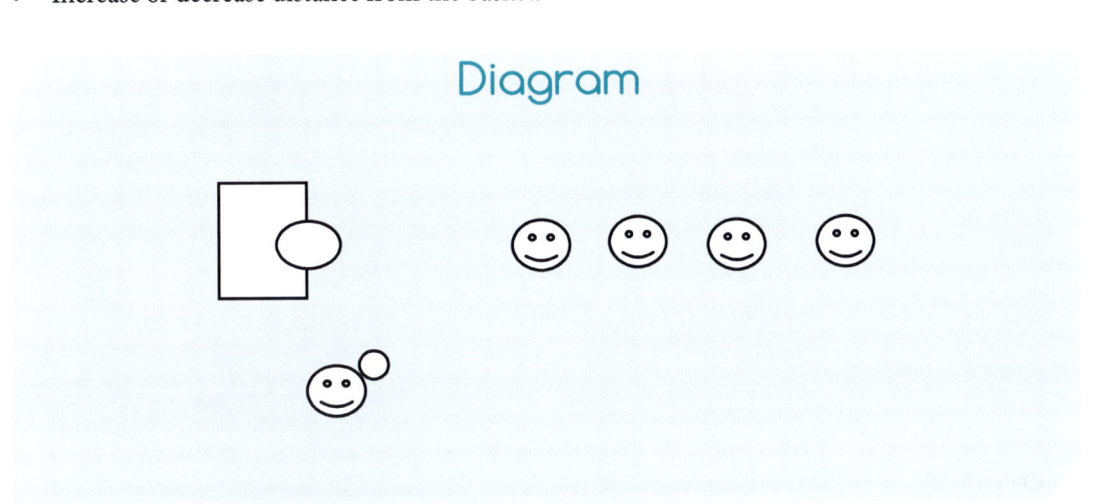

Diagram

Pursuit/Evade

Alphabet Drawing

Recommended Grades:

Grades K2

Equipment:

Pinnies.

Tactical Problems:

Tagging, avoid getting tagged, communication, and using the space available.

Rules of Play:

1. Similar to frozen tag.
2. A couple of students will be taggers while the rest scatter around the gym.
3. When students are tagged, they must stand straight with their arms horizontal ("T").
4. To free someone who is tagged, another student must run behind that person and lightly draw a letter on their back with their fingers.
5. The frozen person must guess what letter was drawn.
6. If guessed correctly, he/she is free.
7. If not, the drawer can try drawing the same letter or a different letter for the person to guess.
8. Taggers cannot tag a person who is drawing on someone else's back.

Safety:

Keep your head up to avoid collisions and appropriate/soft tagging.

Variations/Progressions:

- Increase the number of taggers.
- Draw numbers instead.

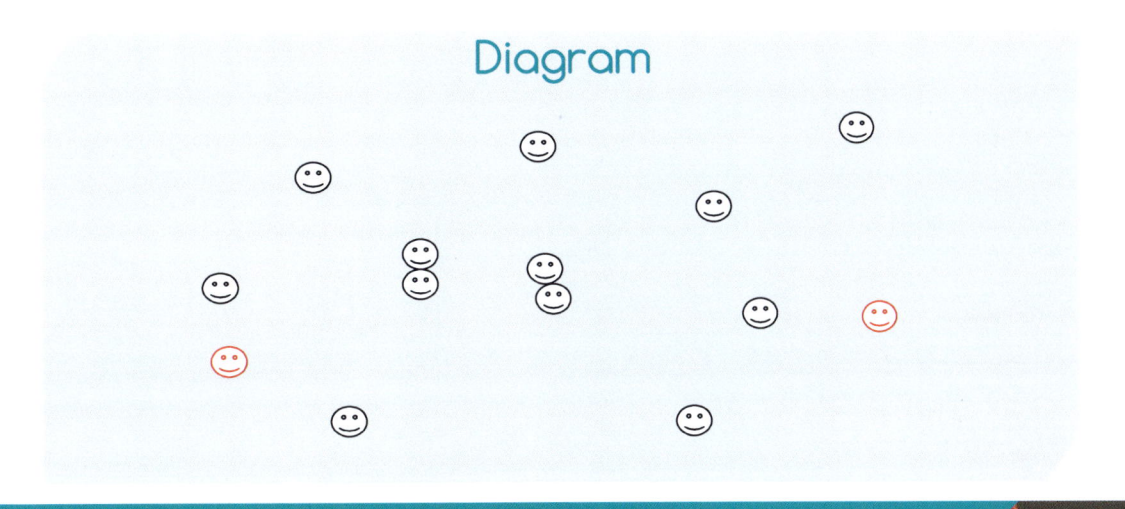

Diagram

Alphabet Tag

Recommended Grades:

Grades K2

Equipment:

Pinnies.

Tactical Problems:

Tagging, avoid getting tagged, communication, and using the space available.

Rules of Play:

1. Similar to frozen tag.
2. A couple of students will be taggers while the rest scatter around the gym.
3. When students are tagged, they must create a letter of the alphabet while standing on their feet.
4. To free someone who is tagged, another student must kneel down in front of the person that is tagged and guess which letter they are.
5. If guessed correctly, he/she is free.
6. If not, they must guess again.
7. Taggers cannot tag a person who is knelt down and guessing the other student's letter.

Safety:

Keep your head up to avoid collisions and appropriate/soft tagging.

Variations/Progressions:

- Increase the number of taggers.
- Create numbers instead.

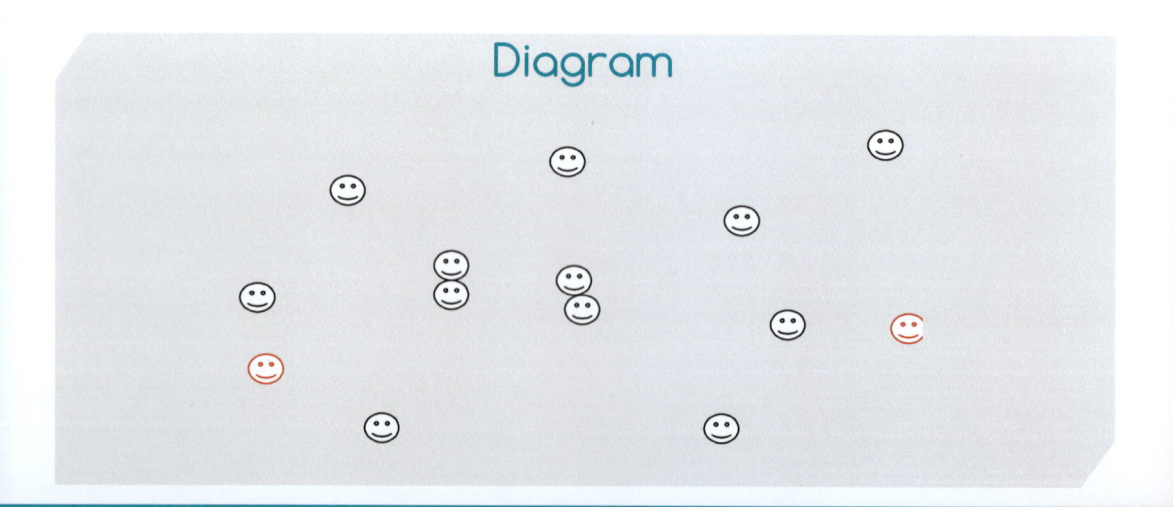

Diagram

Line Tag

Recommended Grades:

Grades K-4

Equipment:

Pinnies.

Tactical Problems:

Tagging, avoid getting tagged, and using the space available.

Rules of Play:

1. Students, including the taggers, have to walk on the lines on the floor.
2. Students try to avoid getting tagged by the designated taggers.
3. Everyone, including those who are "it", can only run on the court lines.
4. The players are not allowed to jump to another line; they have to stay on their line.
5. Students can only tag a student that is on the same line as they are.
6. If a student is tagged, they must sit down and become a block – students, except those who are it, cannot walk past or over the block.
7. Game ends when everyone is tagged or after a certain time limit.

Safety:

Keep your head up to avoid collisions.

Variations/Progressions:

- Add static bases or moveable bases, such as nose and toes base.

- Have taggers use touch noodles – whenever they tag someone, that person now becomes it using the touch noodle.

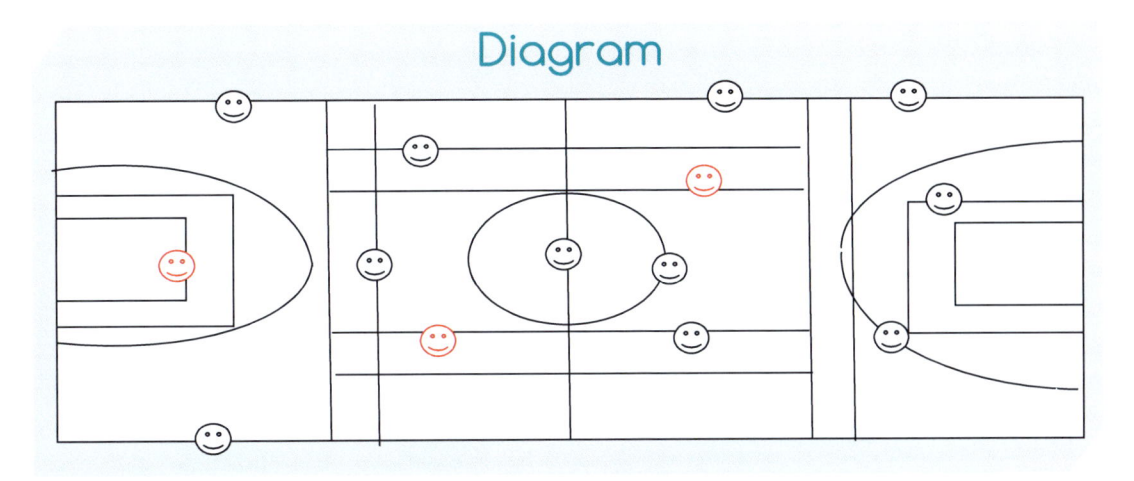

Diagram

89

What Time Is It Mr. Wolf?

Recommended Grades:

Grades K-4

Equipment:

Cones.

Tactical Problems:

Anticipation and using the space available.

Rules of Play:

1. Mr. Wolf will stand 5 meters away from the other players with his/her back turned.
2. The other players call out "What time is it Mr. Wolf?" at which point Mr. Wolf will turn to look at the group and will give a time (i.e. 2 o'clock).
3. Meanwhile, the Wolf and the players behind him will be walking in a forward direction.
4. This continues along with the questioning of "What time is it Mr. Wolf?" until Mr. Wolf responds "DINNER TIME!"
5. Players will then run back to their safety zone as Mr. Wolf attempts to catch one of them.
6. If a player is caught by Mr. Wolf, he or she will also become a wolf for the following round.

Safety:

Keep your head up to avoid collisions with others and be aware of appropriate/soft tagging.

Variations/Progressions:

- Have Mr. Wolf start at the other end of the gym and have only the students walk up to the Mr. Wolf after being given a time.
- Spice things up – Have the teacher play the role of Mr. Wolf!

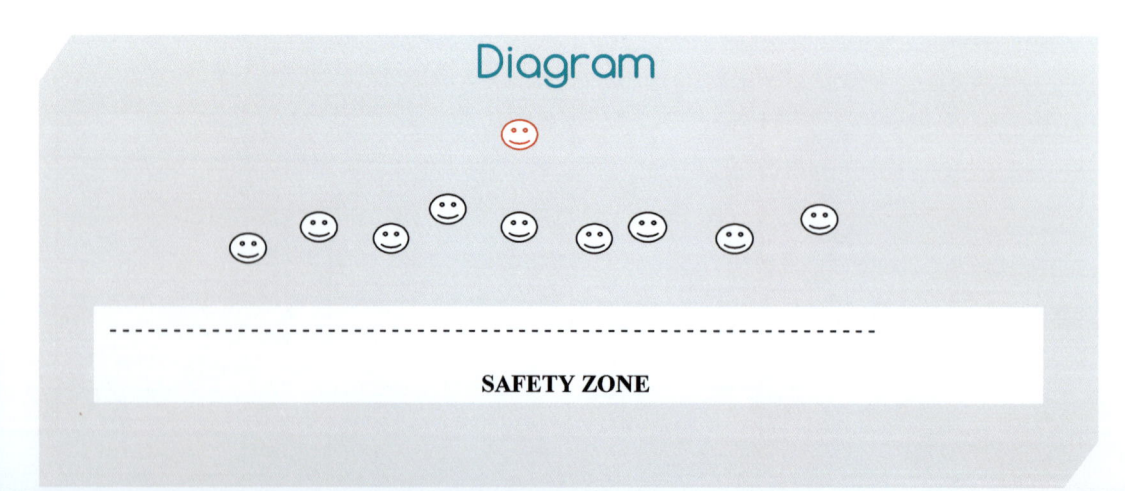

Diagram

SAFETY ZONE

Pass The Pebble

Recommended Grades:
Grades K-4

Equipment:
Beanbag and a container.

Tactical Problems:
Tagging, avoid getting tagged, feinting, using the open space, and communication.

Rules of Play:
1. When the players are standing about with their eyes closed, one goes around dropping a pebble into the hands of one of the players, who will be holding their palms together.
2. When he/she has been completely around the group and has left the pebble in one of the players' hands, he/she will tell the players to open their eyes.
3. The person who has the pebble in their hands will then slyly attempt to slip away and run for the goal.
4. Everyone else tries to catch him/her.
5. The one who succeeds in catching him/her passes the pebble the next time.
6. If no one succeeds, the runner passes the pebble for the next round.

Safety:
Keep your head up to avoid collisions and be aware of appropriate/soft tagging.

Variations/Progressions:
- If the group is too large, divide the group into half and let both groups play their own game at the same time.

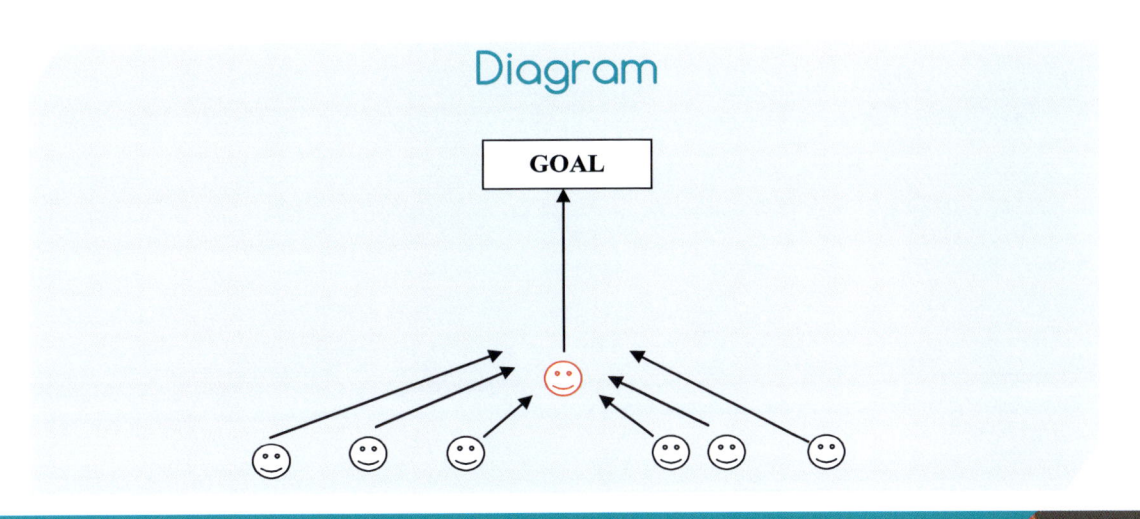

Diagram

Run Sheep Run

Recommended Grades:

Grades K-4

Equipment:

Pinnies, cones, and touch noodles.

Tactical Problems:

Tagging, avoid getting tagged, and using the space available.

Rules of Play:

1. Cones will be spread out in the playing area and will represented trees.
2. 5 students will be hunters(taggers) - they will have touch noodles.
3. The other students will be the sheep.
4. The hunters must hide behind a tree (cone).
5. On the "GO", the sheep will venture off into the forest.
6. When the teacher yells "RUN SHEEP RUN!", the hunters chase and try to touch the sheep that will escape to the safe zone.

Safety:

Keep your head up to avoid collisions and appropriate/soft tagging.

Variations/Progressions:

- Sheep can become hunters instead of waiting on the side.
- Have two safety zones instead of one.
- Introduce different locomotor movements.

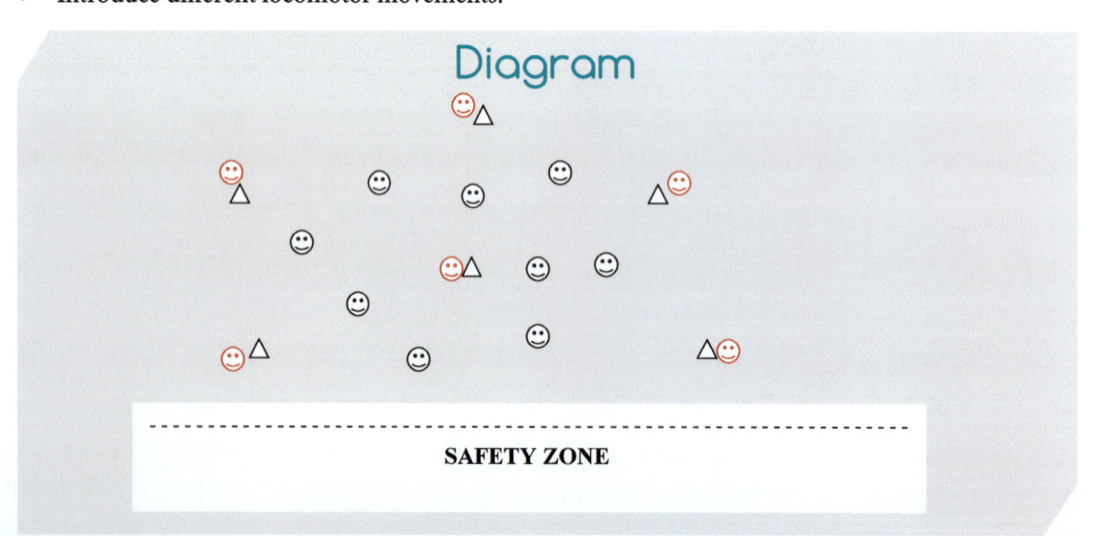

Diagram

SAFETY ZONE

Sharks & Dolphins

Recommended Grades:

Grades K-4

Equipment:

Cones.

Tactical Problems:

Tagging, avoid getting tagged, anticipation, and communication.

Rules of Play:

1. The sharks are in a feeding frenzy and have their backs turned away from the dolphins.
2. In order for a shark to eat a dolphin, they must gently tag the dolphins.
3. The dolphins must swim (run) away as fast as they can without getting caught.
4. On the silent signal, the dolphins will swim towards the sharks until a distance of 5-10 feet is reached.
5. When the instructor yells out "GET BACK!" the sharks chase the dolphins as they swim back to their headquarters (safety zone).
6. If a shark catches a dolphin, that dolphin becomes one of the sharks.

Safety:

Keep your head up to avoid collisions and be aware of appropriate/soft tagging.

Variations/Progressions:

- Start only with two or three sharks instead of separating the class in two.
- Introduce different locomotor movements.

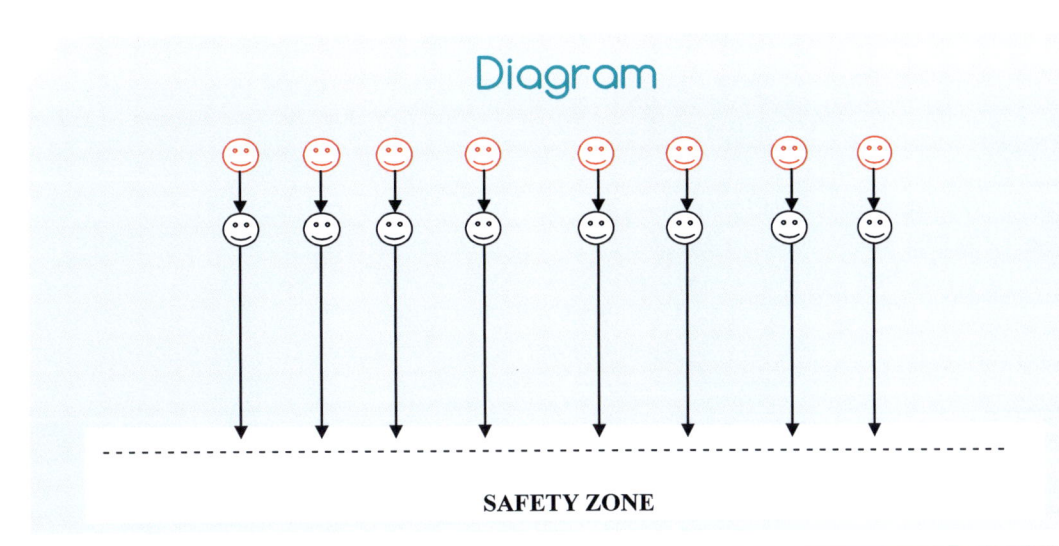

Diagram

SAFETY ZONE

Clothes-Pin Tag

Recommended Grades:

Grades K-6

Equipment:

Clothes-Pins.

Tactical Problems:

Tagging, avoid getting tagged, and using the space available.

Rules of Play:

1. Hand any number of clothes-pins to all the students.
2. Students will pin them to their backs and start in a scattered position on the playing area.
3. On the signal, everyone runs around snatching clothes-pins from one another.
4. When a student snatches another student's clothes-pin, they kneel down to attach their newly acquired clothes-pin.
5. When they are knelt down, they cannot be stripped of a clothes-pin.
6. At the end of the game, the one with the most clothes-pins wins.

Safety:

Keep your head up to avoid collisions, make sure you don't bang your back onto a wall, and appropriate/soft tagging.

Variations/Progressions:

- Introduce different locomotor movements.

- Have each student start with 5 clothes-pins. Every newly acquired clothes-pin will be attached to their abdomen. If a student loses all 5 of his original clothes-pins from his back, they sit out until the time limit is reached or they are put back into the game with new clothes-pin. This continues until there are no more clothes-pins available.

Diagram

Everyone Is IT

Recommended Grades:

Grades K-6

Equipment:

None needed.

Tactical Problems:

Tagging others, avoid getting tagged, and use of open space.

Rules of Play:

1. This game is one that has no end until the instructor whistles the end of the game.
2. There is no expected winner as players run around tagging others and might get tagged as well since no one in particular is designated as "it".
3. When a person gets tagged, he/she will stand in place with his/her hands in front with palms up.
4. Anyone could come up to free that player by touching that person's hands and saying three times "You're free".
5. While they are freeing the player, they are on "base" and therefore cannot be touched.

Safety:

Appropriate/soft tagging and keeping your head up to avoid collisions when running.

Variations/Progressions:

- Bases could be added - Either moveable bases, static bases, or nose and toes base (touching both nose and toes with both hands)
- Also, if players are not helping each other in defrosting, players can auto defrost by performing a set number of a physical skill (i.e. jumping jacks).

Diagram

Giants, Wizards, & Elves

Recommended Grades:

Grades K-6

Equipment:

Cones.

Tactical Problems:

Tagging others, avoid getting tagged, and anticipation.

Rules of Play:

1. Players must be divided into two teams and they must face each other in line formation at the mid-point of the playing area.
2. Each team goes to their boundary line & huddles close to decide amongst themselves if they will be giants, wizards, or elves.
3. Giants take elves, elves take wizards, and wizards take giants.
4. Whatever category the team chooses, they must imitate.
5. For instance, if they are giants, they must walk with big steps or raise their arms high in the air…
6. Both teams approach mid-line.
7. Instructor repeats 3 times Giants, Wizards, & Elves, and both teams start acting out their parts.
8. Whoever is the hunter must catch the escapee – if you are caught, you join the other "team".

Safety:

Soft/appropriate tagging.

Variations/Progressions:

- Change the game into a 1 V 1 type of game.
- Perhaps use dogs, cats, and mice for younger children.

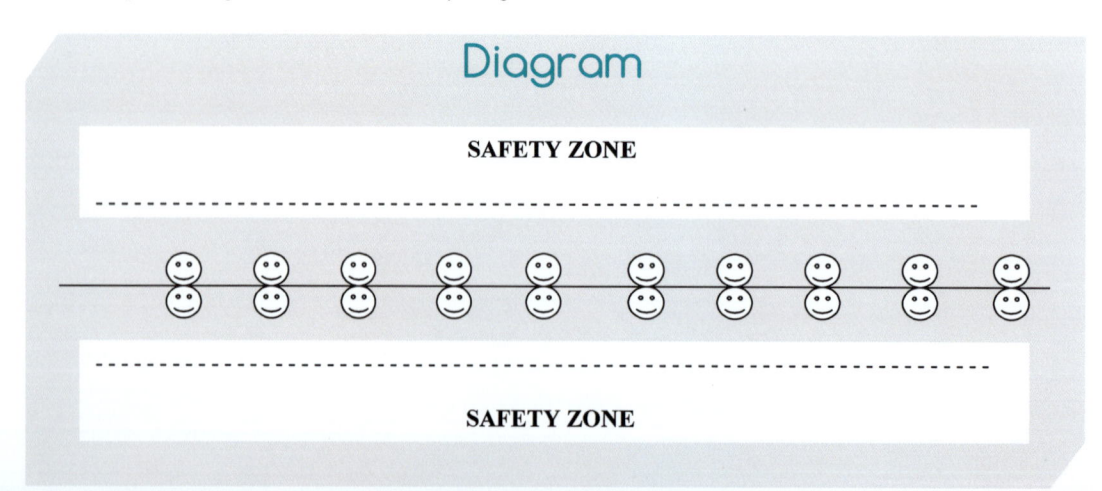

Diagram

SAFETY ZONE

SAFETY ZONE

Hospital Tag

Recommended Grades:
Grades K-6

Equipment:
None needed.

Tactical Problems:
Tagging others, avoid getting tagged by others, and use of open space.

Rules of Play:
1. The basic rules are the same as tag.
2. However, you have "3 lives" so to speak.
3. The first time you get tagged, depending on where you get tagged (i.e. arm), you cannot use that body part anymore.
4. The second time you are tagged, that body part also becomes numb.
5. The third time you get tagged, you are sent to the hospital, which would be any area outside of the playing surface.
6. The game is over when there is only a few people left or if the instructor tells everyone in the hospital to get back in the playing area to restart the game.

Safety:
Keep your head up to avoid collisions and be aware of appropriate/soft tagging.

Variations/Progressions:
- Auto-defrost – Perform a certain number of repetitions of a physical activity to get back into the game after going to the hospital.
- After a certain number of players enter the hospital, they automatically re-enter the game.
- Players cover over their "wounds" the first and second time they are tagged with their hands, but still being able to move their body parts (cannot tag with hands covering wounds). On the third time they're tagged, they are sent to the hospital

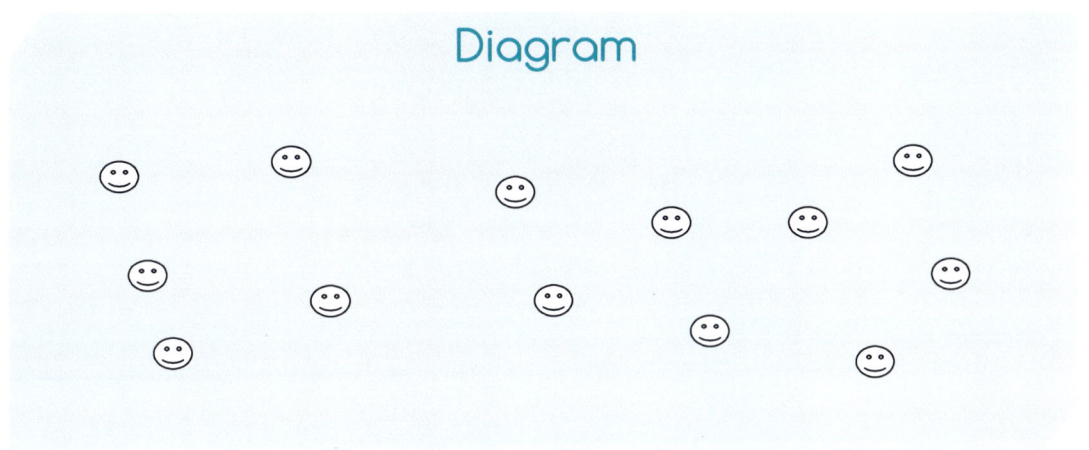

Diagram

Leap-Frog Tag

Recommended Grades:

Grades K-6

Equipment:

Pinnies.

Tactical Problems:

Tagging, avoid getting tagged, and using the space available

Rules of Play:

1. The teacher will assign 2-3 students to be the taggers.
2. The rest of the students will scatter around the gymnasium.
3. When a tagger touches a student, the student must assume the frog position (i.e. squatted/crouched on feet with like a frog with arms next to feet – stay low).
4. The tagged player remains like this until he is rescued.
5. To be unfrozen, a player must "leap-frog" (i.e. jump over) the frozen frog student.
6. Game ends when everyone is tagged or when the time limit has expired.

Safety:

Keep your head up to avoid collisions, ensure that frozen students remain low, and appropriate/soft tagging.

Variations/Progressions:

- Add more taggers.
- Make the playing space larger or smaller.
- Introduce different locomotor movements..

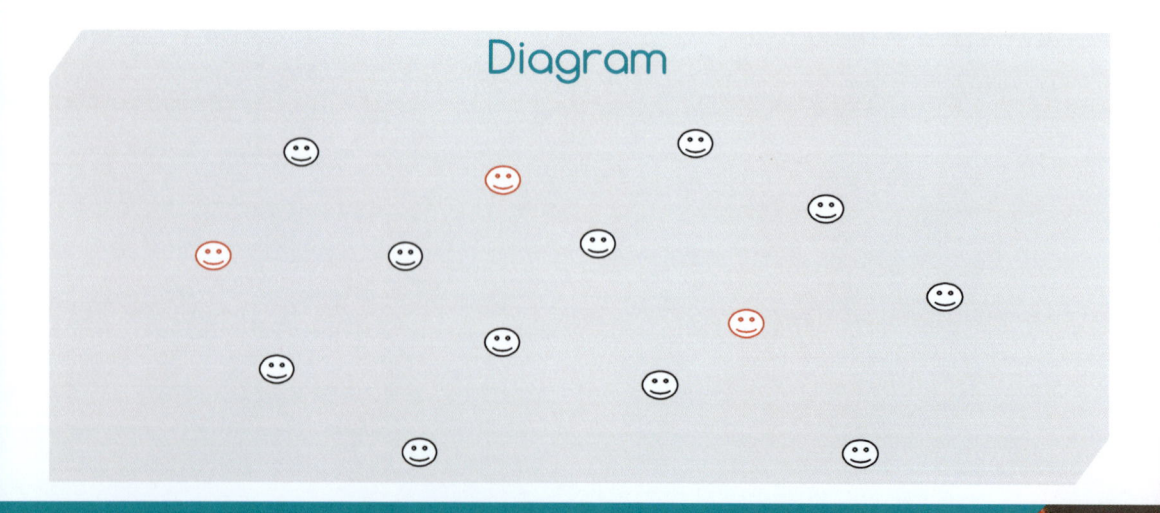

Diagram

Rock, Paper, Scissors Chase

Recommended Grades:

Grades K-6

Equipment:

Cones.

Tactical Problems:

Tagging others, avoid getting tagged, and anticipation.

Rules of Play:

1. Students are paired up and placed across each other from the center line.
2. Students play Rock, Paper, Scissors by putting their "shooting hand" behind their back and then saying "Rock, Paper, Scissors SHOOT".
3. On "shoot", the students show their choice.
4. Rock beats Scissors, Paper beats Rock, and Scissors beats Paper.
5. Winner chases loser to their safety zone.
6. For example, if Rock beats Scissors, Rock chases while Scissors runs to their safety zone.
7. In order to get a point, the winner/chaser must tag the loser/runner before getting to the end line.
8. If the player is not touched, there is no point, and the students return to their starting positions and play again.

Safety:

Appropriate/soft tagging.

Variations/Progressions:

- Introduce a knockout tournament in which winners (best two out of three) continue and the "losers" become part of their cheering squad.
- Rotate partners

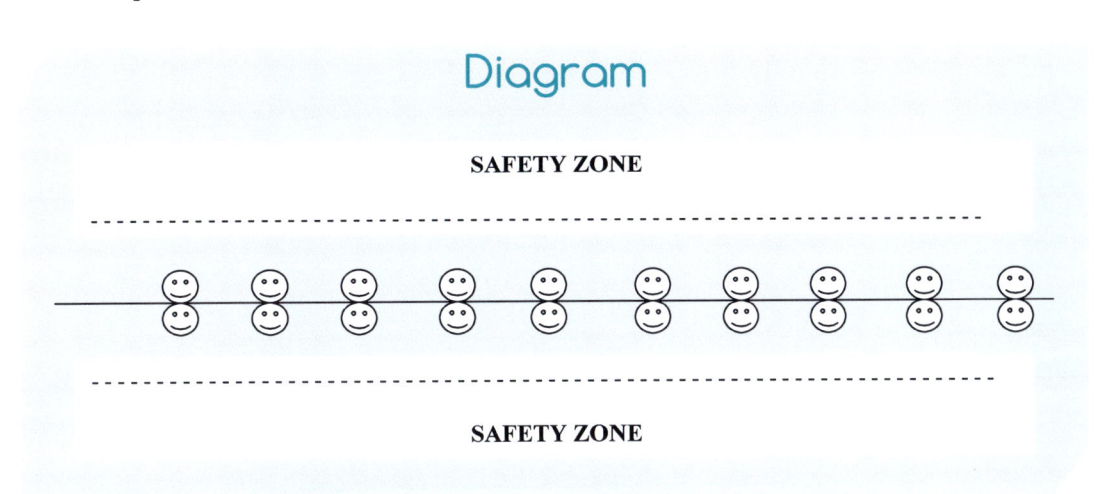

Diagram

SAFETY ZONE

SAFETY ZONE

Scooter Tag

Recommended Grades:

Grades K-6

Equipment:

Scooters and/or pinnies.

Tactical Problems:

Tagging, avoid getting tagged, and using the space available.

Rules of Play:

1. Each student will be given a scooter.
2. Taggers will be given either a different colored scooter or a pinnie.
3. When tagged, the player must perform 5 spins/rotations with his/her scooter to come back into the game.

Safety:

Keep your head up to avoid collisions, watch your hands around other scooters, do not stand on the scooter, and appropriate/soft tagging.

Variations/Progressions:

- Instead of doing 5 spins, take your scooter to the side and perform a physical activity (i.e. 5 jumping jacks).
- Alternatively, to be unfrozen when tagged, another player must circle around him/her once..

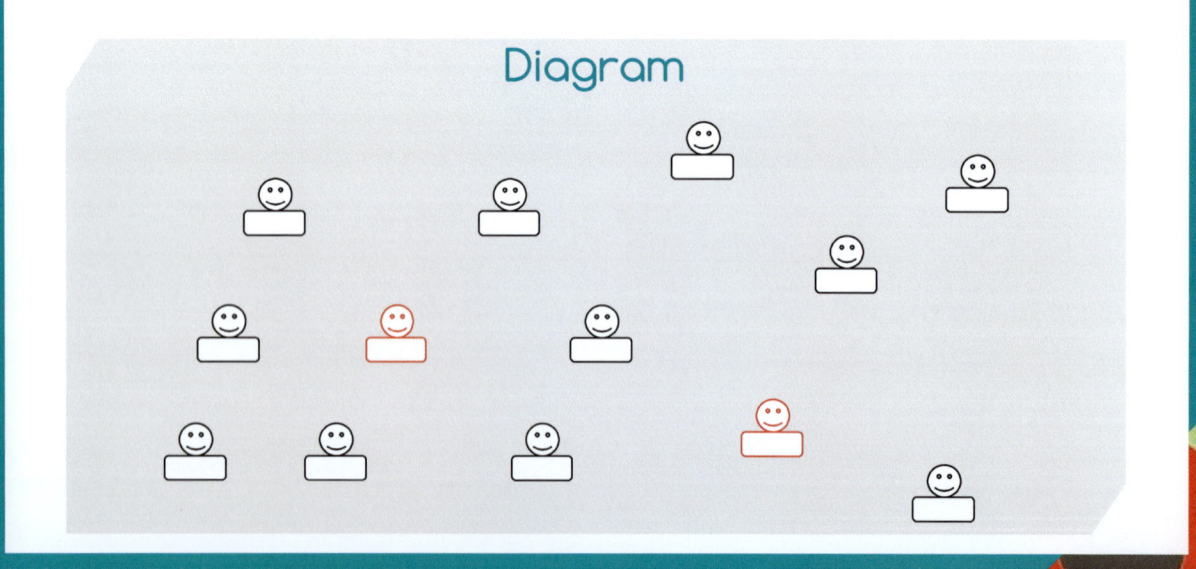

Diagram

Toilet Tag

Recommended Grades:

Grades K-6

Equipment:

Pinnies.

Tactical Problems:

Tagging, avoid getting tagged, and using the space available.

Rules of Play:

1. The teacher will assign 2-3 students to be the taggers.
2. The rest of the students will scatter around the gymnasium.
3. When a tagger touches a student, the student must assume the toilet position (i.e. one knee down, other knee up, and one arm straight up to the side).
4. The tagged player remains like this until he is rescued.
5. To be unfrozen, a player must push down on the student's arm (lightly) while making a flushing sound.
6. Game ends when everyone is tagged or when the time limit has expired.

Safety:

Keep your head up to avoid collisions and appropriate/soft tagging.

Variations/Progressions:

- Add more taggers.
- Make the playing space larger or smaller.
- Introduce different locomotor movements.

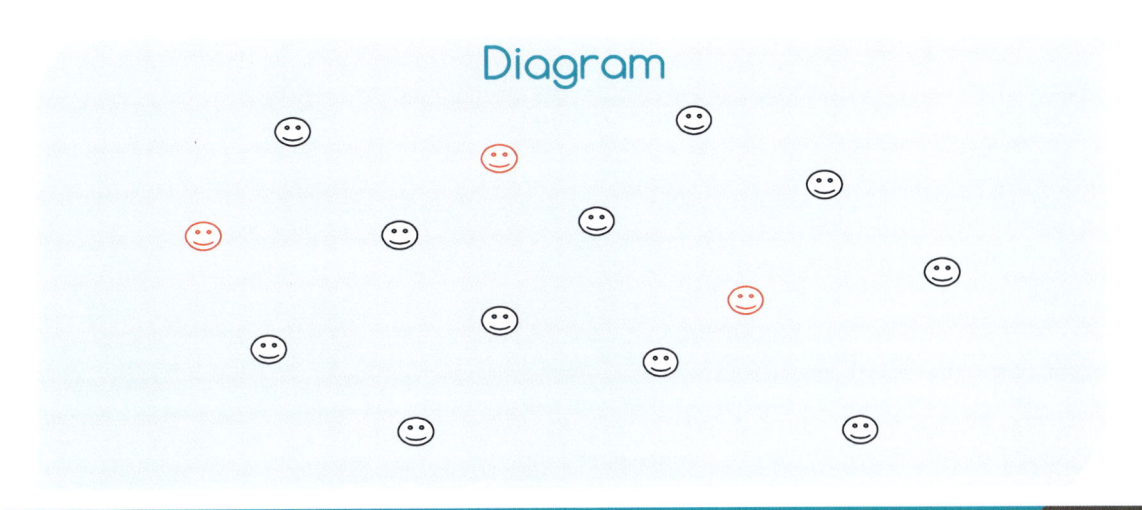

Diagram

Crows & Cranes

Recommended Grades:

Grades 3-4

Equipment:

Cones.

Tactical Problems:

Tagging, avoid getting tagged, anticipating, and reacting.

Rules of Play:

1. Students will be divided into 2 teams: either they will be crows or cranes.
2. Students will line up at the center line.
3. When the teacher calls crows, the crows have to turn around and run to their base before the cranes tag them.
4. When the teacher calls the cranes, the cranes have to turn around and run to their safety zone before the crows tag them.
5. When a student is touched, they must join the other group.

Safety:

Appropriate/soft tagging and ensure students decelerate in their safety zone.

Variations/Progressions:

- Introduce different locomotor movements.
- Have them lie on their stomach or back before calling out either Crows or Cranes.
- Students will have their backs turned away from the opposing team.

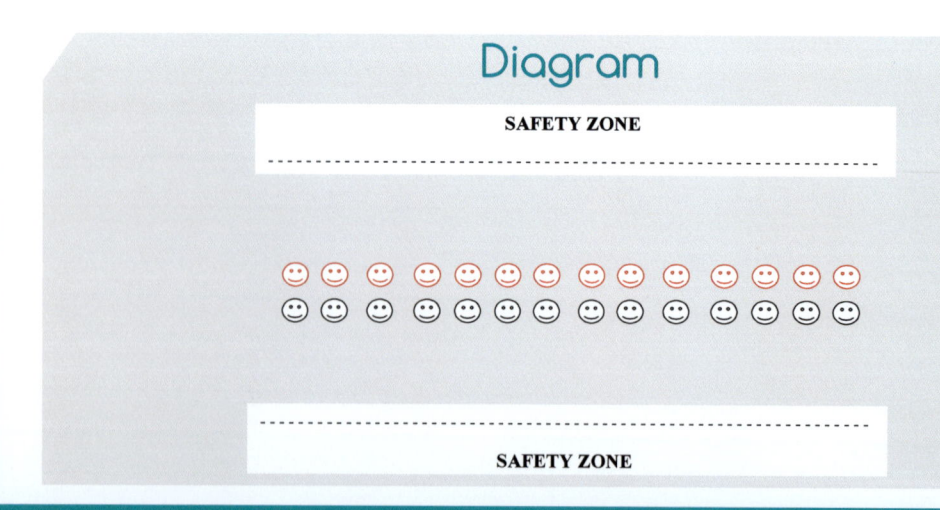

Diagram

SAFETY ZONE

SAFETY ZONE

Kangaroo Ball

Recommended Grades:

Grades 3-4

Equipment:

Soft foam balls and cones.

Tactical Problems:

Communication, using the space available, anticipation, and avoid getting tagged by the ball.

Rules of Play:

1. The students will be working in groups of threes.
2. One student is the "kangaroo" (player in the middle) while the other two students are the "rollers" (players at the end of defined area).
3. The "rollers" face each other approximately 6 feet apart depending on the skill level of the students.
4. The player in the middle—"kangaroo"—will try to avoid being touched by a foam ball rolled back and forth between the two "rollers" by using dodging skills.
5. The "rollers" attempt to touch the kangaroo on the feet with the rolling ball.
6. Once touched by the rolling ball, the "kangaroo" takes the place of one of the "rollers" - usually the one who rolled the ball that touched the "kangaroo".
7. The game then resumes with a new "kangaroo".

Safety:

Be careful not to trip on the ball and keep the ball low.

Variations/Progressions:

- Add another ball in play.
- Allow players to bounce the ball.
- Increase or decrease the distance between the "rollers".

Diagram

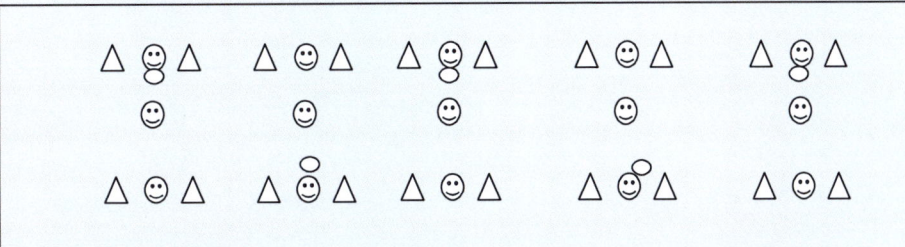

Run Turkey Run

Recommended Grades:

Grades 3-4

Equipment:

Pinnies.

Tactical Problems:

Tagging, avoid getting tagged, and using the space available.

Rules of Play:

1. Place 4 mats at the corners of the gym.
2. Designate a few students to be "it" – they will be the wolves.
3. The mats will be the safety zones for the turkeys.
4. Wolves are not allowed on the mats.
5. When the teacher calls out "Run turkey run", turkeys must leave their current safety zone and run to another mat without getting tagged.
6. If tagged, they put on a pinnie and join the pack of wolves.
7. Play until all turkeys have been tagged or until the time limit has expired.

Safety:

Keep your head up to avoid collisions and appropriate/soft tagging.

Variations/Progressions:

- Remove or add the number of mats in play.
- Introduce different locomotor movements.
- Call out one or two corners at a time instead of all four.

Diagram

Scaredy Cats

Recommended Grades:
Grades 3-4

Equipment:
Pinnies.

Tactical Problems:
Tagging, avoid getting tagged, and using the space available.

Rules of Play:
1. There will be four different colored teams set up at each corner of the gym.
2. In the middle, there will be one or two taggers.
3. The taggers will call out two colors at a time (at first, the teacher will call the colors)
4. For example, if the teacher/tagger calls out: "Blue and Red", these two teams will run as fast as possible and exchange corners.
5. The tagger(s) will try to tag the students as they travel from one corner to another.
6. If someone is tagged, they join the team of taggers.

Safety:
Keep your head up to avoid collisions and appropriate/soft tagging.

Variations/Progressions:
- Add more taggers.
- Increase or reduce the playing area.
- Introduce different locomotor movements.

Diagram

Beaches, Bridges & Boats

Recommended Grades:
Grades 3-6

Equipment:
Pinnies, cones, noodle sticks, and hula-hoops

Tactical Problems:
Tagging, avoid getting tagged, and using the space available.

Rules of Play:
1. Designate 2-3 pirates (taggers).
2. Players may run anywhere on the beach and bridges, but they can only cross the ocean via a boat (hula-hoop).
3. When a player gets tagged, he/she must stand outside the playing area.
4. After 5 players get tagged and leave the playing area, they may all return to play.
5. Switch taggers after a set time limit.

Safety:
Keep your head up, only one person per boat/hula-hoop, and appropriate/soft tagging.

Variations/Progressions:
- Introduce different locomotor movements.
- Add stepping stones as bases scattered around the beach and bridges.

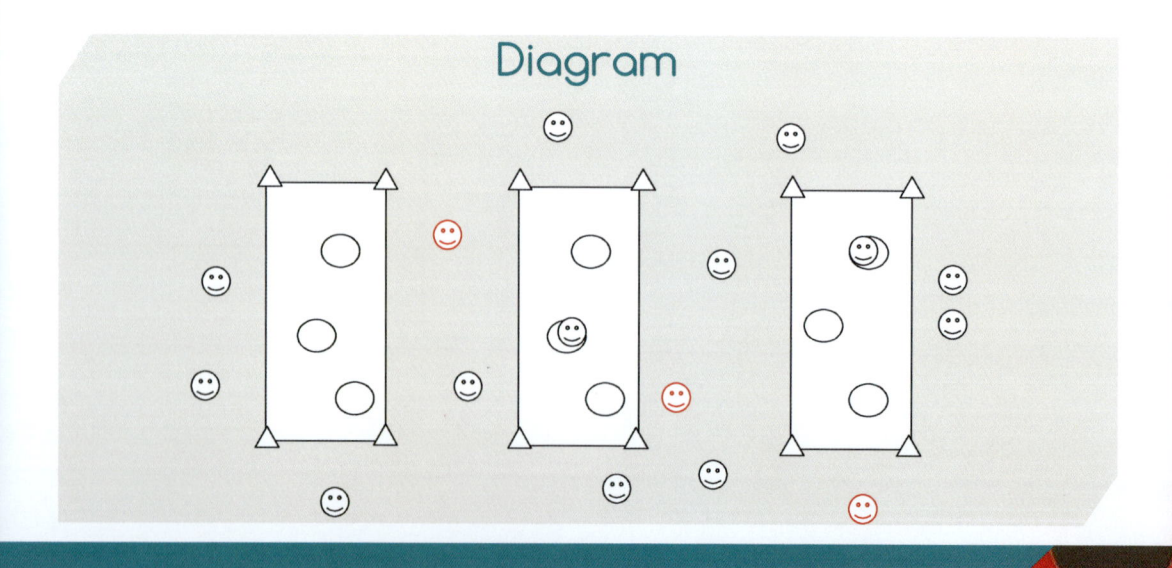

Diagram

Beanbag Tag

Recommended Grades:

Grades 3-6

Equipment:

Beanbags and noodle sticks.

Tactical Problems:

Tagging, avoid getting tagged, change in direction, and using the space available.

Rules of Play:

1. There will be one tagger that will be "it" and will have a noodle stick.
2. The rest of the students will have a beanbag on top of their head.
3. The students with beanbags on their heads must avoid getting tagged while maintaining the beanbag on their head.
4. If they drop the beanbag, they must stop, pick it up, and place it back on their head before continuing.
5. If a student is tagged with or without the beanbag on their head, the tagger and that student switches placed and exchange beanbag and noodle stick.

Safety:

Keep your head up to avoid collisions and appropriate/soft tagging.

Variations/Progressions:

- Introduce different locomotor movements.
- Add more taggers.

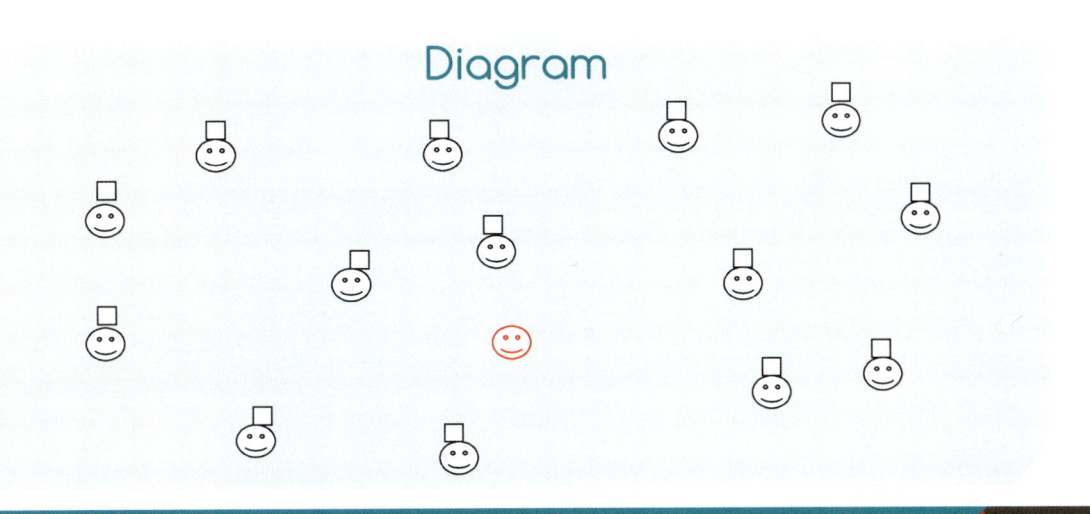

Diagram

Blob

Recommended Grades:
Grades 3-6

Equipment:
None needed.

Tactical Problems:
Avoid getting tagged, tagging others, communication, and use of open space.

Rules of Play:
1. Everyone must run away from the blob.
2. When a person is caught, they must link by holding hands and run together to catch other people in order to enlarge the blob.
3. The blob can split into smaller groups to catch people.
4. When the blog is split into smaller groups, there must be a minimum of 2 people linked together.
5. The only limitation the blob has is that they can only capture people with the people at the ends of the link.

Safety:
Keeping your head up to avoid collisions and appropriate/soft tagging.

Variations/Progressions:
- No splitting of the blob allowed; everyone that is tagged must be linked together.

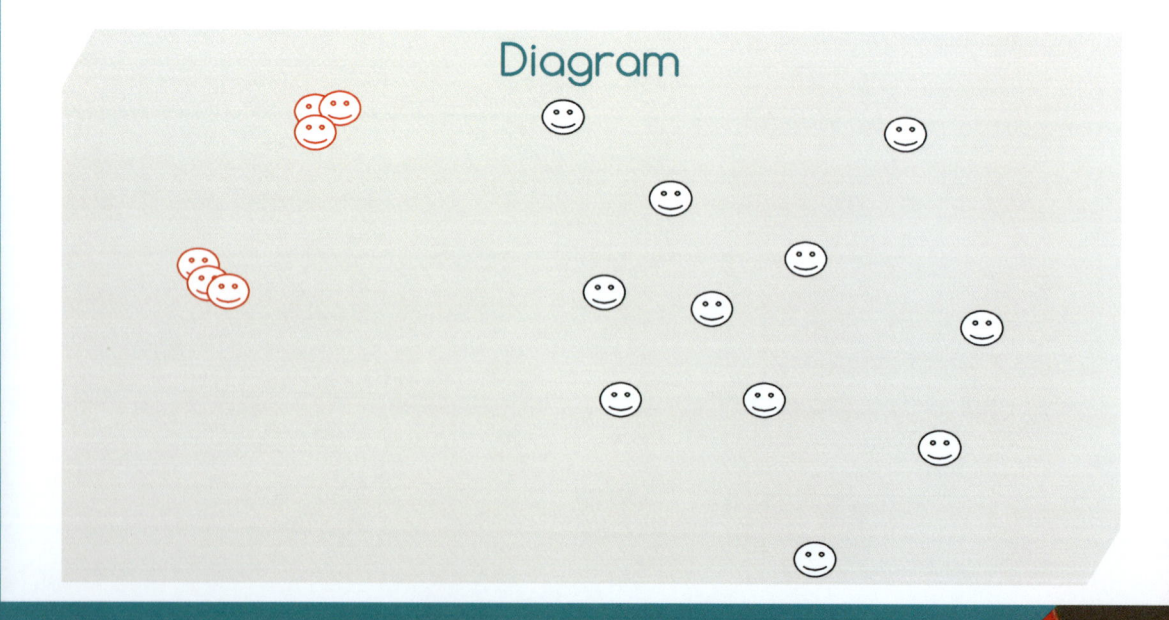

Diagram

Catch the Tail

Recommended Grades:

Grades 3-6

Equipment:

None needed.

Tactical Problems:

Communication, tagging, avoid getting tagged, footwork, and change of speed/direction.

Rules of Play:

1. Similar to triangle tag.
2. Students will be placed in teams of four.
3. Three players form a line holding onto the player's waist or shoulders in front of them with the fourth player (tagger) facing the front of the line.
4. The last player in the line is designated as "it".
5. The goal of the game is to not let the tagger tag the "it".
6. Change taggers and designated player to be tagged after 45 seconds.

Safety:

Appropriate/soft tagging and no pulling.

Variations/Progressions:

- More players in the line.
- Have more than one "it" player.

Diagram

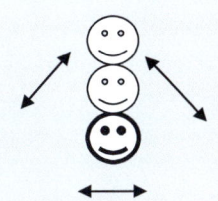

Colorful Teddy

Recommended Grades:

Grades 3-6

Equipment:

Teddy bear (or any other handheld item).

Tactical Problems:

Tagging, avoid getting tagged, and use of open space.

Rules of Play:

1. Students will begin scattered around the playing area.
2. Designate one teddy carrier and designate one teddy chaser.
3. Teddy chaser must touch teddy carrier in order to exchange the possession of the teddy.
4. During this time, other players remain static.
5. Both the carrier and chaser may designate any other static person to complete the task at hand.
6. In other words, if the chaser gets tired, he/she can go next to a static person and now the original chaser becomes a static person while the static person becomes the new chaser.
7. The same idea applies for the carrier.
8. If the chaser tags the carrier, the carrier must transfer the teddy bear and now becomes the chaser after waiting 3 seconds for the other player to run.

Safety:

Keep your head up to avoid collisions with static bases and appropriate/soft tagging.

Variations/Progressions:

- Introduce multiple teddy bears.
- Change the objects used.

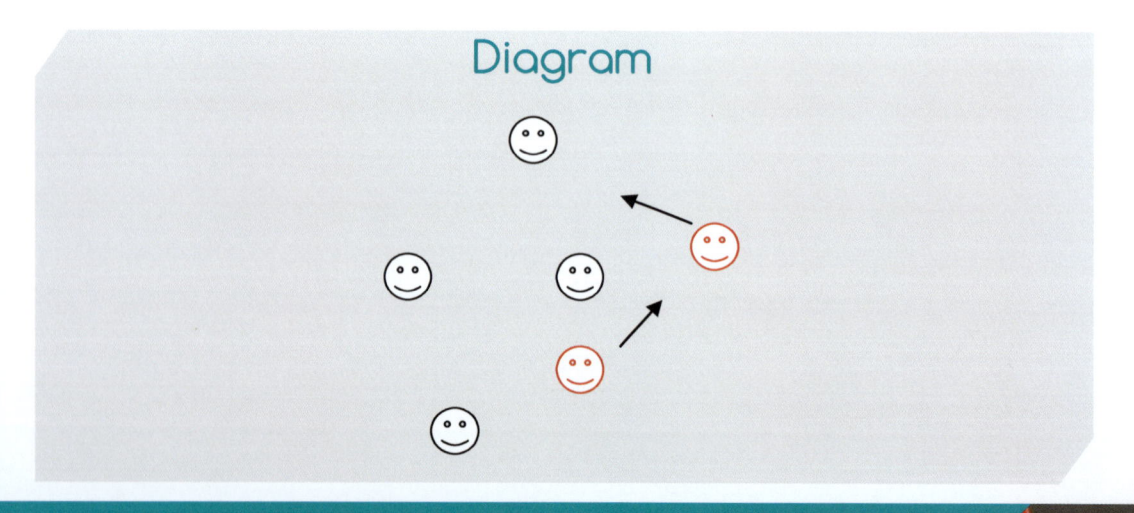

Diagram

Dribble Tag

Recommended Grades:

Grades 3-6

Equipment:

Basketballs.

Tactical Problems:

Stripping the ball away, avoid losing possession of the ball, anticipation, and using the space available.

Rules of Play:

1. Each student will have possession of a basketball.
2. Within the playing boundaries, students will be dribbling a basketball.
3. Each player must keep control of his/her own dribble while at the same time attempting to cause other players to lose control of their ball.
4. If a player loses control of their ball or goes out of bounds, he/she must perform a task (i.e. 10 alternate-hand dribbles) before returning to the game.
5. Start with a large playing area and progressively reduce the playing space.

Safety:

Keep your head up to avoid collisions and be aware of the basketballs in play.

Variations/Progressions:

- Set-up an elimination style game with a set time limit.

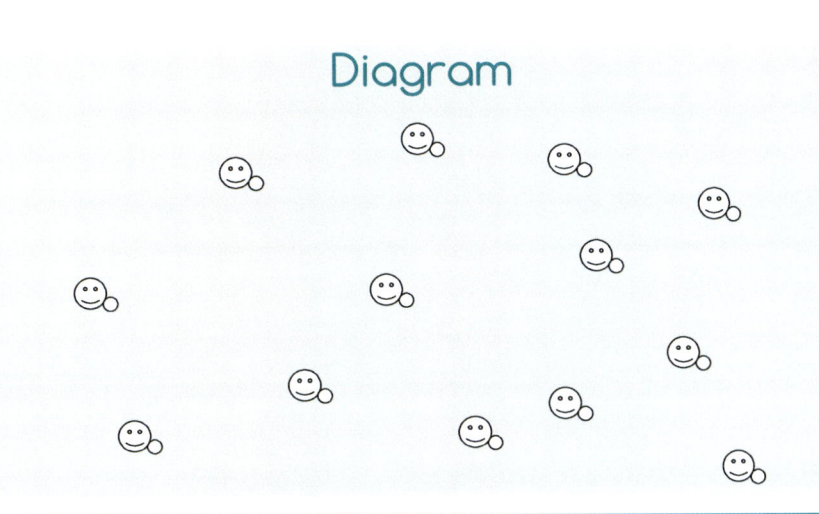

Diagram

Everybody's IT Teams

Recommended Grades:

Grades 3-6

Equipment:

Pinnies.

Tactical Problems:

Tagging, avoid getting tagged, and using the space available.

Rules of Play:

1. The class will be divided in 2 teams.
2. The goal is for one of the teams to tag all the members of the opposite team and remain the last team standing.
3. When a student is tagged, that student must sit down in the place where they got tagged.
4. While they are sitting down, if a student from the opposing team passes by, he/she can tag that person from the sitting down position and return into the game.
5. Play until there is one team remaining or until the time limit is reached.

Safety:

Keep your head up to avoid collisions and appropriate/soft tagging.

Variations/Progressions:

- Remove the team element from the game while maintaining the rest of the rules.
- Make the playing area larger or smaller.
- Have one student from each team act as the "doctor".

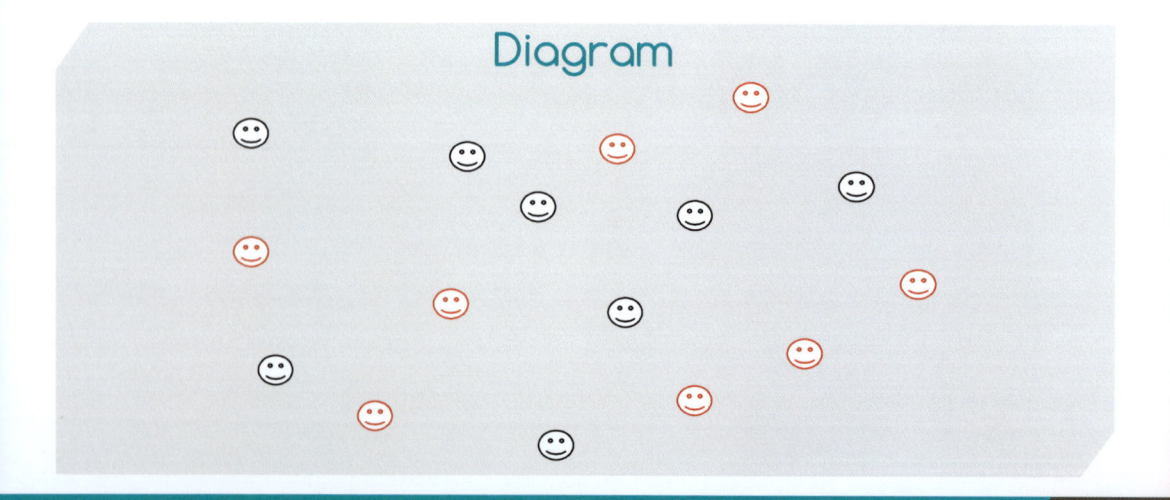

Diagram

Flag Tag

Recommended Grades:

Grades 3-6

Equipment:

Pinnies.

Tactical Problems:

Tagging, avoid getting tagged, and using the space available.

Rules of Play:

1. Players have a pinnie on the side of their shorts.
2. At the signal, they have to run in the playing area and try to take off the pinnie from the short's of another student and drop it on the floor.
3. That player then picks up his pinnie, goes to the side of the playing field, and performs a certain set of a physical activity (i.e. 5 jumping jacks).
4. They then return back into the game.

Safety:

Keep your head up to avoid collisions and appropriate/soft pull of the pinnie when tagging.

Variations/Progressions:

- Each student can have two pinnies – one on each side of their shorts.
- Set a time limit for an elimination style game.

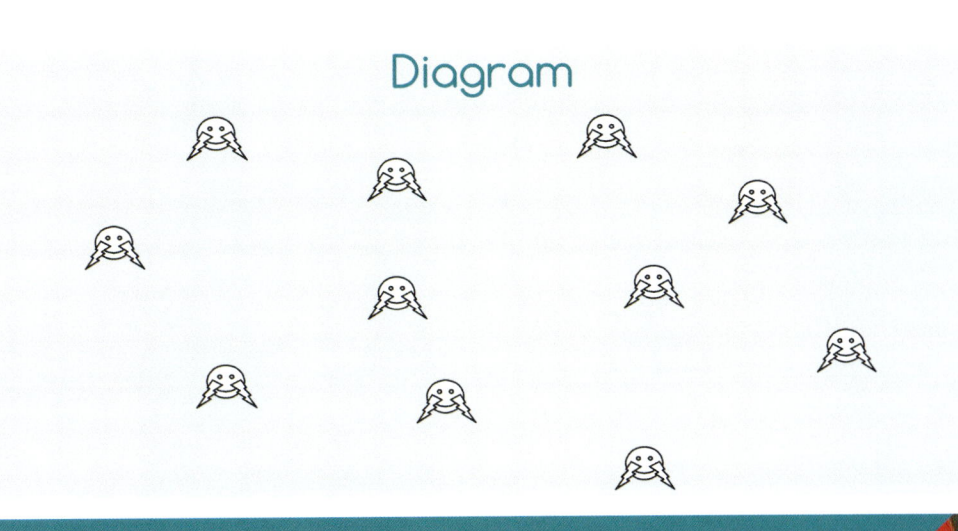

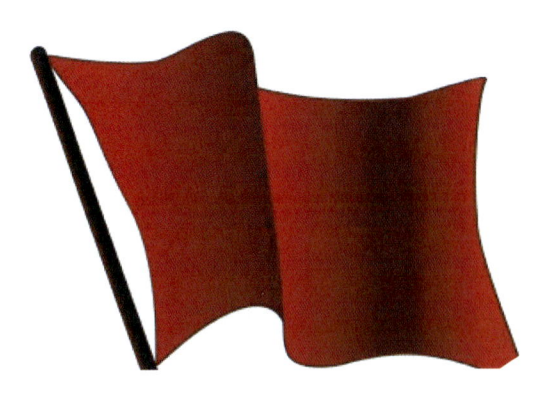

Diagram

Four Kings Tag

Recommended Grades:
Grades 3-6

Equipment:
Pinnies.

Tactical Problems:
Tagging, avoid getting tagged, and using the space available.

Rules of Play:
1. Teacher will give a different colored pinnie to four students – they will be the four kings.
2. At the center of the playing area, there will be a large collection of all four colored pinnies used in the game.
3. The four kings will try to tag the rest of the students in the playing area.
4. When a student is tagged, he/she becomes the king's knight and must run to the center of the field to put on a pinnie of the same color as the king.
5. The knights then also attempt to tag others to recruit students onto their team.
6. Play until everyone is tagged or until the time limit has expired.
7. The king who captures the most knights wins.

Safety:
Keep your head up to avoid collisions and appropriate/soft tagging.

Variations/Progressions:
- Increase or decrease the number of kings in play.
- Reduce or increase the playing area.
- Introduce different locomotor movements.

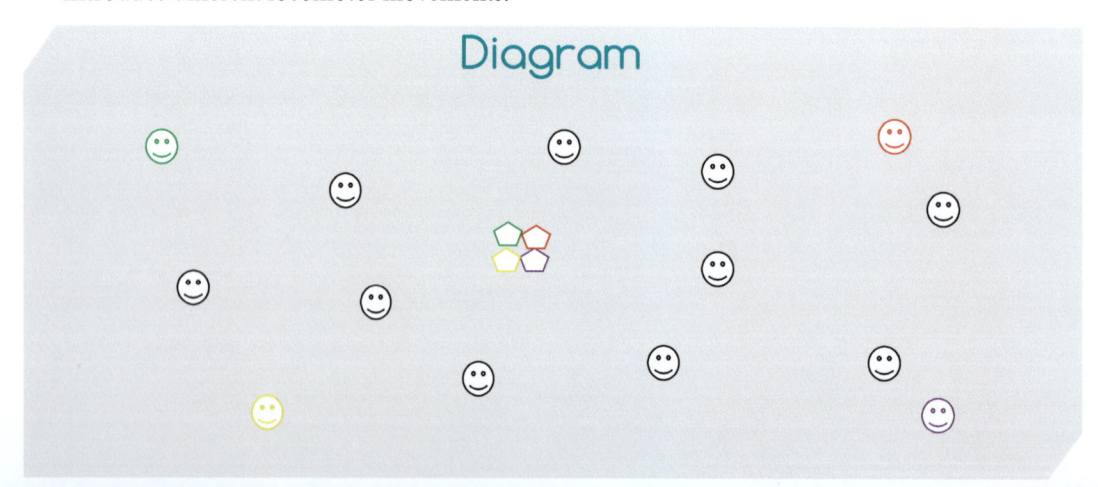

Diagram

Swipe

Recommended Grades:
Grades 3-6

Equipment:
Cones and beanbags.

Tactical Problems:
Throwing opponent off-balance, feinting, and reacting to movement or actions of opponents.

Rules of Play:
1. Everyone lines up on the center line where each player is then paired off with an opponent.
2. Each player tactically tries to earn a point.
3. The player is awarded a point through one of the two following ways.
4. The first way of getting a point is by swiping the beanbag and then making it over to his/her respective safety zone without being touched by the opponent.
5. The second way of getting a point is by tagging the opponent if he/she tries to run off with the beanbag before reaching his/her safety zone.
6. Players must remain behind the center line in their respective zones prior to the beanbag getting swiped.

Safety:
No pushing when chasing opponent and watch your heads when swiping beanbag.

Variations/Progressions:
- Allow players to cross the center line and return to either safety zone after swiping the beanbag.
- Make either the first or second method of earning a point worth double

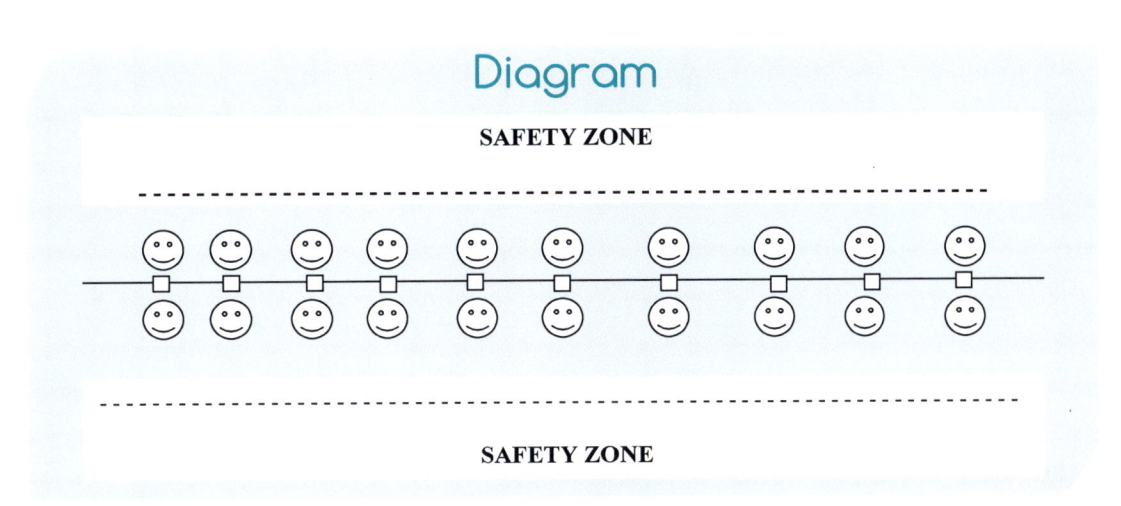

Diagram

SAFETY ZONE

SAFETY ZONE

Tail Tag

Recommended Grades:

Grades 3-6

Equipment:

Pinnies.

Tactical Problems:

Tagging, avoid getting tagged, and using the space available.

Rules of Play:

1. Half the players have a pinnie at the back of their shorts while the other half remain "tail-less".
2. On a "GO" signal, "tailed" players use dodging skills to avoid having their tail snatched.
3. Any tail-less player can snatch a tail from any player with a tail.
4. When a tail-less player snatches a tail, he/she has 5 seconds to attach his/her tail and move into a dodging stance.
5. The newly tail-less players attempt to regain a tail.
6. Students may only have one tail at a time.

Safety:

Keep your head up to avoid collisions and appropriate/soft pull of the pinnie when tagging.

Variations/Progressions:

- Students can have two pinnies – one on each side of their shorts: players with two pinnies try to avoid getting their pinnies removed, players with one pinnie try to avoid getting their pinnie removed while acquiring another, and players without a pinnie simply try to snatch one.
- Set a time limit for an elimination style game

Diagram

Team Ball Tag

Recommended Grades:

Grades 3-6

Equipment:

Pinnies and soft gator skin balls.

Tactical Problems:

Using space, sending and receiving, and communication.

Rules of Play:

1. The game starts with 3 taggers wearing pinnies.
2. They must pass the ball around amongst each other and try to tag the students without pinnies.
3. When someone is tagged, they put on a pinnie and come back into the game as a tagger.
4. Taggers can only pass the ball around; they are not allowed taking any steps.
5. The game ends where there are only 3 players left, who in turn become the new starting taggers for the next game.

Safety:

Keep your head up to avoid collisions and ensure that taggers do not throw the balls at players not wearing pinnies.

Variations/Progressions:

- Allow taggers to take 3 steps.
- Add more balls.
- Make the space smaller or larger.
- Start with more taggers.

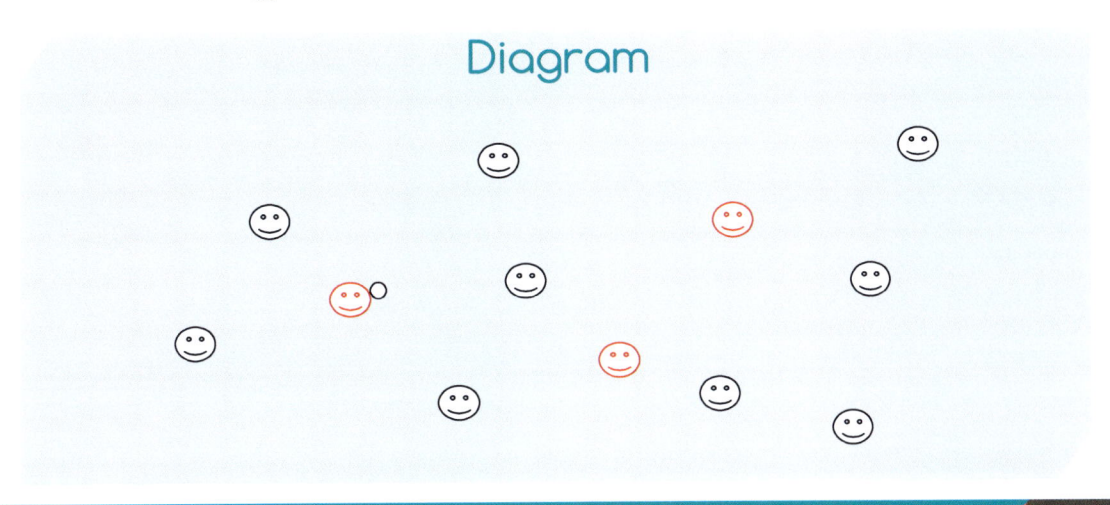

Diagram

Topsy Turvy

Recommended Grades:
Grades 3-6

Equipment:
Pinnies and cones.

Tactical Problems:
Observation, anticipating, and reacting.

Rules of Play:
1. One team will be assigned as "topsies" and the other team will be assigned as "turvies".
2. Topsies will be responsible for turning cones upright while turvies will be responsible for knocking down cones with hands only.
3. There is no defense in this game, which makes observing the other team's actions a must.
4. This also creates the necessity for quick movement.
5. Furthermore, it is a good idea for the teams to adjust cones where there is no opposition nearby.
6. There's usually a time limit involved that lasts roughly a couple of minutes or so.
7. The winner is decided after the time limit by the number of cones upright and how many cones are knocked over.

Safety:
Keep your head up and make sure that the cones are not kicked.

Variations/Progressions:
- Add or reduce the number of cones.
- Introduce different locomotor movements.

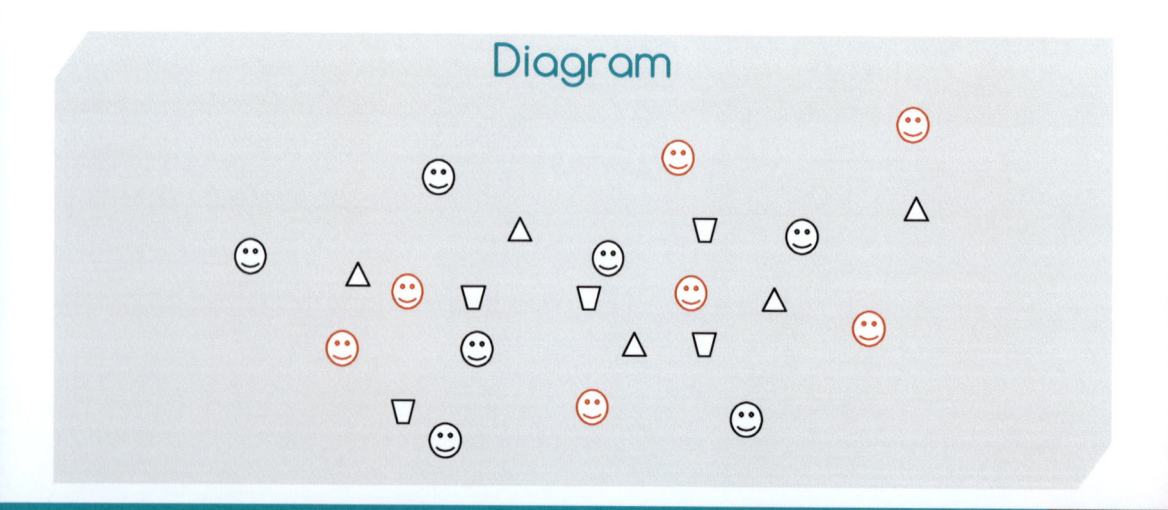

Diagram

Triangle Tag

Recommended Grades:

Grades 3-6

Equipment:

None needed.

Tactical Problems:

Tagging, avoid getting tagged, and footwork (shuffle).

Rules of Play:

1. Students will be placed in teams of four. 2. Three players form a triangle with the fourth player remaining outside. 3. There is one designated person in the triangle that is meant to be tagged. 4. The teammates all shuffle in a circular motion either to the right or to the left to protect the designated person from being tagged.
5. Change taggers and designated player to be tagged after 45 seconds.

Safety:

Appropriate/soft tagging and no pulling.

Variations/Progressions:

- More players in the triangle – could form a square or a circle.

Diagram

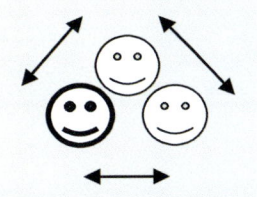

Tusker Tag

Recommended Grades:

Grades 3-6

Equipment:

Noodle sticks.

Tactical Problems:

Tagging, avoid getting tagged, communication, and using the space available.

Rules of Play:

1. The entire class will be paired up into teams of 2.
2. One team will be the taggers, each holding a noodle stick.
3. To tag other students, the tusker team must touch another team with the noodle sticks.
4. Once a team is tagged, they are frozen and they must raise their hands to form a bridge in which other teams have to run through in order to unfreeze and free them.
5. If a pair of students is running around and their hands come apart, they become frozen and must wait until a team runs underneath their arms.

Safety:

Keep your head up to avoid collisions and appropriate/soft tagging.

Variations/Progressions:

- Add more tusker teams (tagging teams).
- Make the playing area smaller or larger.
- Instead of becoming frozen, pairs of students become a tusker team as well and grab a noodle stick each to join the tagging team.

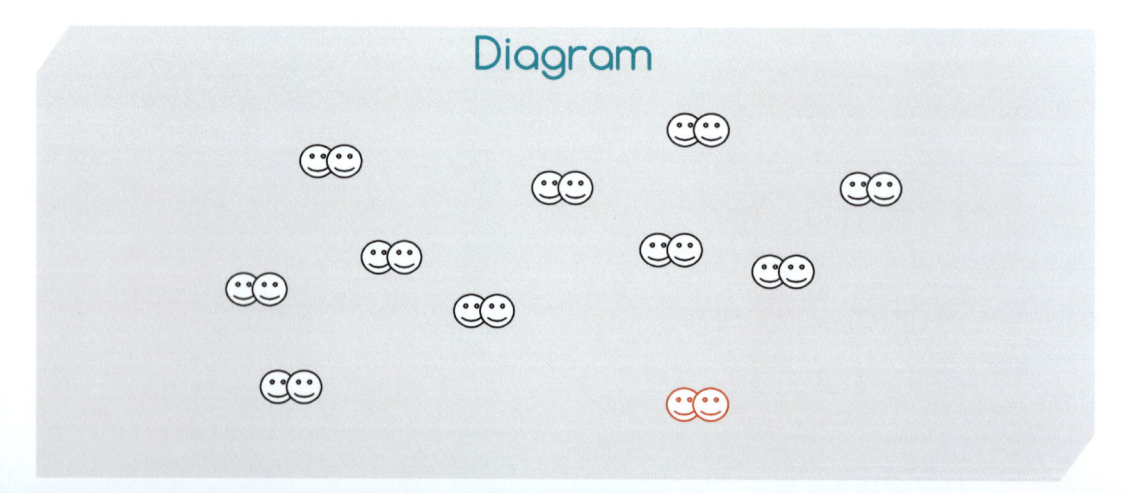

Diagram

Zombie Tag

Recommended Grades:

Grades 3-6

Equipment:

Soft gator skin balls and hula hoops.

Tactical Problems:

Tagging, avoid getting tagged, and using the space available.

Rules of Play:

1. Players must try to get a hold of the "zombie balls".
2. Once they have possession of the ball, they are not allowed to move and must try to hit another player by throwing the ball between his/her legs, much like the football hut.
3. If a player is hit by the ball, they in turn become a zombie.
4. A zombie puts one foot in a hula-hoop.
5. They can move around the playing area in an attempt to tag someone, who will then take the zombie's place.
6. Another alternative is to touch all 4 walls or to grab hold of the zombie ball in order to be "dezombified".

Safety:

Keep your head up to avoid collisions, be aware of the ball at all times, and appropriate/soft tagging.

Variations/Progressions:

- Alter the way students may throw the ball.
- Increase or decrease the number of balls in play.
- Allow for a certain number of steps with the ball.

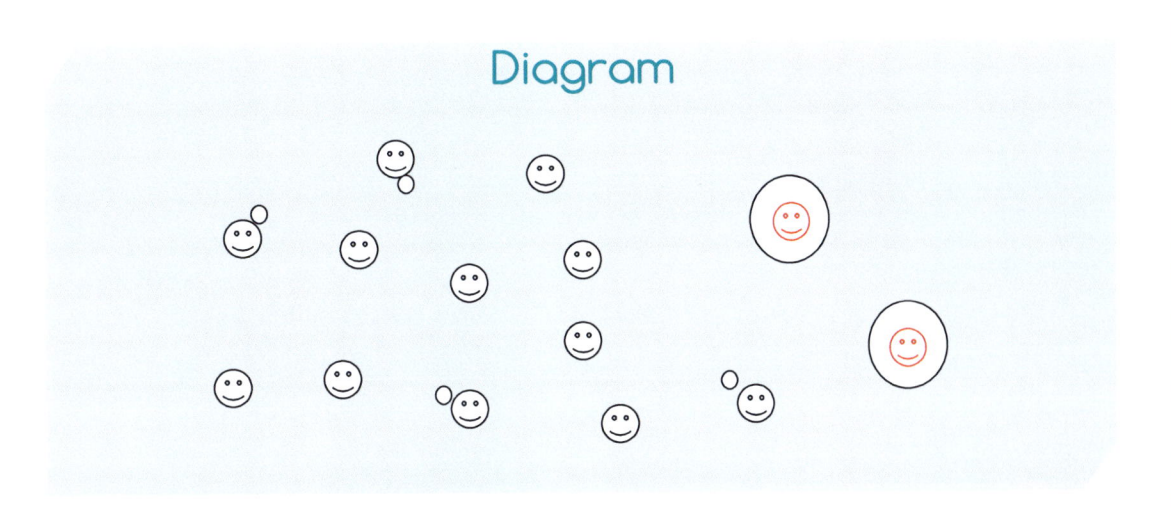

Diagram

Cops and Burglars

Recommended Grades:

Grades 5-6

Equipment:

Cones and a soft gator skin ball.

Tactical Problems:

Tagging, avoid getting tagged, feinting, and accurate passing and receiving.

Rules of Play:

1. At "go", robbers will attempt to enter the diamond store and steal the diamond.
2. Robbers in the diamond store are considered safe, but can only stay in there for 5 seconds.
3. Robbers can run or pass the ball to their teammates in order to reach the safe zone.
4. If the ball is dropped, the cop team wins that round.
5. Cops exit their police station and run after the robbers, even before a robber enters the diamond store.
6. If cops exit the police station, they must touch a robber; otherwise they become robbers on the next round.

Safety:

Keep your head up to avoid collisions and appropriate/soft tagging.

Variations/Progressions:

- Introduce different locomotor movements.
- Have the robbers designate a diamond snatcher prior to the round beginning.
- Have more than one store.

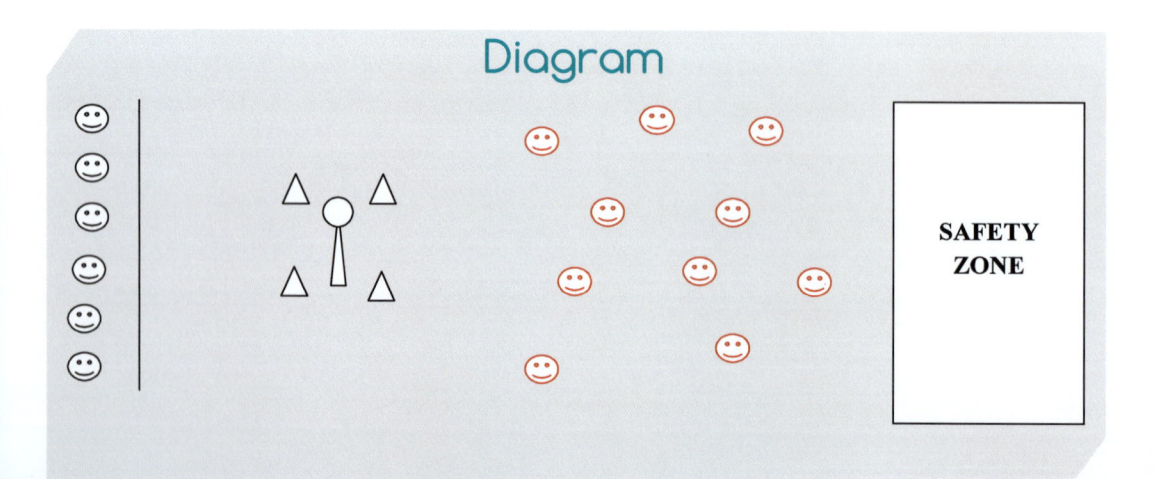

Diagram

SAFETY ZONE

Leg Ball

Recommended Grades:

Grades 5-6

Equipment:

Soft gator skin balls.

Tactical Problems:

Tagging, avoid getting tagged, and hitting a target.

Rules of Play:

1. Free-For-All – Students are on their own (no teams).
2. Each student tries to "tag" the other students with the ball.
3. To throw the ball, the student must be facing backwards and throw the ball between his or her legs.
4. Once you get touched by a ball in the air, the student is "out".
5. Students go to the side line and do 10 jumping jacks to get back into the game.

Safety:

Aim low with the ball and keep your head up to avoid collisions.

Variations/Progressions:

- Students can perform another physical activity (i.e. push ups, sit ups) to come back in.
- Students that get knocked out must stay out until 5 students are out – then they can come back in.
- Introduce a time limit.

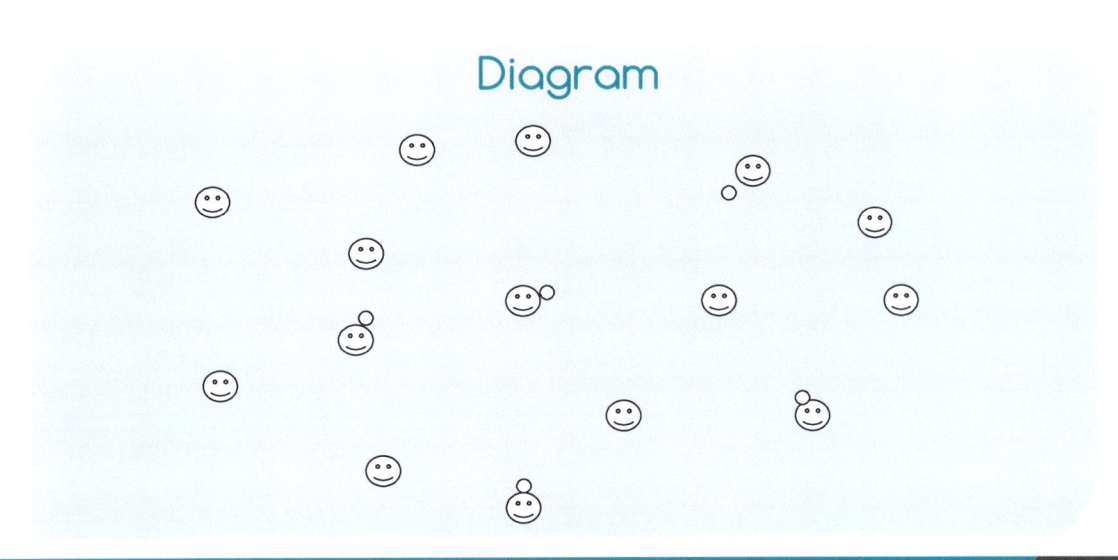

Diagram

Streets & Alleys

Recommended Grades:
Grades 5-6

Equipment:
None needed.

Tactical Problems:
Tagging, avoid getting tagged, footwork, anticipating, and using the space available.

Rules of Play:
1. Students will line up in 4 equal rows, spaced out, facing the same direction, and arms spread out so that their fingers are just touching the hands of the person to the left and right of them.
2. Streets are formed when players' arms form long sections while alleys are formed as shorter sections.
3. Teacher will choose a cop to chase a robber.
4. During the game, the teacher will call out either "Streets" or "Alleys" and thus the players forming the walls must turn and face the correct direction.
5. If the robber is caught, choose a different cop and robber.
6. Choose a different cop and robber every 30 seconds.
7. Call "Streets" or "Alleys" more or less often depending on the ease the cop and/or robber are having in the game.

Safety:
Keep your head up, appropriate/soft tagging, and watch out not to hit anyone when you turn from the Streets position to the Alleys position and vice versa.

Variations/Progressions:
- Add more cops/robbers.
- Introduce breaks in the walls

Diagram

STREETS

ALLEYS

Team Flag Tag

Recommended Grades:
Grades 5-6

Equipment:
Pinnies.

Tactical Problems:
Tagging, avoid getting tagged, communication, and using the space available.

Rules of Play:

1. Players will be divided into 4 teams – each will be given different colored pinnies.
2. Students will tuck in their respective team's pinnies in their shorts with most of it hanging out.
3. The objective of the game it to pull off the pinnies from the players of the other teams while at the same time defending your own pinnie from being pulled off.
4. All teams are against each other with the last team left in the playing space winning.
5. This is a knockout game - if a student's pinnie is pulled out that student is out of the game until one team is left.
6. Teams must work together to stay in the game and protect each other from the other opponents..

Safety:
Keep your head up to avoid collisions and appropriate/soft pull of the pinnie when tagging.

Variations/Progressions:
- More teams can be added.
- Each player may have two pinnies instead of one

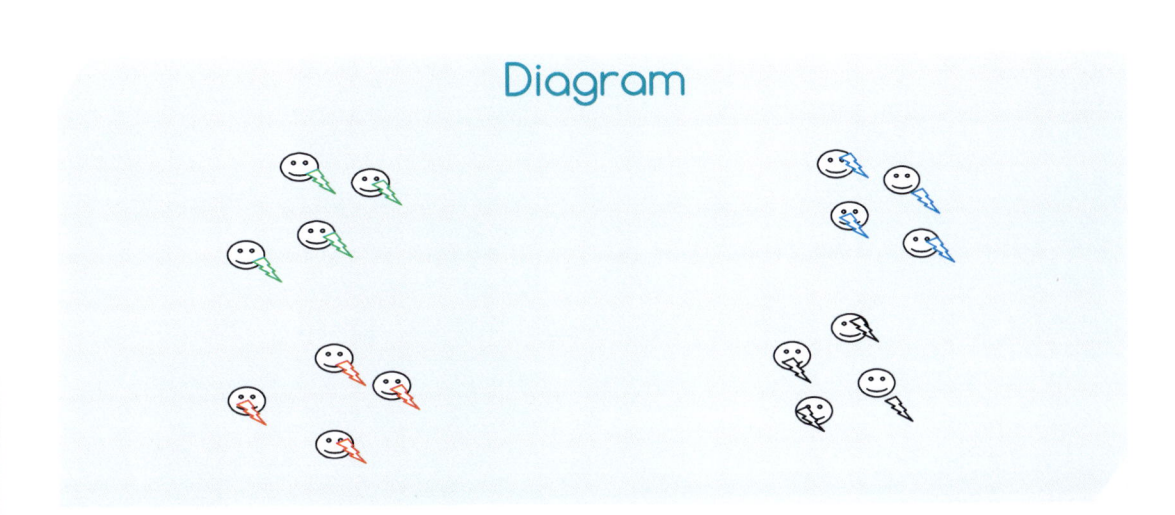

Diagram

Under the Leg

Recommended Grades:

Grades 5-6

Equipment:

Semi-deflated beach balls.

Tactical Problems:

Using the space available, tagging, and avoid getting tagged (by the ball).

Rules of Play:

1. Students will scatter around the playing area, which in itself is a shared space and not divided.
2. Two semi-deflated beach balls will be thrown into play.
3. When a student grabs hold of a beach ball, they are not allowed to locomote.
4. To tag another player, he/she must throw the ball underneath his/her legs.
5. When hit, players must go outside the boundaries and wait for a total of 5 players to be out before returning into the game.

Safety:

Keep your head up to avoid collisions and aim below the neck region.

Variations/Progressions:

- Number of balls in the game.
- Introduce jumping jacks (or another activity) as a way of returning into the game.

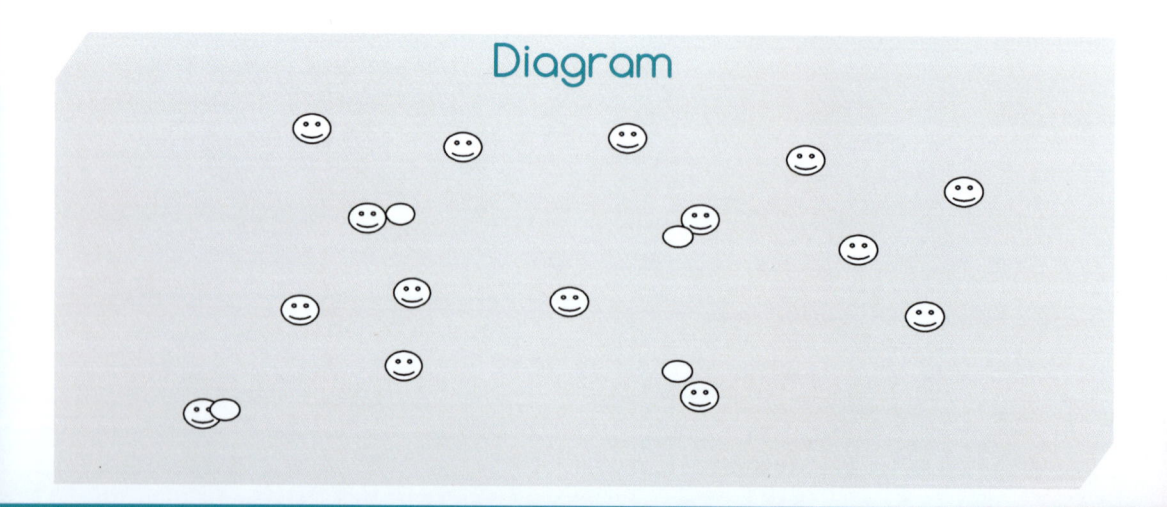

Diagram

Striking/Fielding

Beat The Leader

Recommended Grades:
Kindergarten – Grade 4

Equipment:
Tennis balls and buckets.

Tactical Problems:
Placement of the ball in the field and fielding positions.

Rules of Play:
1. The teacher (or a designated student) will be the leader with a bucket filled with tennis balls.
2. Remaining students will spread out around the area and act as fielders.
3. The leader will toss the balls as high and as quick as possible in all directions.
4. Students can catch/retrieve the ball and must run to return the ball back into the bucket.
5. If the thrower empties the bucket at any time, he/she wins.
6. Change the leader.

Safety:
Ensure that students keep their heads up and are aware of all the balls in play.

Variations/Progressions:
- Fielders must perform different locomotor movements.
- Have more than 1 leader.
- Have 2 buckets – 1 for the throwers and 1 for the retrievers with a time limit.

Diagram

Fire At Will

Recommended Grades:

Grades K-4

Equipment:

Bucket, cones, soft balls, and a bat.

Tactical Problems:

Placement of the ball in the field and fielding positions.

Rules of Play:

1. Divide students so that there is 1 leader/batter (teacher or assigned student) and numerous fielders.
2. A perimeter will be set up with cones.
3. Fielders must stay behind their boundary line.
4. The leader/batter will begin the game by picking a soft ball up from the bucket behind him and striking it into play.
5. When a fielder retrieves the ball, he/she will have to run around one side of the cones and place the ball back into the bucket before continuing forward and back to the fielding area.
6. As such, this game becomes a "Beat The Leader" style of game where the leader/batter can strike the balls with the striking instrument or may also throw and kick the balls.

Safety:

Ensure students do not collide while attempting to retrieve the same ball at once and be careful for students running around the perimeter – ensure there is enough room.

Variations/Progressions:

- Add a leader/batter.
- Increase or decrease the size of the playing area.

Diagram

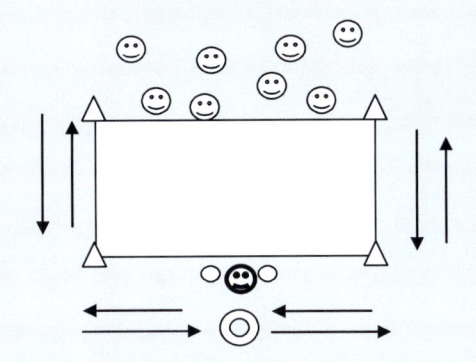

Incoming

Recommended Grades:
Grades K-4

Equipment:
Container/Bin, tennis balls, and hula-hoops.

Tactical Problems:
Placement of the ball in the field, sprinting, and quick and accurate sending and receiving skills.

Rules of Play:
1. The first player runs towards the team's designated bin.
2. When he/she collects a ball, he/she must first step in the hoop, and attempts to return one ball to her/his corner by hitting it with his/her hand.
3. The team members field the ball and then pass it to one another before the last person in line places it in a hoop located in their corner.
4. The batter then runs to the back of her/his line and tags the next player on the team to go.
5. This process continues until the bin of balls is empty.
6. First team to complete the task is the winner.

Safety:
Be aware of the ball at all times.

Variations/Progressions:
- Change the type of ball being used.
- Add a batting instrument.
- Introduce different locomotor movements.

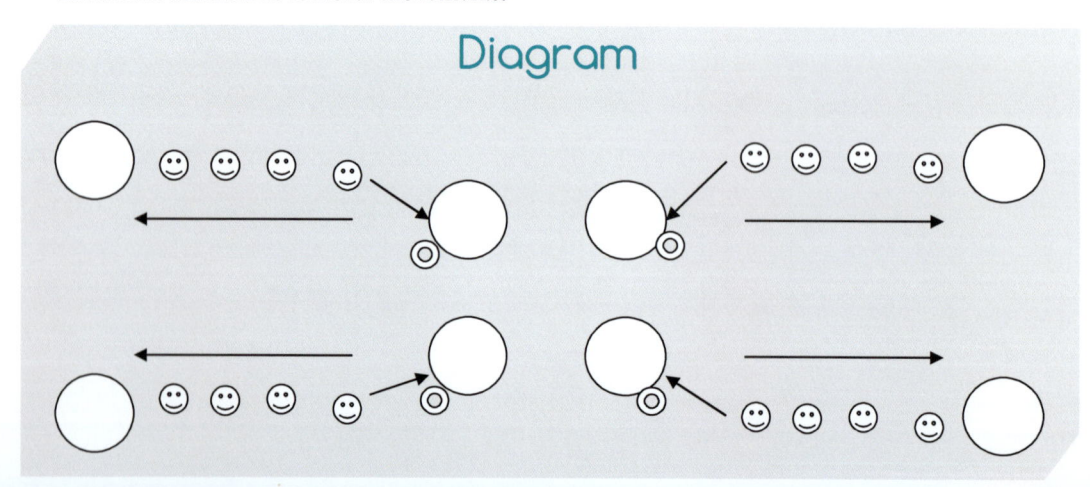

Diagram

Buckets

Recommended Grades:
Grades K-6

Equipment:
Soft balls and large baskets/bins.

Tactical Problems:
Fielding positions.

Rules of Play:

1. Divide students into teams of 4.
2. Each student of each team will be numbered between 1 – 4.
3. The teacher begins with a full basket of soft balls in the center of the playing area.
4. Each team of 4 places a basket somewhere on the boundaries of the playing area.
5. The teacher will then empty the basket as quickly as possible by either tossing or rolling the balls.
6. Player #1 must pick up a ball and return to his/her team's basket.
7. The team will form a circle around the basket.
8. The person with the ball passes it starting to the left or right of the circle.
9. When the ball goes back to the player that retrieved the ball, he/she puts it in the basket.
10. If the ball is dropped, the passing restarts.
11. The next numbered player goes to retrieve a ball.
12. Play until there are no more balls in play – team with the most balls wins.

Safety:
Ensure students use the space available to them and keep their heads up to avoid collisions.

Variations/Progressions:
- Use different equipment.
- Increase or decrease the size of the playing area.
- Use different manipulation techniques.

Diagram

3 Ball

Recommended Grades:
Grades 3-4

Equipment:
Container, various balls, and cones.

Tactical Problems:
Placement of the ball in the field, base running, and quick and accurate sending and receiving skills.

Rules of Play:
1. 2 teams will set up, one on the field, one sitting at the side with the batter up and ready to go.
2. The batter will have various types of balls at his disposal: tennis balls, oversized footballs, dodgeballs, etc. He/she then 3 of these objects wherever he/she would like.
3. After the third item is thrown, he/she may start running around the bases.
4. As for the outfielders, they are not allowed to move until that 3rd ball is tossed.
5. The team in the field then passes the objects to their teammates with the goal of placing all the objects back into the box.
6. Once all the objects are in the box, you stop counting the number of bases the player has run around.
7. Each time a runner makes it back to home, the team gets a point.

Safety:
Keep your head up to avoid any collision with the fielding team, be aware of the balls at all times, and communicate.

Variations/Progressions:
- Add more bases than the standard
- Introduce different locomotor movements.

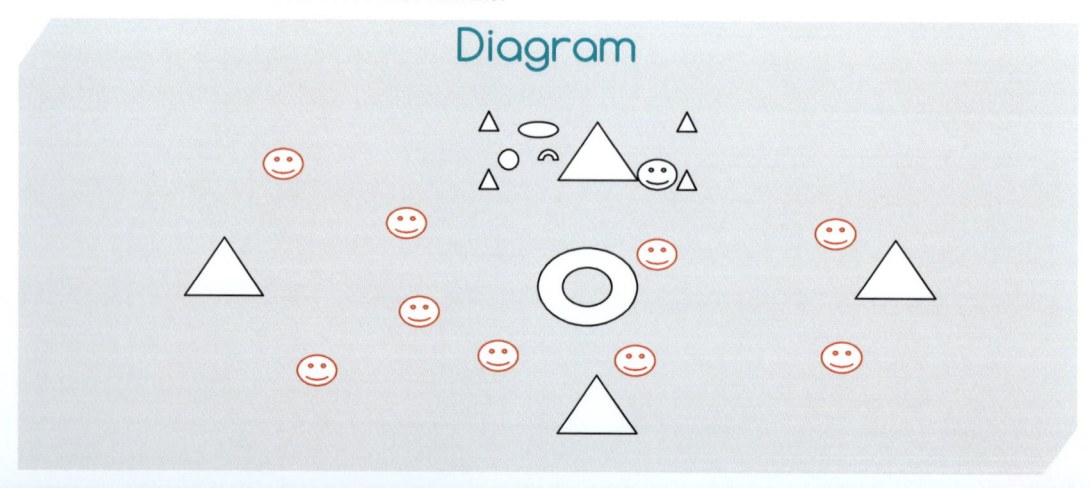

Diagram

Back and Forth

Recommended Grades:
Grades 3-6

Equipment:
Tees, cones, batting instruments, and soft balls.

Tactical Problems:
Placement of the ball in the field, covering bases, base running, and fielding positions.

Rules of Play:

1. Students will be divided into pairs or into small groups.
2. Each pair/group will have a tee, a cone, a bat, and a soft ball.
3. One player begins as the batter and hits the ball off the tee, also home base.
4. The cone will be set up a certain distance in front of the batter serving as a base.
5. Batter attempts to get to the base and back home (scoring 1 point) as many times as possible before the fielding player returns the ball to home and places the ball on the tee.
6. A player is out if a fly ball is caught or if the ball is returned to home base while the batter is between both bases.
7. Batter's turn is over once 5 consecutive hits are made or 2 outs are achieved.

Safety:
Ensure students are spaced out around the playing area and are aware of the balls in play.

Variations/Progressions:
- Allow the fielder the ability to return the ball to whichever is closest – the tee or the cone.
- Increase or decrease the distance between the tee and the cone.
- Add more bases.
- Fielder pitches the ball.

Diagram

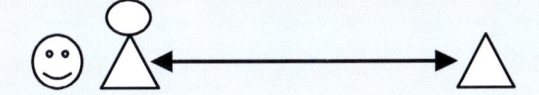

Base Running

Recommended Grades:
Grades 3-6

Equipment:
Tees, bases, soft balls, and baseball bats.

Tactical Problems:
Placement of the ball in the field, covering bases, fielding positions, forcing play, and base running.

Rules of Play:
1. Divide students into 2 teams.
2. One team will start at bat while the other team will be the fielding team.
3. Play begins with the first batter hitting the ball off the tee.
4. To score a point, he/she must make it to first base and his/her entire batting team must form a line behind him/her.
5. Points are only scored when a line is formed behind the single base and not at home plate – batting team must also run and form a line at home plate when returning from the base in order to proceed.
6. To stop the batting team, the fielders must field the ball and throw it at "home", only after everyone has touched the ball once.

Safety:
Use a soft ball, make sure there is enough space provided for the batter, and ensure that fielders call out to who the pass is intended for.

Variations/Progressions:
- Have a pitcher.
- Batting team must score runs using different locomotor movements.

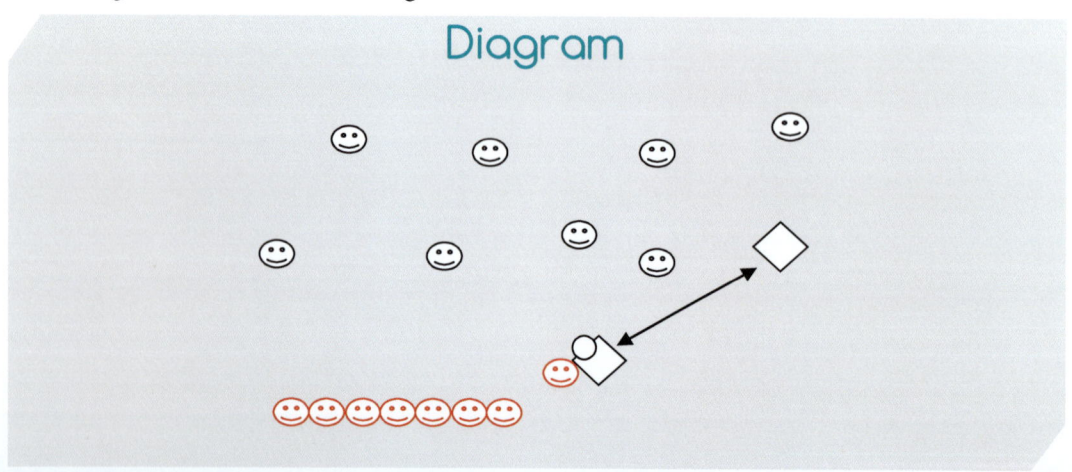

Diagram

Beanbags

Recommended Grades:

Grades 3-6

Equipment:

Beanbags, bases, and hula-hoops.

Tactical Problems:

Placement of the beanbag on the field, decision making, covering bases, base running, fielding positions, and quick and accurate receiving and sending skills.

Rules of Play:

1. Divide students into 2 teams.
2. Players from the fielding team position themselves in the infield/outfield and the players from the batting team line up in a straight line across home base, each holding different color beanbags.
3. The batting team will begin the game by all throwing the beanbags into play.
4. As a team, the batting team must run around the bases.
5. The fielders must collect the beanbags, place them in the correctly colored hula-hoop, and yell "Stop!"
6. Fielders can only take 3 steps with the beanbag.
7. A point is awarded to the batting team if they score and they continue to "bat" for up to 2 more additional turns.
8. If the fielding team gains the point, they switch roles with the batting team.

Safety:

Ensure students keep their heads up to avoid collisions and that beanbags are not thrown at people.

Variations/Progressions:

- Increase or decrease distances between the bases.
- Do not allow fielders to take any steps with the beanbags.

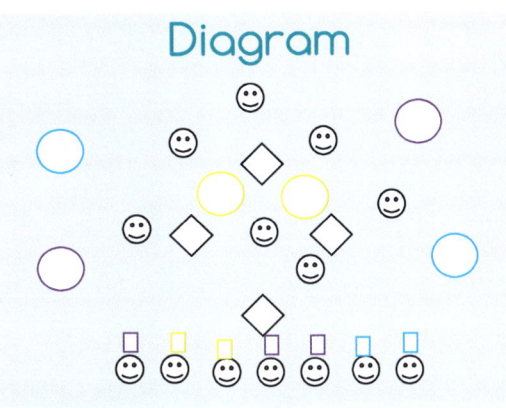

Diagram

Belly Flop

Recommended Grades:

Grades 3-6

Equipment:

Mats (crash mats), hula-hoops, soft balls, and bats.

Tactical Problems:

Placement of the ball in the field, decision making, covering bases, base running, fielding positions, forcing play, staying on offense, and quick and accurate sending and receiving skills.

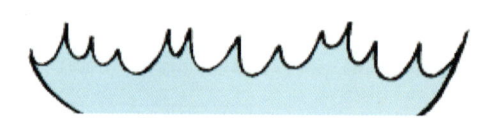

Rules of Play:

1. Divide students into 2 teams.
2. There will be a hula-hoop placed as the home base and 3 crash mats for 1st, 2nd, and 3rd base.
3. The pitcher throws the ball and bounces it before it reaches the hula-hoop.
4. When the batter makes contact, he/she runs to the bases and must "belly flop" or "dive" on the base.
5. He/she can stay on the base or continue to move to the next base by first rolling before running and "belly flopping" once more to the next base.
6. Regular softball rules – caught fly ball is an out and the game is played with 3 outs.

Safety:

Ensure that the mats used are safe and ensure that students do not over exaggerate the belly flop.

Variations/Progressions:

- Go through the entire batting order once before switching.
- Use different striking and fielding instruments.
- Increase or decrease the distances between the bases.

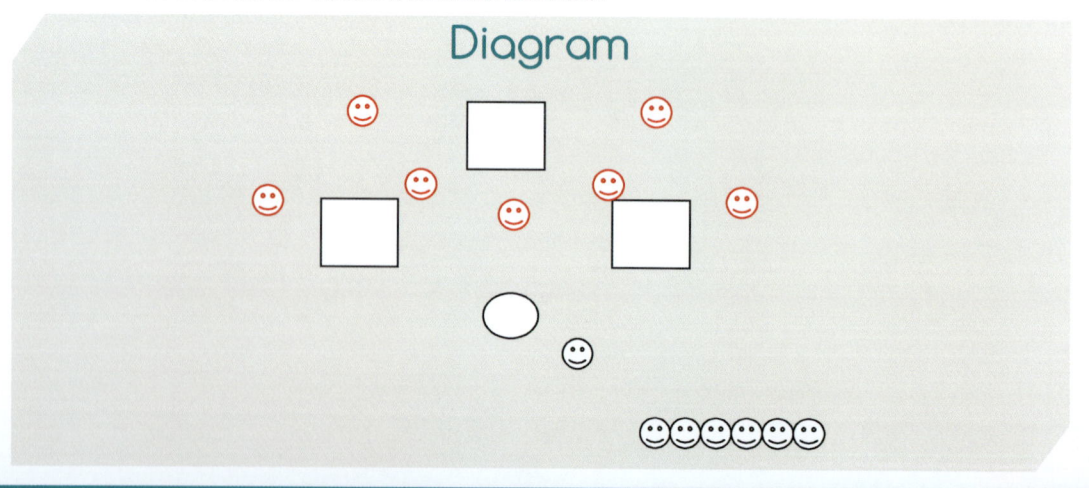

Diagram

Boot It

Recommended Grades:
Grades 3-6

Equipment:
Buckets, various balls, and bases.

Tactical Problems:
Placement of the ball on the field, covering bases, base running, fielding positions, and forcing play.

Rules of Play:

1. Divide students into teams of 6 – 2 teams on one field.
2. One team will field while the other will bat.
3. 3 balls will be placed in a bucket next to home plate.
4. The 1st batter in line will kick each of the 3 balls and then run around the bases.
5. If a ball is caught in the air, the player holds the ball high in the air.
6. Otherwise, other kicked balls must be retrieved and placed in the bucket.
7. A runner is out if all the balls are caught/returned and he/she is off a base.
8. More than one runner is allowed per base.
9. Runs are scored when players return home.

Safety:
Ensure students call out for a fly ball in order to avoid collisions and ensure there is enough room between the batter and the batting team.

Variations/Progressions:
- Add or remove balls from the mix.
- Fielders are not allowed to go after the balls until all 3 balls are kicked.
- Increase or decrease the distances between the bases.

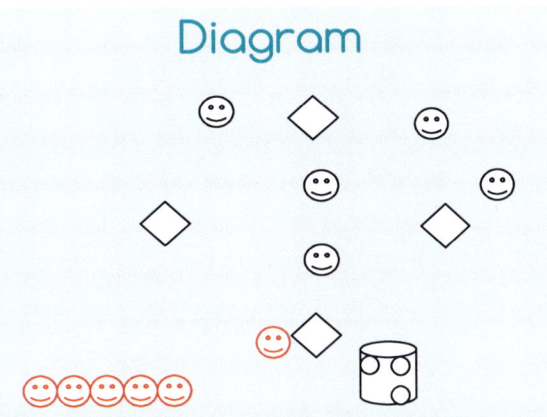

Diagram

Chuck the Chicken

Recommended Grades:

Grades 3-6

Equipment:

Pinnies and rubber chickens.

Tactical Problems:

Placement of the chicken on the field, decision making, fielding positions, keeping turn for as long as possible, and accurate receiving and sending skills.

Rules of Play:

1. Divide students into 2 teams.
2. The 1st team will be lined up with the 1st player in line holding a rubber chicken.
3. The fielding team will be scattered around the playing area.
4. The 1st player of the throwing team will send the rubber chicken anywhere in the playing area while yelling "Chuck the chicken!"
5. During this time, the player from the throwing team will run around the line as many times as he/she can, scoring a point for his/her team each time a whole turn is made around the group.
6. Meanwhile, the fielding team will attempt to retrieve the plush.
7. When a player from the fielding team retrieves the plush, the remaining players must form a line behind him/her and begin to pass the rubber chicken to the other players, first passing left, then passing right, so on and so forth until it reaches the last player who yells "Stop!"
8. Repeat with teams switching roles – play until a certain score or time limit is achieved.

Safety:

Ensure students keep their heads up to avoid collisions.

Variations/Progressions:

- Pass the object between the legs and over the head.

Diagram

Cone 3s

Recommended Grades:

Grades 3-6

Equipment:

Cones and a soft foam balls.

Tactical Problems:

Base running and quick & accurate sending.

Rules of Play:

1. Students will be divided into pairs.
2. Each pair will have a station set up with 3 cones and 1 soft foam ball resting on the middle cone.
3. One cone will be closer to the middle while one cone will be further from it with both partners standing on either one of them.
4. Partner at home base walks toward middle cone, walks around it, and then sprints for home.
5. Partner at farthest cone begins to run towards the middle cone only once the other player begins to go around the middle cone.
6. Once the partner from the farthest cone reaches the middle cone, he/she picks up the ball from the top of the cone and attempts to throw the ball at the home plate cone before the runner is able to get back.
7. Switch roles often.

Safety:

Ensure students are given adequate spacing between playing areas and that throwers do not aim for the student, but instead aim for the cone.

Variations/Progressions:

- Increase or decrease distances between cones.
- Introduce different locomotor movements.
- Introduce tagging.

Diagram

Cross Country Smack The Round Thing

Recommended Grades:

Grades 3-6

Equipment:

Container, cones, batting instruments (i.e. baseball bat, tennis racket), and a soft ball.

Tactical Problems:

Placement of the ball on the field, base running, forcing play, holding runner on base, and quick and accurate sending and receiving skills.

Rules of Play:

1. There are 2 teams playing in a very large space.
2. The game will start with one batter on deck while the other players are occupying a base - the fielding team will space themselves out.
3. The instructor will pitch and when the ball is hit, everyone on the bases must move on to as many bases as they can before the outfielders make 3 passes, place the ball inside the bucket in the middle, and yell "STOP!".
4. Everyone must bat once before teams switch roles.
5. The bat must stay inside the box after the hit is made or else the hit doesn't count.

Safety:

Keep your head up to avoid collisions with your team or the fielding team and be aware of the ball at all times.

Variations/Progressions:

- Increase or decrease the number of bases in play.
- Increase or decrease the minimum number of passes requirement.
- Change the type of ball used.

Diagram

Danish Longball

Recommended Grades:

Grades 3-6

Equipment:

Batting instruments (baseball bat, tennis racket, etc.), cones, and a soft gator skin ball.

Tactical Problems:

Placement of the ball in the field, holding runner on base, and quick and accurate sending and receiving skills.

Rules of Play:

1. There are 2 teams playing in a very large space.
2. One team will be at bats with the other players sitting on the bench while the fielding team will space themselves out.
3. The instructor will pitch and when the ball is hit, the batter must make his/her way to the safety zone, where he/she has the option to stay in there or to attempt to run back to the batting zone.
4. He/she must do this without getting hit by the ball that the outfielders have caught/recovered.
5. The fielding team can run with the ball or pass it off to teammates.
6. Everyone must bat once before teams switch roles.
7. The bat must stay inside the box after the hit is made or else the hit doesn't count.
8. A point is equal to one trip to the safety zone and back to the batting zone.

Safety:

Aim low with the ball, call for the ball, and be aware of the ball at all times.

Variations/Progressions:

- Add another safety zone.
- Change the type of bat/ball used.

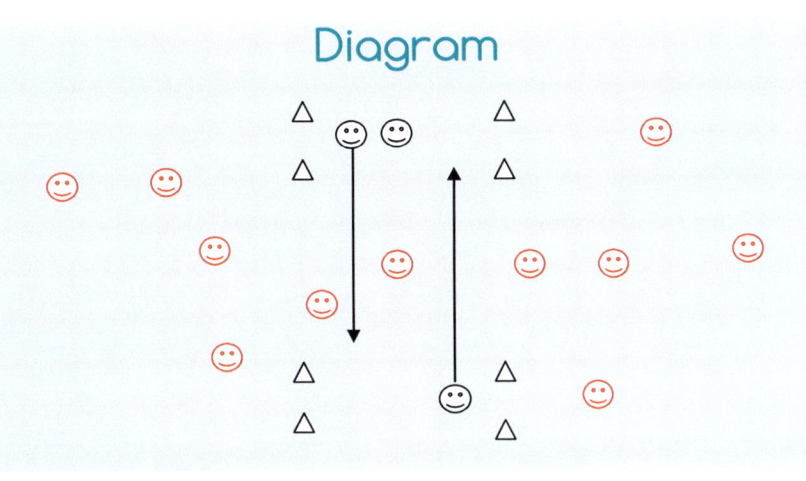

Diagram

Four Quarters

Recommended Grades:
Grades 3-6

Equipment:
Ropes, cones, hula-hoops, rackets, and tennis balls.

Tactical Problems:
Placement of the ball in the field, covering bases, base running, fielding positions, forcing play, and quick and accurate receiving and sending skills.

Rules of Play:
1. Divide students into small groups (4 – 6 students).
2. Place 4 ropes so that they divide 4 quarters of the playing field.
3. At the end of these ropes, cones will be placed.
4. In each playing quarter, there will be 2 hula-hoops – one for the pitcher and one for the hitter with the rest of the players spread out in the outfield.
5. The pitcher will toss a tennis ball to the batter who will then make contact with the ball with a racket.
6. As the fielding team attempts to get the ball back to the pitcher, the runner will run as many times as he can from one cone to the other.
7. Every time a cone is touched, 1 point is earned.
8. Switch roles after each hit – players keep track of their own score..

Safety:
Ensure students are adequately spaced out from the other 3 quarters of the playing field.

Variations/Progressions:
- Introduce different locomotor movements for the batter.
- Increase or decrease the distance between the cones.
- Use different striking and fielding implements.

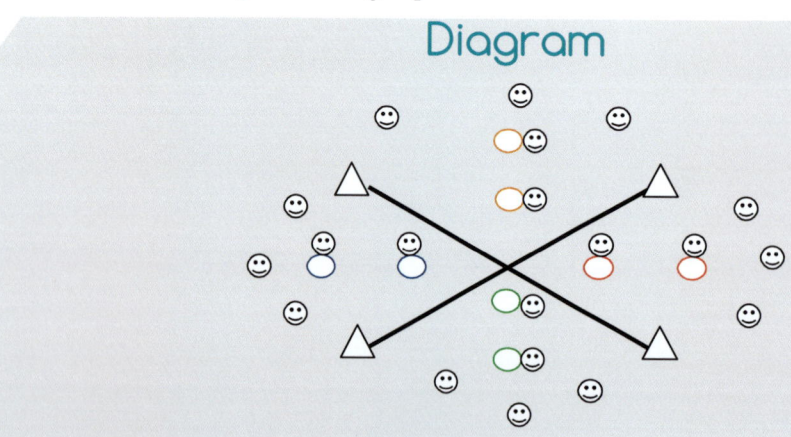

Diagram

Go Home

Recommended Grades:
Grades 3-6

Equipment:
Soft foam balls and bases.

Tactical Problems:
Covering bases, base running, holding runner from stealing, and quick and accurate sending skills.

Rules of Play:
1. Divide students into small groups in each of the 4 bases – there will also be students set up in the middle with soft foam balls at their disposal.
2. The goal of the game is for the groups to score points by running from their starting base (home base) and returning back home by running through all the bases.
3. The players in the middle attempt to hit the students with the ball below the waist.
4. If a player is hit, he/she must raise his/her hand and return to his/her home base before running again.
5. Play until a certain time limit or score limit is reached and switch roles.

Safety:
Ensure students aim below the waist with the ball and that students do not suddenly stop running with players behind them.

Variations/Progressions:
- Create a relay-type activity with groups of 4 – 1 player on each base.
- Add or remove the number of throwers.
- Increase or decrease the distances between the bases & the # of bases.

Diagram

Hockey Bases

Recommended Grades:

Grades 3-6

Equipment:

Cones, hula-hoops, hockey sticks, and beanbags.

Tactical Problems:

Placements of the beanbags on the field, covering bases, base running, fielding positions, forcing play, and quick and accurate receiving and sending skills.

Rules of Play:

1. Divide students into small groups (4 – 6 students).
2. Depending on the number of students in a group, set up different colored beanbags next to the batting area with equivalent colored hula-hoops on the playing surface.
3. Two cones will also be set up next to the batting area for the batter to make runs.
4. Batter will use the hockey stick to send the beanbags into the field and then run from cone to cone.
5. Fielding team can only start collecting beanbags once the last beanbag is sent.
6. Beanbags must be brought back to the appropriate colored hula-hoop.
7. The batter stops running once all the beanbags are collected and earns 1 point for every cone that he/she passes.
8. Rotate players.

Safety:

Ensure students keep the beanbags on the floor and do not shoot them in the air.

Variations/Progressions:

- Increase the number of beanbags/hula-hoops in play.
- Use different striking and fielding implements.
- Fielding team can only take 3 steps with the beanbag (or no steps at all).

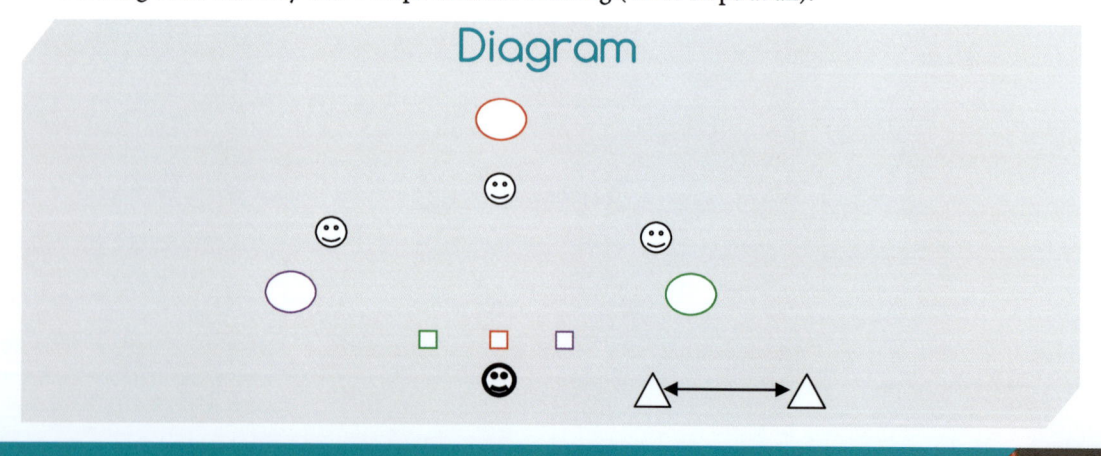

Diagram

Home Run

Recommended Grades:

Grades 3-6

Equipment:

Tees, cones, bats, and wiffle balls (or other appropriate balls).

Tactical Problems:

Placement of the ball on the field and fielding positions.

Rules of Play:

1. Divide students into 2 teams – batting and fielding.
2. The first player of the batting team will strike the wiffle ball in an attempt to get it as far as possible.
3. The fielding team will attempt anything to stop this from happening.
4. 3 cones will be placed – at the three-point marker (1 point), half court (2 points), and the opposite three-point marker (3 points) with the opposite wall being worth 5 points.
5. If the fielding team knocks down the ball, the ball is counted where it stopped in terms of points earned.
6. If a ball is caught in the air, no points are awarded.
7. Go through the entire batting order before switching roles.

Safety:

Ensure there is sufficient distance between the fielding team and the batter and ensure players keep their heads up to avoid collisions.

Variations/Progressions:

- Change the point system.
- Play outdoors.
- Add cones.

Diagram

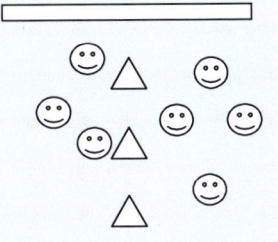

In The Trash

Recommended Grades:
Grades 3-6

Equipment:
Trashcan/basket/bucket, cones, bases, bats, and soft balls.

Tactical Problems:
Placement of the ball in the field, covering bases, base running, fielding positions, forcing play, and quick and accurate receiving and sending skills.

Rules of Play:
1. Divide students into 2 teams – batting and fielding.
2. Regular softball rules with a few tweaks.
3. The batter must strike the ball after one bounce – pitched by the pitcher.
4. When the batter makes contact with the ball, he/she must first run to a "trashcan" to place his/her bat.
5. The fielding team can get a player out by catching it in the air, throwing to the appropriate base, or tagging the player with the ball.
6. Everyone bats in the inning before switching roles.

Safety:
Ensure students do not throw their bats towards the "trashcan"..

Variations/Progressions:
- Increase or decrease the distance between the "trashcan" and 1st base.
- Increase or decrease the distances between the bases.
- Use different striking and fielding implements

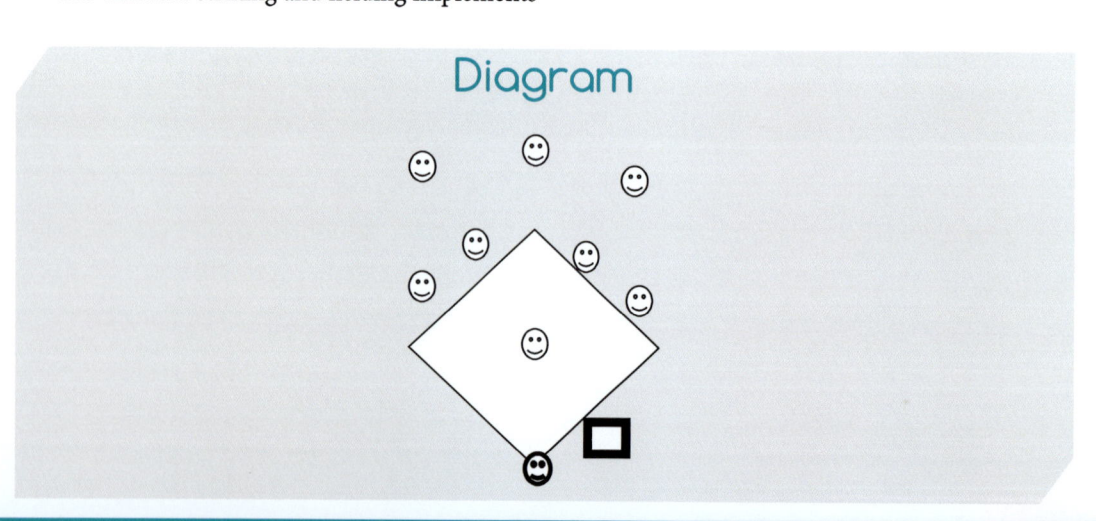

Diagram

Kick Galore

Recommended Grades:

Grades 3-6

Equipment:

Cones, hula-hoops, and soft balls

Tactical Problems:

Placement of the ball in the field, covering bases, base running, fielding positions, forcing play, keeping turn for as long as possible, and quick and accurate receiving and sending skills..

Rules of Play:

1. Divide students into groups of 8 – 10 (Two teams of 4 – 5 in each game).
2. The first batter of the batting team will kick 3 balls into the playing field.
3. Once the 3rd ball is kicked, the entire batting team runs from home base and to the opposite cone as many times as possible.
4. To avoid confusion, runners may only run back to the next cone once all players have crossed the imaginary line (i.e. no runner can start running towards the next cone until all players are behind the respective cone).
5. The fielding team must pick up the objects, pass them to one another (no steps allowed), and place them in a hula-hoop near home base.
6. A run is scored only when the entire batting team returns back to home base.
7. Switch roles once every player of the batting team has gotten the chance to kick.

Safety:

Ensure students from the fielding team keep their distance from the batting team and that the runners run without trampling one another.

Variations/Progressions:

- Introduce different locomotor movement.
- Increase or decrease the distance between the cones

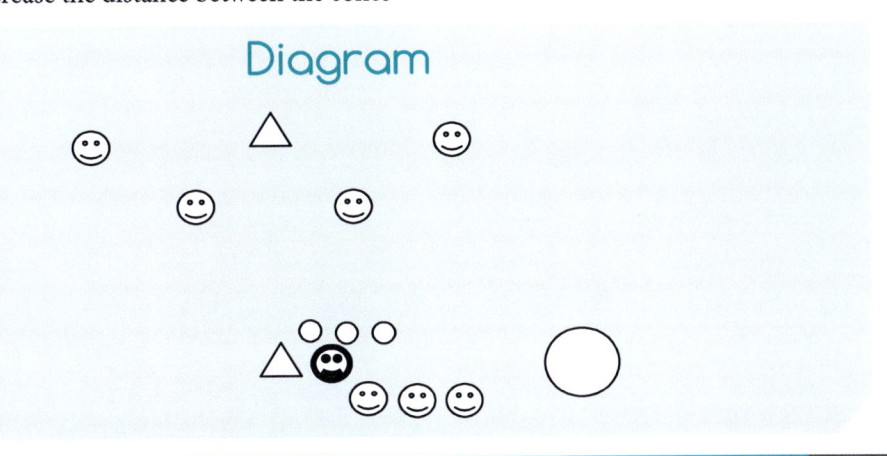

Diagram

147

Kickball (Soccer-Baseball)

Recommended Grades:

Grades 3-6

Equipment:

A soft ball and 4 bases or mats.

Tactical Problems:

Placement of the ball in the field, covering bases, base running, forcing play, and sending and receiving skills.

Rules of Play:

1. There will be two teams – one will be the kicking team lined up next to the wall and the fielding team on the field.
2. Pitcher will roll the ball to the kicking team – there are no strikeouts.
3. Game could be played with 3 outs or going through the kicking order.
4. Regular softball rules in terms of getting players out (pop fly, touching the appropriate base with ball possession, or tagging the player with the ball).
5. One player per base.

Safety:

Keep your head up to avoid collisions and keep your eye on the ball.

Variations/Progressions:

- Make students kick with their non-dominant foot.
- Increase or decrease the playing area.

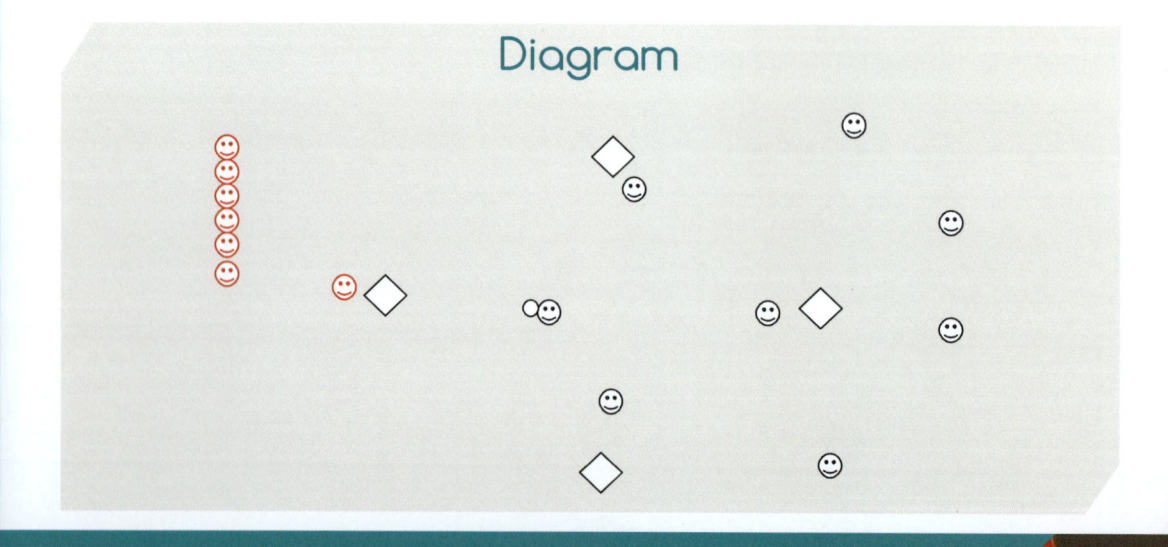

Diagram

Mini-Baseball

Recommended Grades:

Grades 3-6

Equipment:

Cones, batting instrument, soft ball, and placemats for the bases.

Tactical Problems:

Placement of the ball in the field, sprinting to base, and quick and accurate sending and receiving skills.

Rules of Play:

1. 3 versus 3 baseball.
2. The batter will strike the ball he/she pitched to himself/herself into the zone occupied by the 1st outfielder indicated by the two cones.
3. The batter must then run to first base before the 1st outfielder fields the ball and passes it to the first baseman.
4. If the batter makes it to 1st base, his/her team gets a point.
5. After each bat, the 3 outfielders will rotate positions (i.e. 1st baseman becomes 1st outfield to field the ball).
6. Teams will switch roles after 2 full batting rotations have been made.
7. Note: To avoid collision, there will be two bases for the batter and the fielder.

Safety:

Keep your head up to avoid collision with the fielding team and getting hit by the ball.

Variations/Progressions:

- Add a second base.
- Increase or decrease the distance between the cones indicating the zone occupied by the 1st outfielder.
- Add a tee.

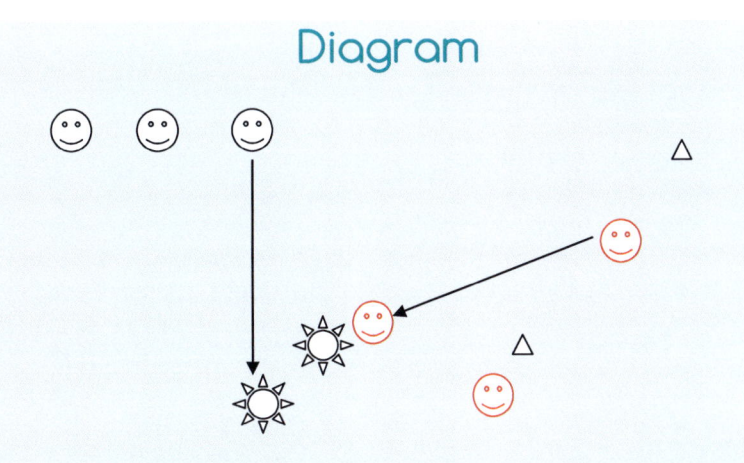

Diagram

Multi-Ball

Recommended Grades:

Grades 3-6

Equipment:

Buckets, tennis balls, and bases (recommended: score sheets).

Tactical Problems:

Placement of the ball in the field, decision making, covering bases, base running, fielding positions, and accurate receiving and sending skills.

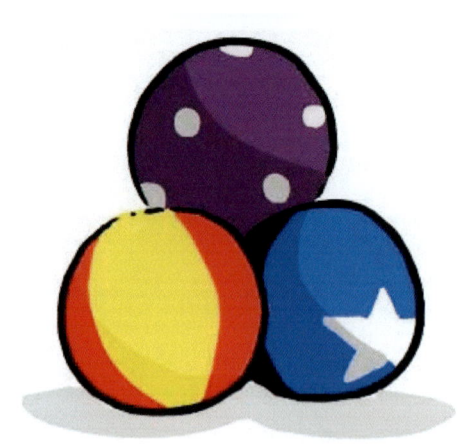

Rules of Play:

1. Organize students into small teams (6 – 8 players).
2. One player from the batting team will carry 10 tennis balls (alternatively, can use a tennis racket).
3. He/she will "bat" the balls all at the same time and begin running around the bases while the fielding team attempts to collect the balls and bring them back to the bucket in the middle.
4. If the batter is in between bases when all the balls are collected, he/she is out.
5. If a batter achieves a home run, he/she earns 4 points for his/her team.
6. If a batter stops at any of the other bases, he/she could only score a certain number of points when they return to home base.
7. For example, if the runner stops at 1st base, he/she could only earn 1 point (2nd base = 2 points, 3rd base = 3 points).
8. Switch roles when all players have batted once.

Safety:

Ensure that there is sufficient space between playing areas and that all players are aware of the balls in play.

Variations/Progressions:

- Different locomotor movements between bases.
- Use fewer balls and deny the ability of the fielding team to move around.

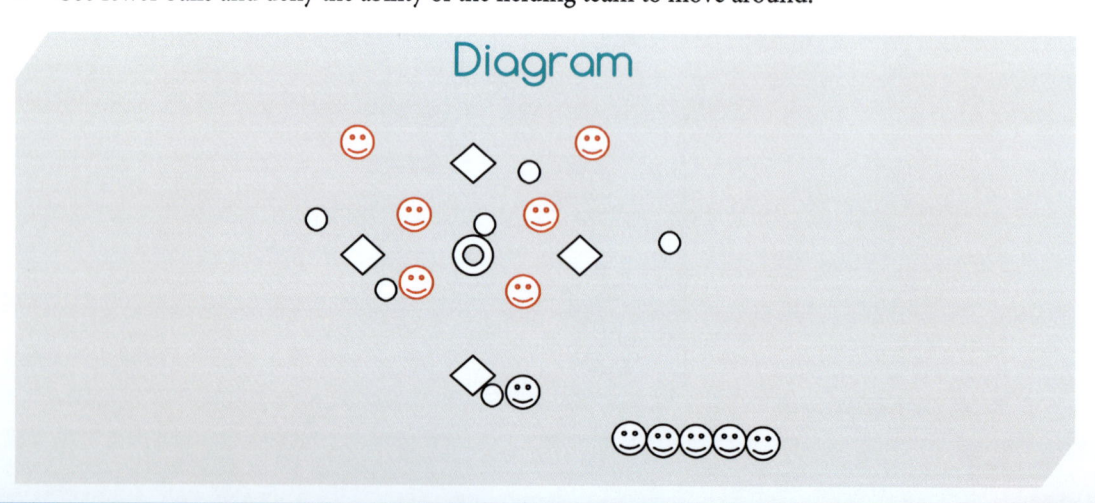

Diagram

No Man's Land

Recommended Grades:

Grades 3-6

Equipment:

Tennis balls and cones.

Tactical Problems:

Placement of the ball in the field, fielding positions, and accurate receiving and sending skills.

Rules of Play:

1. Divide students into groups of 6 (3 V 3 games).
2. Each team will have a goal on their end of the court marked by cones.
3. Each team will also have a throwing line – in between these throwing lines is "No Man's Land", an area where players may not enter.
4. One player begins the game with the tennis ball and attempts to get the ball past the other 2 defenders into the goal below waist height in order to earn a point.
5. The opposing team attempts to defend their goal using fielding techniques.
6. Alternatively, if a ball is caught before it bounces by the opposing team, the player earns a point for his respective side.
7. Play until a certain time limit or score limit is reached.

Safety:

Ensure student's do not throw the ball in No Man's Land and that the area of No Man's Land is appropriate to the age and ability of the group.

Variations/Progressions:

- Use actual nets.
- Increase the size of the teams.
- Increase or decrease the size of No Man's Land

Diagram

Protector

Recommended Grades:
Grades 3-6

Equipment:
Wicket, polyspots, and soft balls.

Tactical Problems:
Placement of the ball in the field, covering bases, base running, fielding positions, keeping turn for as long as possible, and quick and accurate receiving and sending skills.

Rules of Play:
1. Divide students into small groups (6 – 8 students).
2. Place a wicket in the center that the batter must defend.
3. Polyspots will be positioned at an equal distance from the wicket in a circle formation with a fielding player standing on each one.
4. The fielding team/bowlers will bowl a soft ball using an underarm throw in an attempt to hit the wicket, only from the polyspot location.
5. The batter will attempt to hit the ball with an open hand and then run to one marker and come right back.
6. The bowling is continuous, the batter cannot protect the wicket with his/her body, and the fielders may only bowl from the polyspot markers.
7. A ball could be recovered from inside the circle, but it massed be passing to a teammate on the fielding team before being bowled.
8. Switch roles after a certain number of hits or when the wicket is hit.

Safety:
Ensure students do not throw the ball purposely at the batter.

Variations/Progressions:
- Introduce a striking implement.
- Increase or decrease the distance of the circle to the wicket.

Diagram

Throw & Run

Recommended Grades:
Grades 3-6

Equipment:
Soft balls and bases.

Tactical Problems:
Placement of the ball in the field, covering bases, base running, fielding positions, forcing play, keeping turn for as long as possible, and quick and accurate sending and receiving skills.

Rules of Play:
1. Divide students into 2 teams (or more if more than 1 game is running).
2. One team will be fielding while the other team will take turns batting.
3. The pitcher will throw a ball to the batter, but instead of batting, the batter must catch the ball with his/her bare hands and then throw it into the field.
4. The ball is then in play and regular softball rules apply.
5. Runners on base can only proceed to the next base once the ball is thrown from the batter.
6. Rotate when every player has batted or when 3 outs are achieved.

Safety:
Ensure students keep their heads up and are aware of the ball in play at all times.

Variations/Progressions:
- Change the type of ball used.
- Modify the softball rules.

Diagram

Toss Away

Recommended Grades:

Grades 3-6

Equipment:

Cones and beanbags.

Tactical Problems:

Placement of the beanbag in the field, covering bases, base running, and fielding positions.

Rules of Play:

1. Divide students into 2 teams – 1 at each endline of the playing area.
2. Players of the attacking team will have a beanbag each.
3. Cones will be scattered around the gymnasium.
4. The goal of the game is for the attacking team to score a point by first throwing their beanbag and then knocking down the cones with their hands.
5. This task must be complete prior to the fielding team retrieving the beanbags and making it to the opposite endline.
6. A point is earned if the attacking team knocks down all the cones before the fielding team retrieves the beanbags or if the fielding team retrieves the beanbags before all the cones are knocked down.
7. Reverse roles every round.

Safety:

Ensure students keep their heads up to avoid collisions.

Variations/Progressions:

- Introduce a throwing line in which the beanbag must cross.
- Increase or decrease the number of cones.
- 2 beanbags per player of the attacking team.

Diagram

Triangles

Recommended Grades:
Grades 3-6

Equipment:
Cones, bats, and soft balls.

Tactical Problems:
Placement of the ball in the field, covering bases, base running, fielding positions, forcing play, keeping turn for as long as possible, and quick and accurate receiving and sending skills.

Rules of Play:
1. Divide students into small groups (6 – 8 students).
2. Cones are arranged in a triangle formation with an additional cone in the middle for the designated pitcher.
3. A ball is pitched to a batter, who begins positioned at any of the 3 points, and places the ball into the field.
4. The batter runs around the 3 cones (triangle) and earns a point for each cone he/she passes.
5. The batter is out if the fielding team catches a fly ball, touch the base in which the batter is running to with the ball, or tags the runner with the ball.
6. The cone in which the batter stops running at becomes the new home base and is where the ball is pitched to.
7. After 3 pitches or an out, whichever comes first, players rotate positions so that there is a new batter and a new pitcher.

Safety:
Ensure students keep their heads up to avoid collisions and ensure that the ball is not thrown at the runner, but instead held to tag the player.

Variations/Progressions:
- Fielding team cannot move with the ball.
- Increase or decrease the distance between the cones.

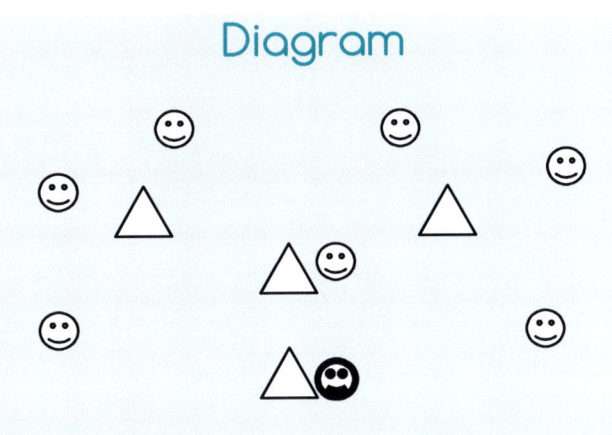

Diagram

Two By Four

Recommended Grades:

Grades 3-6

Equipment:

Tees, cones, bats, and soft balls.

Tactical Problems:

Placement of the ball in the field, covering bases, base running, fielding positions, forcing play, and quick and accurate receiving and sending skills.

Rules of Play:

1. Divide students into groups of 8 – 10 (teams of 2).
2. One team of 2 will be the batters while the remaining players are the fielders.
3. Both batters will have a tee set up along with their proper bat.
4. There will be 2 lines of 4 cones spaced out parallel to one another (8 cones total).
5. Both batters hit their balls at the same time, run along their respective lines, and if they reach the end of the line, they run back.
6. Each cone is worth 1 point and both batters add their scores to get a collective one.
7. The batters must stop running once the fielders have placed both balls back on the tees.
8. Each batter gets between 2 – 3 hits (4 – 6 total between the 2 batters).
9. Switch roles.

Safety:

Ensure students are adequately distanced from the batter and keep their heads up to avoid collisions.

Variations/Progressions:

- Use different striking and fielding implements.
- Fielders must all get a touch with one of the balls prior to returning them to the tee.

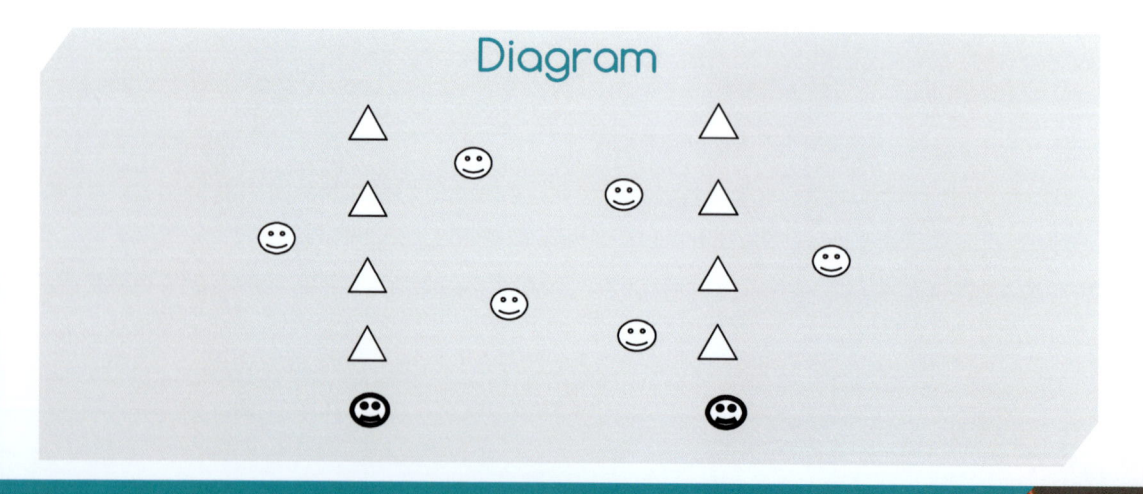

Diagram

500

Recommended Grades:
Grades 5-6

Equipment:
Bats and softballs.

Tactical Problems:
Placement of the ball in the field, fielding positions, and accurate sending and receiving skills.

Rules of Play:

1. Teacher or an assigned student will start at bat with the remaining players taking up fielding positions in the infield & outfield as they wish.
2. The batter begins play by batting a ball towards the outfielders and into play.
3. The fielders attempt to become the first player to collect 500 points.
4. 200 points for catching a fly ball, 100 points for catching a ball on the first bounce, and 50 points for fielding a grounder cleanly.
5. Switch batters after a fielder earns 500 points.
6. Fielders start back at 0 when a new player goes to bat.

Safety:
Ensure students keep their heads up to avoid collisions and are aware of the ball in play.

Variations/Progressions:
- Use different equipment for striking and fielding.
- Increase or decrease the surface of the playing area.
- Adjust the point scoring scheme.

Diagram

Blast It!

Recommended Grades:

Grades 5-6

Equipment:

Bases, baseball bat, and a soft ball.

Tactical Problems:

Placement of the ball in the field, covering bases, base running, throwing, and catching.

Rules of Play:

1. There will be a batting team and a fielding team.
2. Batting team will be lined up against the wall and the fielding team will be spread out around the playing area.
3. A pitcher will pitch the ball to the first batter in line.
4. Upon contact, the goal of the batting team is to gain points by running all four bases (one point).
5. The fielding team is trying to stop them by either catching the ball in the air or making five passes to different teammates – a dropped ball does not count as a pass.
6. Change roles after every batter has gone

Safety:

Keep your eye on the ball, keep your head up to avoid collisions, and give the batter enough room to swing.

Variations/Progressions:

- Allow runners to stay on base.
- Increase or decrease the distance between the bases.
- Increase or decrease the number of passes to be made between the fielding team.

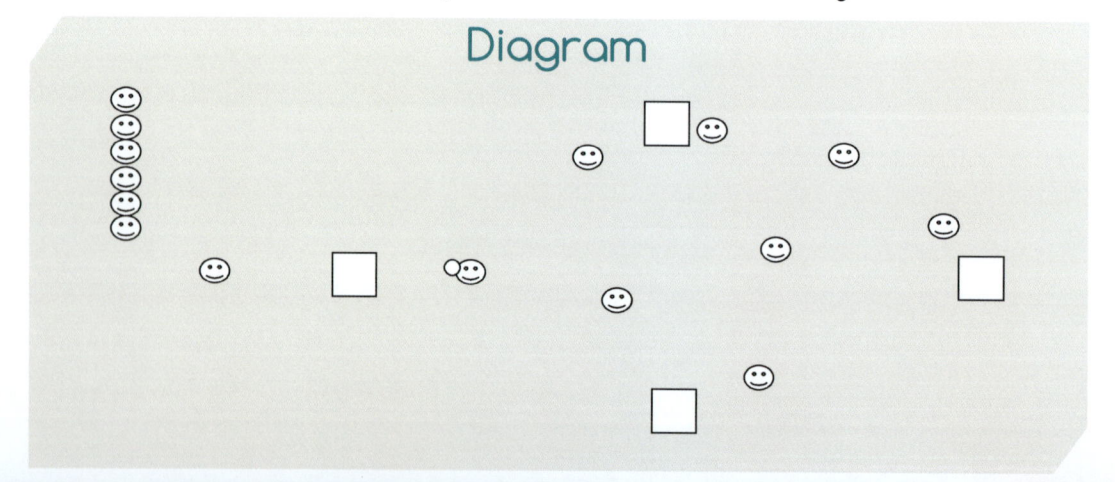

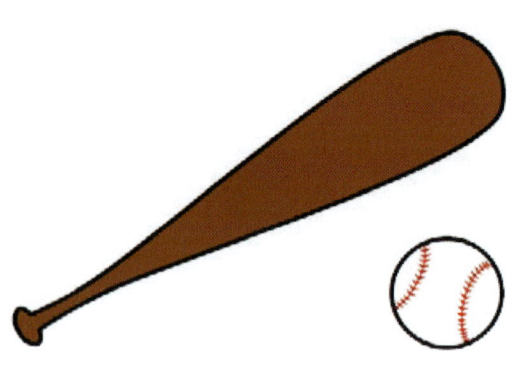

Diagram

Frisbee Ball

Recommended Grades:

Grades 5-6

Equipment:

Frisbees and bases.

Tactical Problems:

Placement of the frisbee in the field, decision making, covering bases, base running, fielding positions, forcing play, and quick and accurate sending and receiving skills.

Rules of Play:

1. Divide students into 2 teams.
2. The 1st player of the batting team will have a frisbee, proceed to launch it into the playing area, and run around the bases.
3. If the frisbee is caught, the batter is out.
4. If the frisbee is not caught, in order to stop the runner, the frisbee must be thrown towards the pitcher.
5. If the pitcher catches the frisbee when the batter is off a base, he/she is out.
6. A point is earned every time a player returns home.
7. Switch roles after each batter has had the chance to launch the frisbee.

Safety:

Ensure that the batting team is distanced enough from the batter/thrower and that the fielders are aware of the frisbee at all times.

Variations/Progressions:

- Use regular softball rules with 3 outs.
- Play indoors.
- Add a minimum number of passes that must be made before sending the frisbee to the pitcher.

Diagram

Ground Cone

Recommended Grades:

Grades 5-6

Equipment:

Tees, soft balls, and cones.

Tactical Problems:

Placement of the ball in the field, fielding positions, and keeping turn for as long as possible.

Rules of Play:

1. Divide students into small groups (4 – 6).
2. The goal of the game is to strike the balls into open space without them being caught.
3. One player starts off as the batter while the other three players will have an upside down cone in which they will use to attempt to catch the ball out of the air.
4. If the batter succeeds in getting the ball to touch the ground, he/she gets 1 point.
5. If a fielder catches a ball, he/she gets 1 point (not the entire fielding team).
6. Note: Draw a line or designate an area in which the ball must cross to be considered good.
7. Once the ball has been caught a total of 3 times, one of the fielders will switch with the batter.
8. This continues until everyone in the group has had a turn batting.

Safety:

Ensure there is enough space between groups and that fielders do not collide.

Variations/Progressions:

- Introduce a different point system.
- Allow 2 batters to go at once.

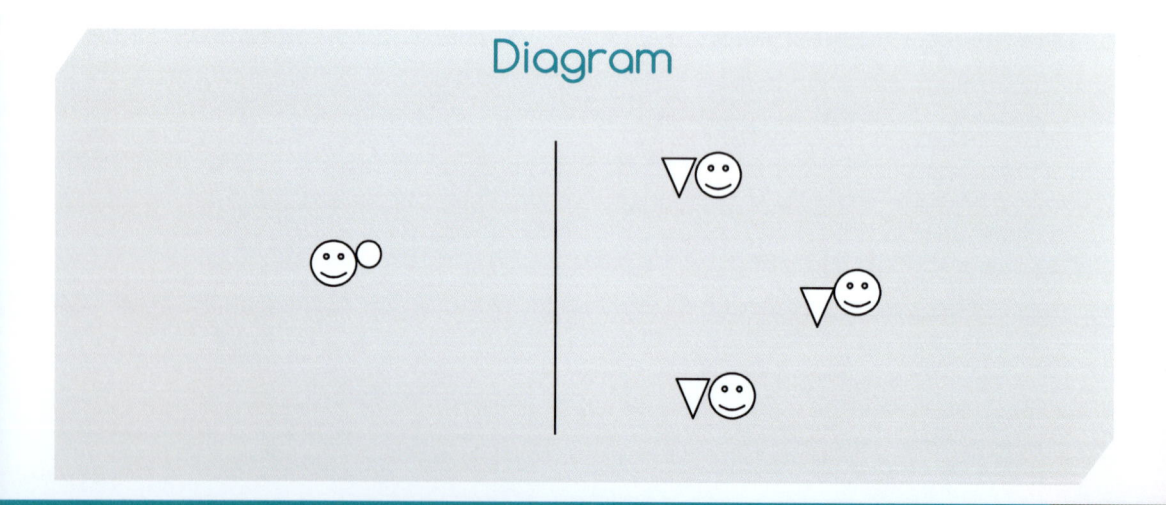

Diagram

Hoop Softball

Recommended Grades:

Grades 5-6

Equipment:

Tees, hula-hoops, baseball bats, and soft balls.

Tactical Problems:

Placement of the ball in the field.

Rules of Play:

1. Divide students into pairs (or into small groups).
2. Each pair of students will have their own playing area.
3. The goal of the game is to score more points than your partner by hitting the soft balls into the designated hula-hoops.
4. Partners will decide where to place the hula-hoops and how many points each will be worth.
5. The player has between 5 – 10 attempts before switching with his/her partner.
6. Players not batting will retrieve the balls for the batter.
7. Play for a certain number of rotations.

Safety:

Ensure a safe distance between playing areas.

Variations/Progressions:

- Have the fielder try to prevent the ball from entering a hoop.
- Add or remove the number of hula-hoops in play.
- Increase or decrease the distance of the hula-hoops to the batter

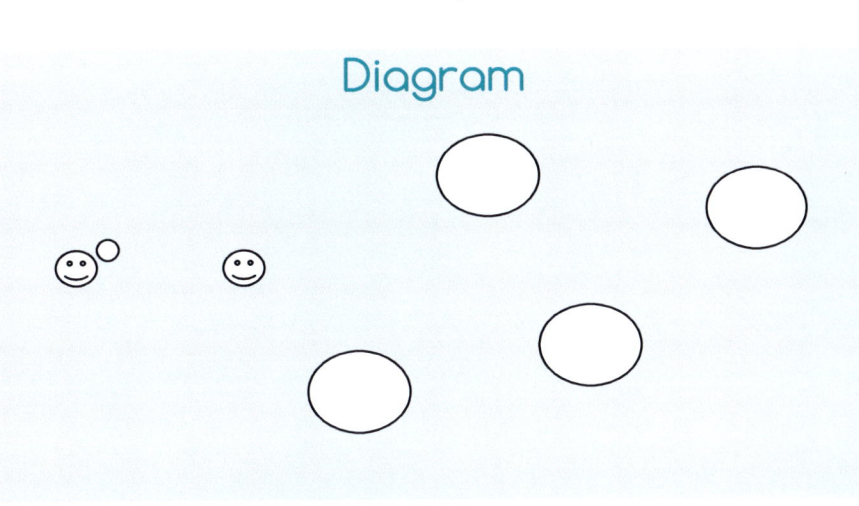

Diagram

Kickball Knockdown

Recommended Grades:

Grades 5-6

Equipment:

Large containers, lots of gator skin balls, and lots of cones.

Tactical Problems:

Placement of the ball on the field, base running, and quick and accurate sending and receiving skills.

Rules of Play:

1. Class is divided into 2 teams.
2. A certain number of boxes are placed in the outfield.
3. The cones will be scattered all over the playing surface and each player on the batting team will possess one ball.
4. When given the command, the batting team's players will kick the ball from behind a designated line and will then run out and try to knock over all the cones with their hands.
5. At this point, the outfielders are trying to collect the balls into the baskets.
6. Whichever team completes their respective task first gets the point.
7. Roles are reversed after a point is awarded.

Safety:

Communicate with teammates when passing the ball and keep your head up to avoid collisions between the fielding team and the batters.

Variations/Progressions:

- Increase the number of boxes if task is too easy for batters.
- Reduce the number of cones if task is too easy for fielders.
- Split the batting group into two

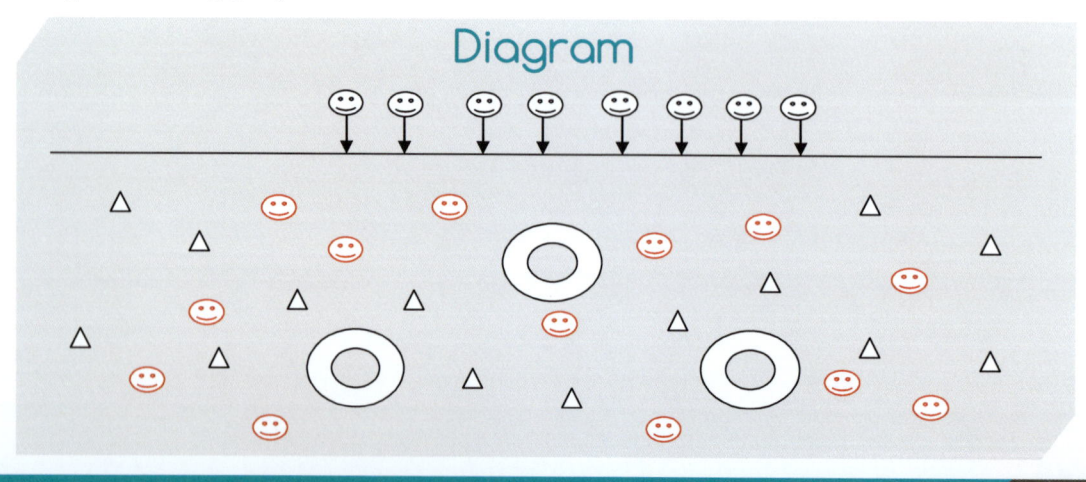

Diagram

Kin-Ball

Recommended Grades:

Grades 5-6

Equipment:

Pinnies and Omnikin balls.

Tactical Problems:

Placement of the ball in the field, decision making, fielding positions, keeping ball for as long as possible, and quick and accurate receiving and sending skills.

Rules of Play:

1. Divide students into teams of 4 – there will be 3 teams playing at once (minimum).
2. Players of the defensive teams will form a square around the ball in which 1 player from each team will position himself/herself at one corner of the square.
3. When a team is striking the ball, 3 of the players stabilize the ball (usually 2 players on one side and 1 player on the other) and the hitter runs up and launches the ball forward.
4. Just before striking the ball in an upward motion, the player must call out "OMNIKIN" along with a color of one of the teams.
5. The team that gets called out must catch the ball before it hits the floor.
6. If the team succeeds, it is the team's turn to hit the ball (after stabilizing it).
7. If not, the other 2 teams get a point and it is still the hitting team's turn to hit.

Safety:

Ensure students keep their heads up and stay crouched when holding the ball for the hitter.

Variations/Progressions:

- Increase or decrease the size of the playing area.
- Introduce a 4th team.

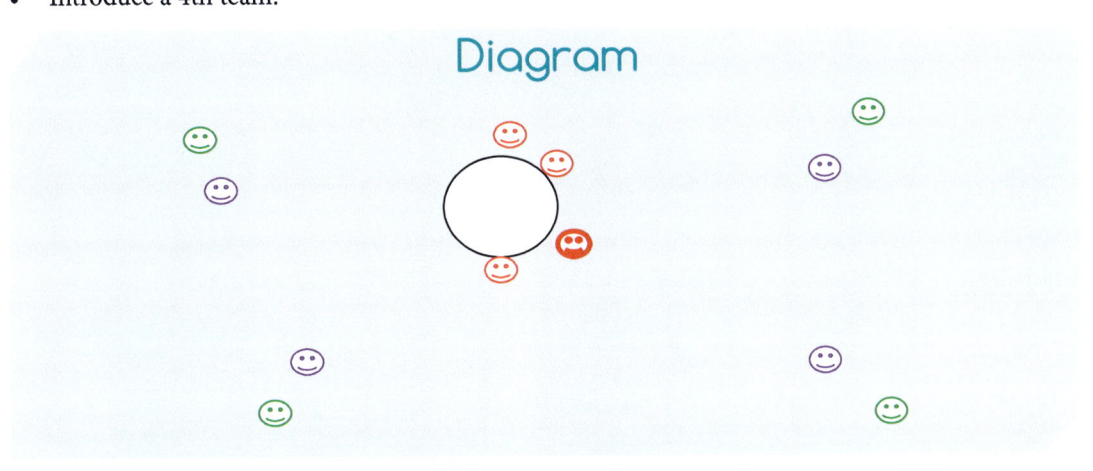

Diagram

No Team

Recommended Grades:

Grades 5-6

Equipment:

Softball, bases, gloves, and a bat.

Tactical Problems:

Placement of the ball in the field, covering bases, base running, fielding positions, forcing play, staying on offense, keeping turn for as long as possible, quick and accurate receiving and sending skills.

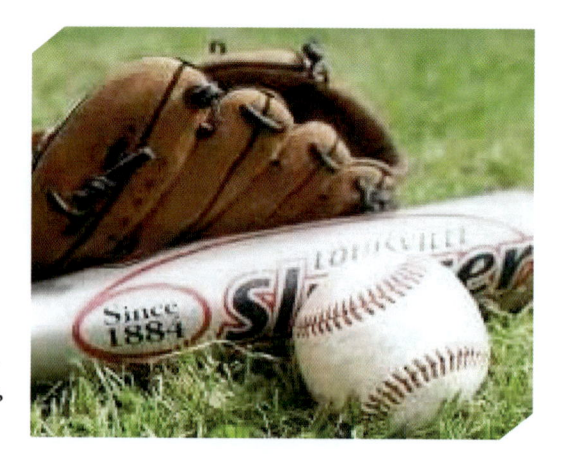

Rules of Play:

1. Fielders will position themselves as follows: right field, center field, left field, shortstop, 3rd base, 2nd base, 1st base, pitcher, and catcher.
2. The remaining players will start as batters.
3. Same rules as baseball/softball.
4. If a batter gets out, he/she moves to the right field position and everyone rotates one position – catcher goes to the back of the batting line.
5. If a batter makes it on base, he/she stays there and waits for the next person to bat.
6. Players keep track of their own runs as the goal is to make it back to home base.

Safety:

Ensure students keep their heads up to avoid collisions and call for the ball.

Variations/Progressions:

- Batters earn runs by hitting the ball and landing it on the field (ground balls equal an out).
- Use a tee.
- Use different striking and fielding equipment

Diagram

One Bounce

Recommended Grades:

Grades 5-6

Equipment:

Cones and tennis balls..

Tactical Problems:

Placement of the ball in the field and fielding positions.

Rules of Play:

1. Divide students into small groups (4 – 6).
2. A cone will be set up where the batter should be and 2 additional cones will be placed roughly 5 – 10 m apart anywhere between 20 – 30 m away from the batter.
3. A ball is dropped by a feeder in front of the batter, who tries to hit the ball at the target (between the 2 cones) below head height after the bounce.
4. A fielder will be positioned in front of the cones and try to stop any balls on the way to the target.
5. A retriever will be positioned beyond the cones and will recover any balls that get past the fielder.
6. If the ball is caught in the air, the batter loses a point.
7. Batter earns a point for every ball that goes through the target zone below head height.
8. Bat between 5 – 10 times before rotating positions.

Safety:

Ensure that there is adequate space between games, the ball is kept low, and that the feeder moves after dropping the ball.

Variations/Progressions:

- Introduce more fielders.
- Increase or decrease the distance between the cones.
- Increase or decrease the distance from the cones

Diagram

T-Ball

Recommended Grades:
Grades 5-6

Equipment:
Tee for the ball, batting instrument, and placemats to act as bases for both the batter and the fielding team.

Tactical Problems:
Placement of the ball in the field, base running, and quick and accurate sending and receiving skills.

Rules of Play:
1. The batter that comes up is expected to strike the ball off the tee.
2. Afterwards, the batter must run around a certain number of bases.
3. At the same time, the fielding team is trying to gain possession of the ball and pass the ball around their respective bases amongst themselves before the batter has time to reach the final base.
4. If the batter reaches the last base before the outfielders do, the batter's team is rewarded with a point.
5. Teams switch roles when everyone has bat once.
6. Note: There are two sets of bases placed on the field: one for the batter and another for the fielders.

Safety:
Keep your head up to avoid collisions, call for the ball, be aware of the ball at all times.

Variations/Progressions:
- Add or remove the number of bases.
- Increase or decrease the distance between the bases.

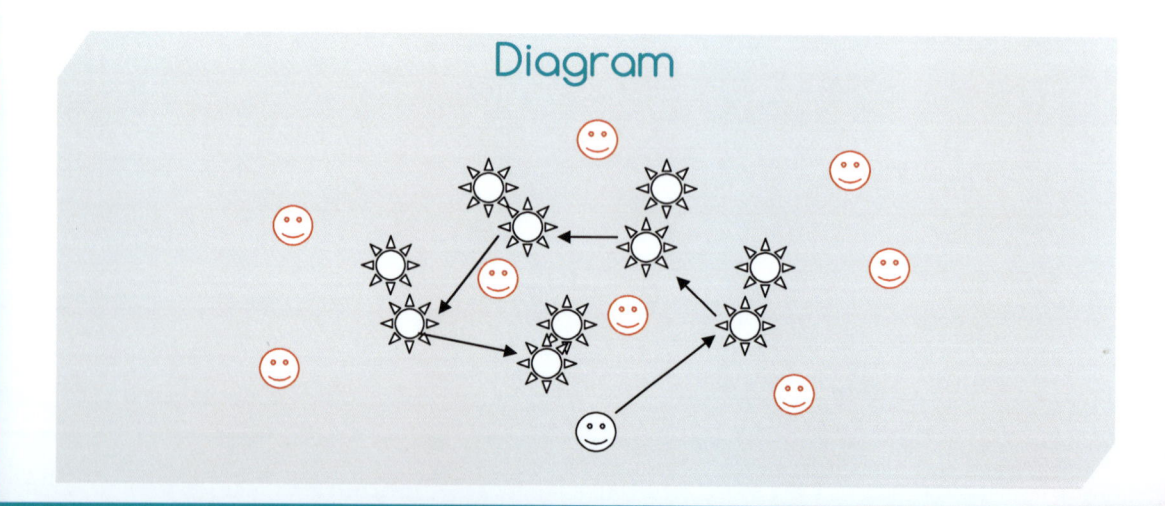

Diagram

Wacky Softball

Recommended Grades:

Grades 5-6

Equipment:

Soft and hittable ball, batting instruments, and bases.

Tactical Problems:

Placement of the ball in the field, covering bases, base running, and accurate sending and receiving.

Rules of Play:

1. Two teams on the field – fielding team and batting team.
2. There will be 5 bases in total, including home plate (4 bases + home plate).
3. Maximum 3 pitches , which will be pitched by a player from the batter's team.
4. 1st base = close to batter, 2nd base = normal position, 3rd base = behind pitcher, 4th base = normal position for 3rd base, but significantly further from home plate.
5. No outs – go through batting order.
6. More than one person on base allowed.
7. Must run with final batter.
8. Must hit player with the ball to get him/her out.

Safety:

Keep your head up to avoid collisions and aim below the waist.

Variations/Progressions:

- Change the positioning of the bases.
- Change the batting instruments.
- Do not allow more than one person on each base

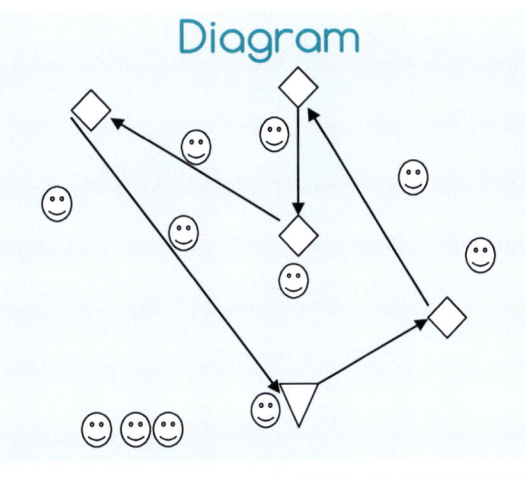

Diagram

Target/Miscellaneous

Garbage Day

Recommended Grades:

Kindergarten – Grade 4

Equipment:

Volleyball net, bean bags, and soft foam balls.

Tactical Problems:

Sending, receiving, and travelling.

Rules of Play:

1. Students will be divided into two teams.
2. A volleyball net will be set up in the middle.
3. Each team will have a set number of bean bags and soft foam balls on their side of the court.
4. When the game starts, the goal is to have the "cleaner" court – this is done by getting rid of the bean bags and soft foam balls.
5. Bean bags must slide under the net while soft foam balls will be tossed over the net.
6. The team with the cleaner court after the specified time limit wins.

Safety:

Keep your head up to avoid collisions and ensure students are sliding the bean bags UNDER the net.

Variations/Progressions:

- Increase or decrease the number of objects on the court.
- Increase or decrease the size of the playing area.
- Introduce different locomotor movements.

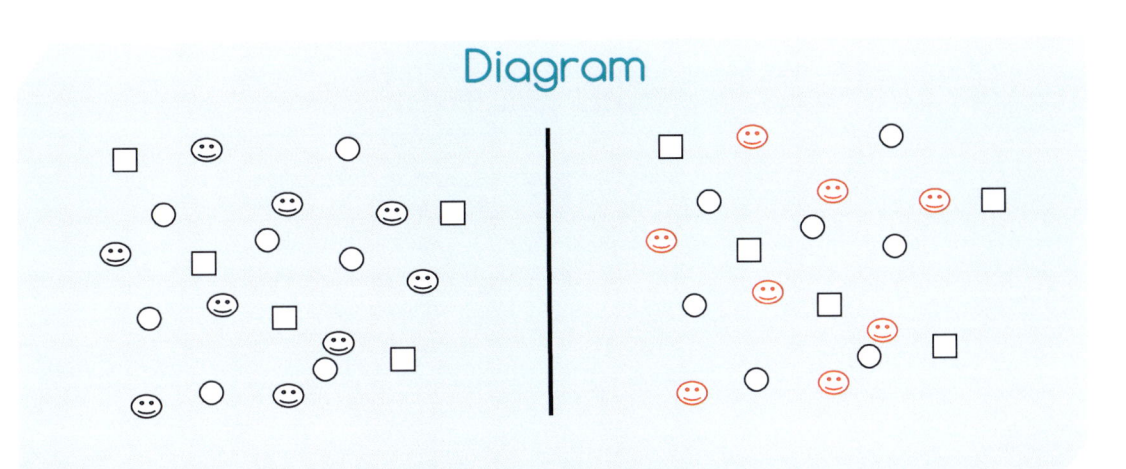

Diagram

Olympic Toss

Recommended Grades:
Grades K-4

Equipment:
Hula-hoops and beanbags.

Tactical Problems:
Hitting a target.

Rules of Play:

1. Divide students into groups of 4 – 8.
2. Set up 4 different colored hula-hoops a certain distance from the throwing (boundary) line.
3. Each student will have an assortment of different colored beanbags at their disposal.
4. The leader will call out a color – the players must throw the correctly colored beanbag in the correctly colored hoop.
5. Beanbags have to stay in the hula-hoop – if not, the student must go pick-up the beanbag and wait for that color to be called out again.

Safety:
Ensure that there is room between the throwers and between the other teams.

Variations/Progressions:
- Add obstacles.
- Encourage different types of throwing.
- Increase or decrease the distance to the hula-hoops.

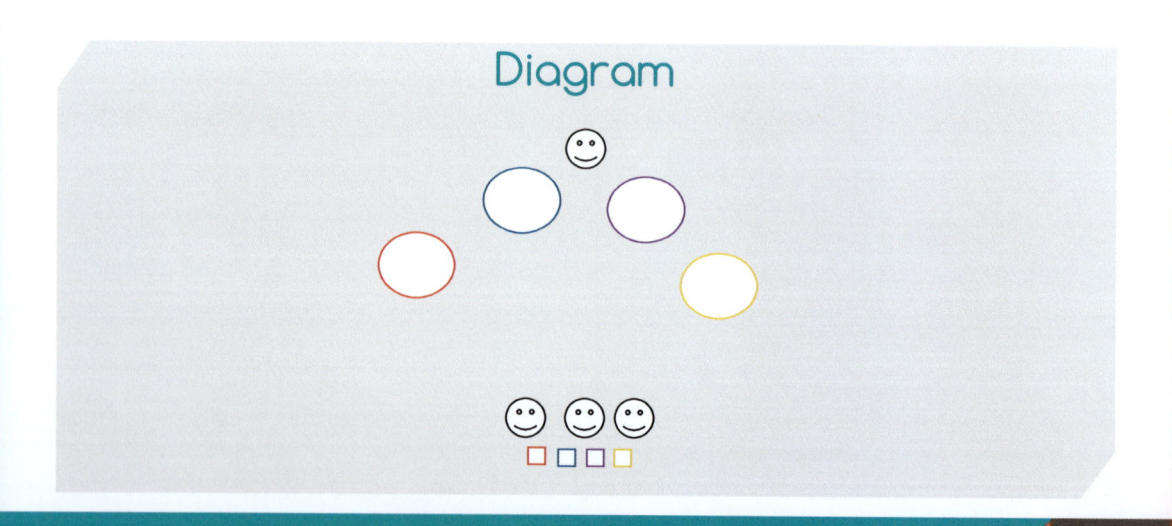

Diagram

Parachute Turn

Recommended Grades:

Kindergarten – Grade 4

Equipment:

Parachute.

Tactical Problems:

Cooperation and synchronization.

Rules of Play:

1. Students will stand holding one side of the parachute.
2. Spin clockwise slowly – spin counter-clockwise slowly.
3. When the instructor calls out "Freeze", students will have to put the parachute down and take 5 steps back.
4. At this point, the instructor will call out an action for the students to perform (i.e. 10 push-ups).
5. Return back to the mat and perform the same actions as step #2, but much faster.
6. Repeat.

Safety:

Ensure that students have enough space between one another and that if anyone doesn't feel well spinning, assure them that they could stop at any time.

Variations/Progressions:

- Mix up the actions according to the group.
- Include other motions with the parachute instead of just turning.

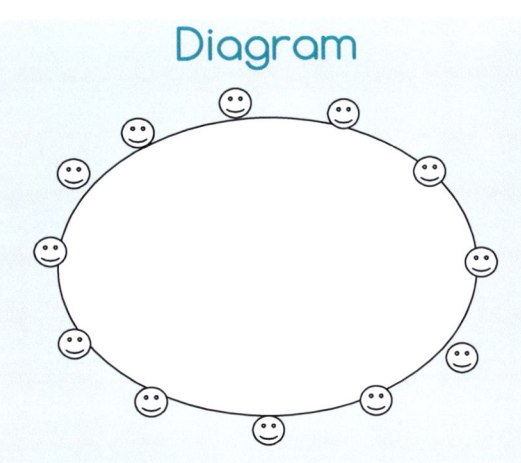

Diagram

Popcorn
Recommended Grades:
Kindergarten – Grade 4
Equipment:
Parachute and almost any type of ball.
Tactical Problems:
Cooperation and communication.

Rules of Play:
1. Simple and short game.
2. Students line up and grab hold of one side of the parachute with both hands.
3. Either while kneeling or standing, students will warm up by slowly waving the parachute.
4. Eventually, the students will speed up until they are going full force.
5. At this point, the balls will be introduced and thus will be "popping" throughout the activity.
6. Good idea to designate a few students to pick up the loose balls and reintroduce them into the parachute.

Safety:
Adequate space between students.

Variations/Progressions:
- Students can rotate clockwise or counter-clockwise

Diagram

Switch Dodge

Recommended Grades:

Kindergarten – Grade 4

Equipment:

Dodgeballs.

Tactical Problems:

Hitting a target and evading.

Rules of Play:

1. Students will be divided into 2 teams.
2. Regular dodgeball rules; however, if a student from one team gets hit, he/she must join the other team.
3. He/she does this by going on the other side, touching the end wall, and returning on the opposite team.
4. Continue until all the players from the other team are eliminated or the time limit has been reached.
5. Ensure that students do not purposely attempt to be hit by the other team.

Safety:

Keep your head up to avoid collisions and aim below the waist.

Variations/Progressions:

- Increase or decrease the size of the playing area.
- Introduce a time limit.

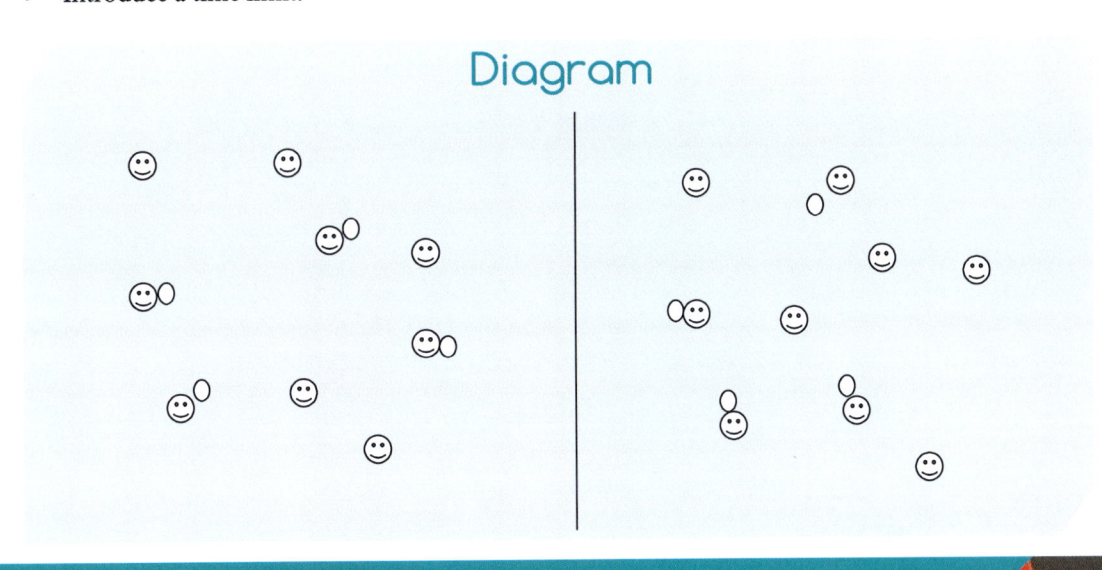

Diagram

21

Recommended Grades:

Kindergarten – Grade 6

Equipment:

Beanbags, cones, hula-hoops, and mats.

Tactical Problems:

Sending away, releasing, and hitting a target.

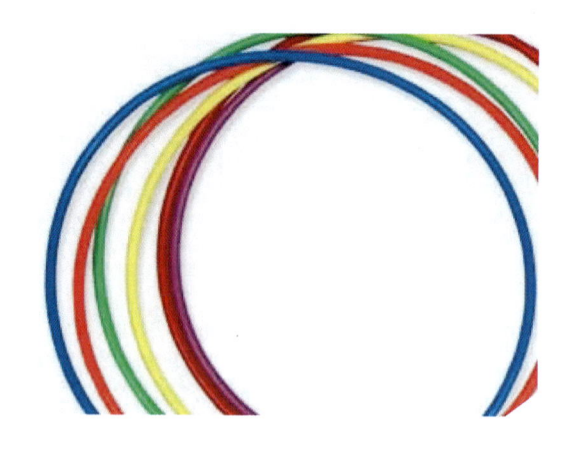

Rules of Play:

1. Divide students into pairs or into small groups.
2. For each group, set up a mat with a hula-hoop on top of it.
3. Set up 3 cones – 5 steps, 10 steps, and 15 steps away.
4. Each person will have a beanbag.
5. Alternating turns, each player will attempt to get his/her beanbag into the hula-hoop from one of the three distances.
6. Points are awarded in the following manner – 5 steps (x1), 10 steps (x2), 15 steps (x3).
7. Multiply the above with – landing on the mat (x1), landing in the hula-hoop (x2).
8. Example: Thrown from 15 steps and lands in hula-hoop – 3X2 = 6 points.

Safety:

Ensure that there is enough space between players.

Variations/Progressions:

- Use different objects (i.e. frisbee, etc.).
- Introduce a time limit.
- Remain seated during the activity.

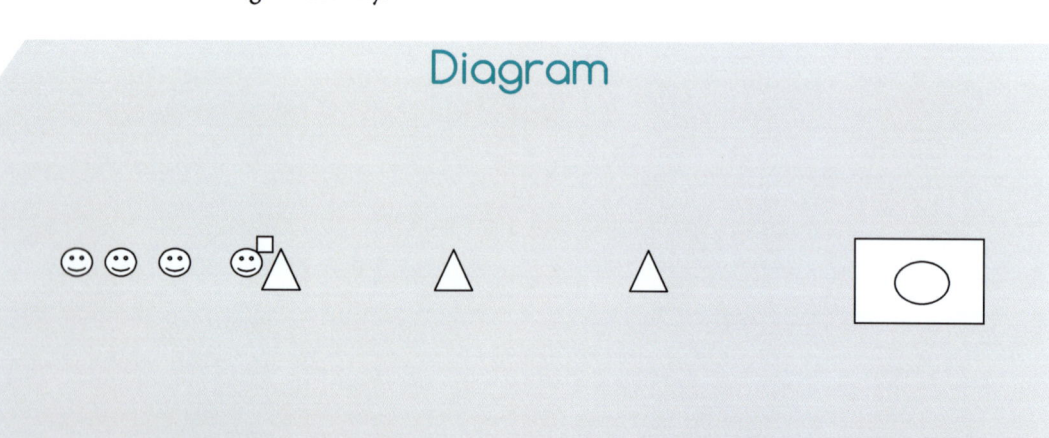

Diagram

Protect The Pin

Recommended Grades:
Kindergarten – Grade 6

Equipment:
Sponge ball and a bowling pin.

Tactical Problems:
Hitting a target and shuffling.

Rules of Play:

1. Divide students into small groups.
2. Within each group, form a circle.
3. One of the players will be at the center of the circle protecting a single bowling pin.
4. Goal of the game is for the circle to knock down the bowling pin while the defender's goal is to protect the pin from being knocked over.
5. If the thrower knocks down the pin, he/she replaces the person in the middle.
6. Encourage passing the ball around to the teammates in the circle.

Safety:
Ensure that there is enough space between players and aim low with the ball.

Variations/Progressions:
- Use a cone and use a soft foam ball instead.
- Increase or decrease the distance to the bowling pin.
- Add another defender.

Diagram

One Pin

Recommended Grades:

Grades 1-4

Equipment:

Bowling pins and beanbags.

Tactical Problems:

Hitting a target.

Rules of Play:

1. Divide students into pairs.
2. Each student will have a bowling pin.
3. Set up the bowling pins a certain distance away from one another.
4. Players take turns sliding the beanbag on the floor attempting to hit the opponent's pin.
5. If the pin is knocked down, the player puts it back upright and continues with his/her turn.
6. Play until a certain time limit or score limit is reached.

Safety:

Ensure the beanbag is "rolled" and not thrown.

Variations/Progressions:

- If the opponent's "roll" is short, the opponent can pick up the beanbag from where it is stopped and "roll" from there.
- Increase or decrease the distance to the target.
- Use different equipment..

Diagram

Direct Hit

Recommended Grades:
Grades 1-6

Equipment:
Beanbags, hula-hoops, and cones.

Tactical Problems:
Hitting a target.

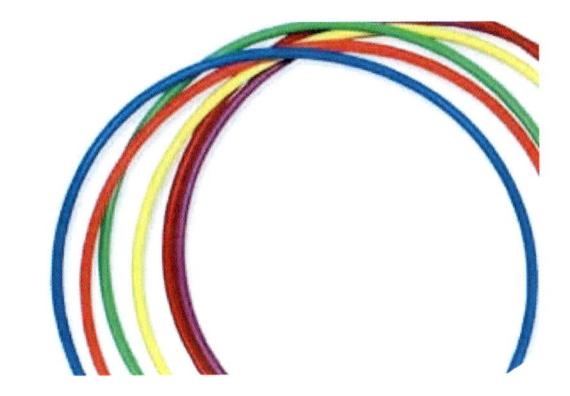

Rules of Play:

1. Divide students in 1 v 1 games or 2 v 2 games (or more).
2. Place a cone in the middle of a hula-hoop.
3. Create two lines – one 5 feet away and the other 10 feet away.
4. Goal of the game is to have the most points after 10 attempts at the cone.
5. Points are awarded as follows: 1 point for landing in the hoop, 2 points for hitting the cone, and 3 points for a beanbag that stays on the cone without knocking it over.
6. Points are doubled if thrown from the 10 foot line.

Safety:
Ensure that there is throwing room for the thrower and space between the different games going on at once.

Variations/Progressions:
- Use different objects.
- Increase or decrease the distance to the target.

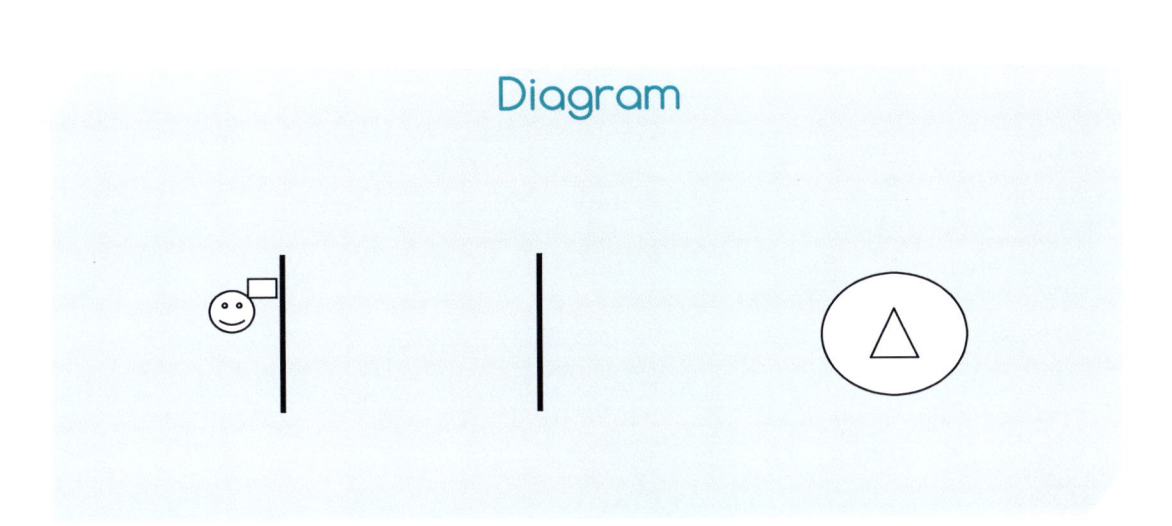

Diagram

Dr. Dodgeball

Recommended Grades:

Grades 1-6

Equipment:

Soft foam balls.

Tactical Problems:

Hitting a target, sending, receiving, shuffling, change of speed, and change in direction.

Rules of Play:

1. Students will be divided into two teams in their respective sides of the court.
2. On each team, there will be 1 or 2 "doctors".
3. If a player is hit by the ball, he/she must sit on the floor where he/she was hit.
4. For that player to return to the game, the "doctor" must simply touch his/her back with his/her finger.
5. Evidently, the doctor doesn't want to be exposed – teammates should work together to create a diversion so as to not alert them to who the "doctor" is.
6. Play until a certain time limit is reached or until one team has no more players.

Safety:

Keep your head up to avoid collisions, aim below the waist, and be aware of the balls at all times.

Variations/Progressions:

- Introduce scooters in which the doctors must carry injured teammates to the side before allowing them to return (doctors cannot be eliminated).
- Increase or decrease the size of the playing area.
- Use your own dodgeball rules.

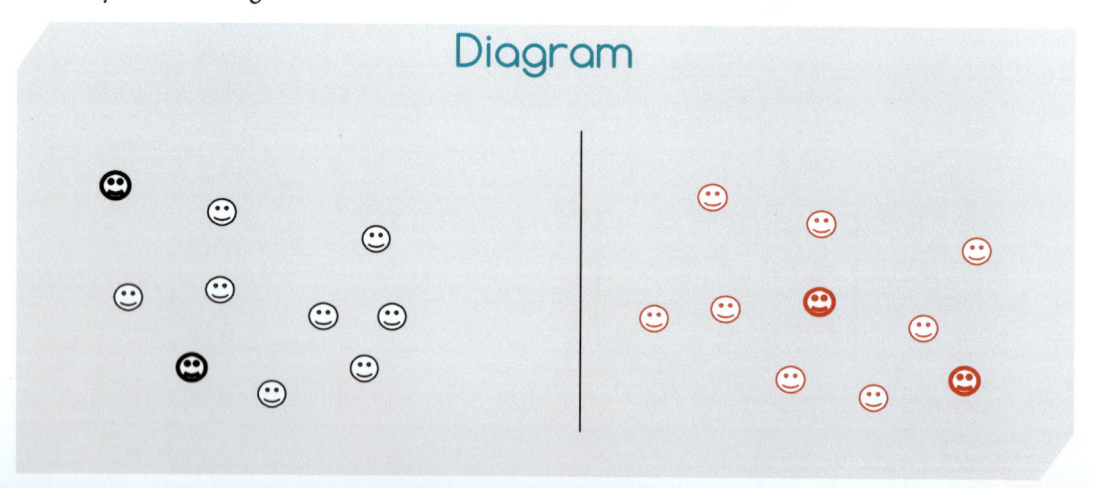

Diagram

Knock It

Recommended Grades:
Grades 1-6

Equipment:
Cones or bowling pins, and soft foam balls.

Tactical Problems:
Hitting a target.

Rules of Play:
1. Students will be divided into pairs.
2. Each pair will have 4 cones or bowling pins and a soft foam ball.
3. The cones/pins will be set up 10 – 15 m away in any way the players desire.
4. One partner will stand next to the cones/pins as the thrower gets ready.
5. The partner will point and tell the thrower which cone/pin he/she should knock down first.
6. If another cone/pin is knocked down besides the "target", pick it right up.
7. Count the number of rolls needed to knock down all 4 targets.
8. Switch with your partner.

Safety:
Keep your distance between your station and that of the other players.

Variations/Progressions:
- Use different objects.
- Increase or decrease the distance to the targets.
- Use the non-dominant hand.

Diagram

Roll It Over

Recommended Grades:

Grades 1-6

Equipment:

Big ball, soft foam balls, and cones.

Tactical Problems:

Hitting a target, sending, and receiving.

Rules of Play:

1. Divide students into two teams and mark off a square using cones, lines, or tape.
2. Team #1 will line up on one side of the square with team #2 lined up on the opposite end.
3. Each player will be given a soft foam ball.
4. The goal for each team is to make the large ball cross the other team's line by throwing the smaller foam balls.
5. Players retrieve the balls from the throwing of their opponents.
6. If the ball leaves the square, replace it back in the middle and start over.

Safety:

Maintain space between your teammates and aim low at the ball.

Variations/Progressions:

- Introduce 2 more teams – have each team defend a line of the square.
- Increase or decrease the size of the playing area.
- Play sitting down.
- Use different objects.

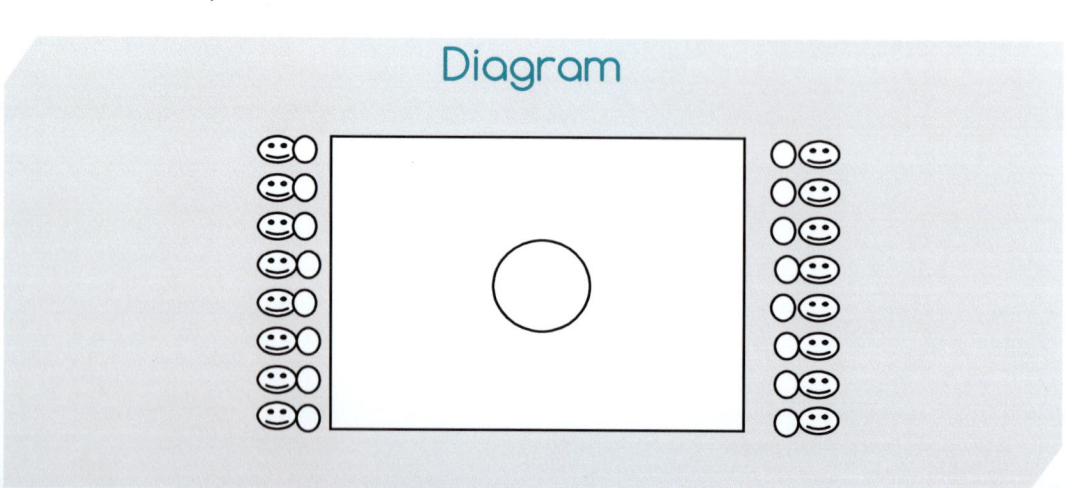

Diagram

Run, Ball, Run!

Recommended Grades:

Grades 1-6

Equipment:

Soft foam ball.

Tactical Problems:

Throwing, catching, change of speed, change in direction, and footwork.

Rules of Play:

1. Students will line up one behind the other facing the same direction.
2. The first student in line will have a soft foam ball.
3. On the instructor's signal, students will run around the boundaries of the playing area while simultaneously passing the ball to the person in back of them.
4. When the ball reaches the last person, he/she will have to speed up in order to become the "leader" of the line and thus moving in front of the first person in line.
5. Repeat.

Safety:

Make sure students have enough space between one another and encourage communication when passing the ball from front to back.

Variations/Progressions:

- Introduce more than one ball.
- Introduce different locomotor movements

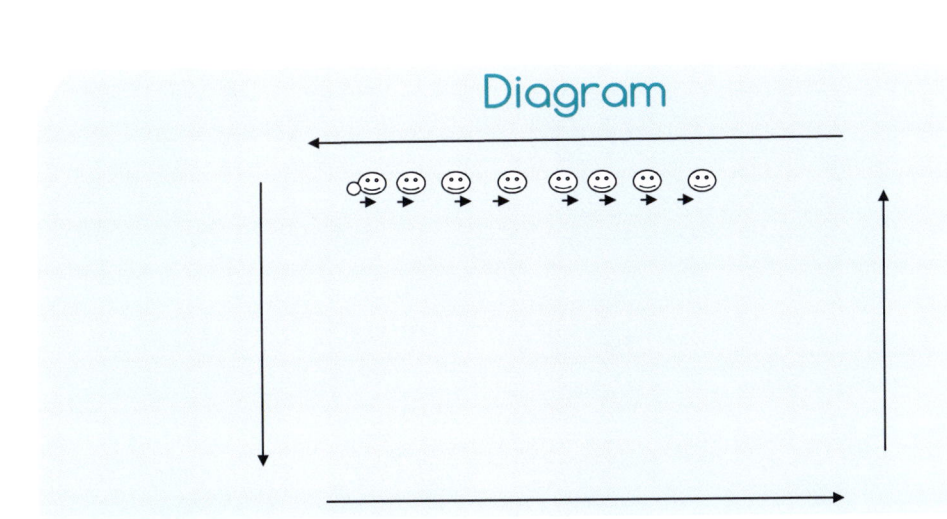

Diagram

Silence

Recommended Grades:
Grades 3-4

Equipment:
Soft foam balls.

Tactical Problems:
Throwing, catching, and non-verbal communication.

Rules of Play:
1. All students spread out around the gymnasium and remain stationary.
2. Start with one ball.
3. The ball will be passed from one student to the next without bouncing.
4. If the ball is dropped, if a bad throw is made or if someone talks and thus is no longer "silent", that student will have to perform an action to return to the game.
5. Actions can be a number of push-ups, jumping jacks, etc.

Safety:
Ensure that you make eye contact with the student you're throwing the ball to.

Variations/Progressions:
- Add more than one ball in play.
- Increase or reduce the size of the playing area.
- Allow movement.

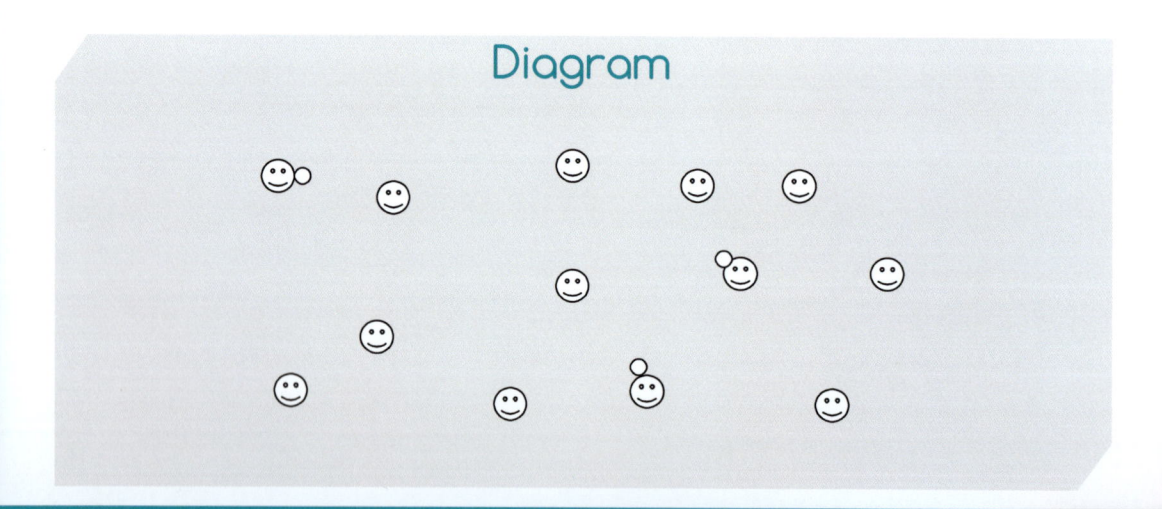

Diagram

Alien vs Human

Recommended Grades:
Grades 3-6

Equipment:
Pinnies and soft foam balls.

Tactical Problems:
Throwing, catching, and hitting a target.

Rules of Play:
1. Students will be divided in two teams.
2. Both teams share the same court.
3. There will be three balls in play.
4. When a player has the ball, he/she is not allowed to move.
5. The player must try to hit a member of the opposing team with it.
6. When a player is hit by a ball, he/she goes to the side of the playing area.
7. In this case, this player can only return to the game when a player of the opposing gets hit and eliminated.

Safety:
Keep your head up to avoid collisions and aim below the waist.

Variations/Progressions:
- Increase or decrease the size of the playing area.
- Increase the numbers of balls in play.
- Modify the dodgeball rules.
- Within the game, you could designate certain color balls for the girls and the other for the boys.

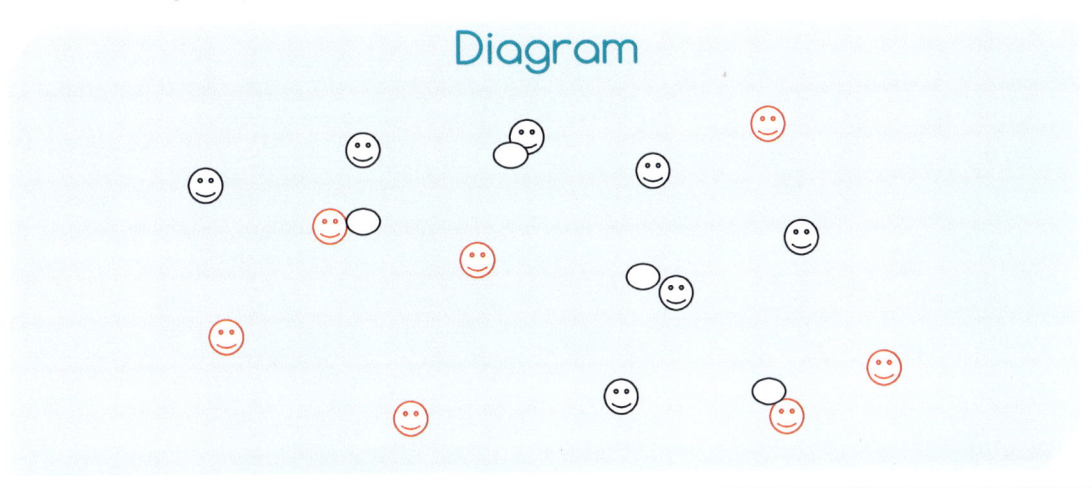

Diagram

Back & Forth

Recommended Grades:
Grades 3 – 6

Equipment:
Pinnies, bowling pins, and soft foam balls.

Tactical Problems:
Hitting a target, prevent own targets from being hit.

Rules of Play:
1. Divided students into two teams separated into their respective halves.
2. An equal number of bowling pins will be set up on both ends of the court.
3. The goal of the game is for the players to roll the ball and knock over the opponent's pins.
4. Balls cannot be thrown or kicked, only rolled.
5. Students must stand 5 feet in front of the pins at all times (use boundary lines as a reference).
6. If there aren't many pins left standing, pause the game to bring the pins up closer to the center line.

Safety:
Ensure that no one throws or kicks the balls.

Variations/Progressions:
- Allow throwing/kicking of the balls.
- Increase or decrease the size of the playing area.
- Allow students to cross the center line (but can be tagged).

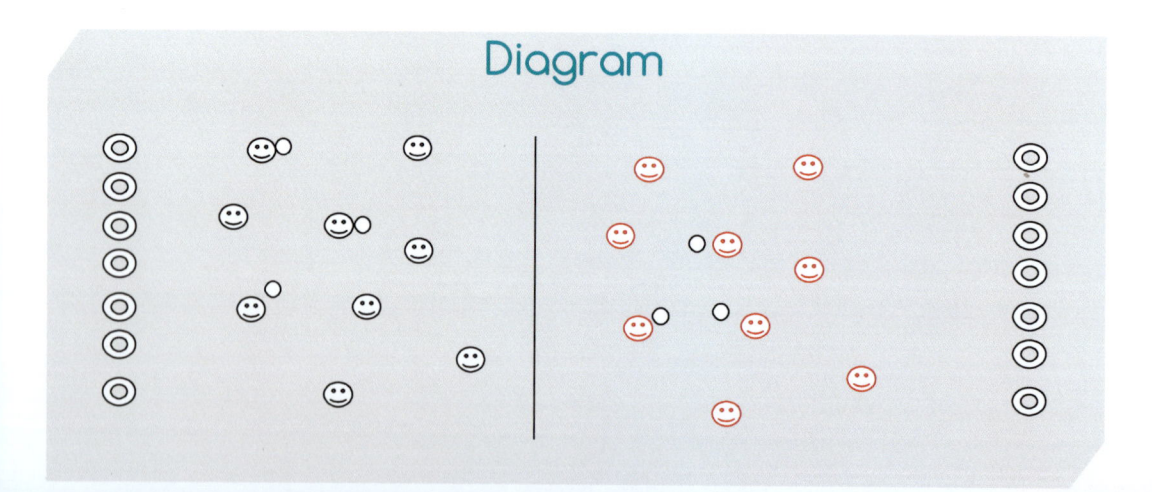

Diagram

Bean Bag Dodgeball

Recommended Grades:

Grades 3-6

Equipment:

Pinnies, bean bags, and bowling pins or noodles.

Tactical Problems:

Hitting a target and preventing own target from being hit.

Rules of Play:

1. Bean bags are used to knock over bowling pins that are set up on the opposing team's side of the playing area.
2. Bean bags cannot be thrown aerially; bean bags must slide on the floor to hit the targets.
3. If a player from the opposing team gets struck by the bean bag on their feet, they must go outside of the playing area and perform a physical skill (i.e. 10 push ups) before coming back into the game.
4. The game ends when all the bowling pins are knocked down on one side of the playing area.

Safety:

Make sure that students keep the bean bags on the floor and do not throw them in the air.

Variations/Progressions:

- Students hit by bean bags don't automatically come in – must stay out until teacher's signal to come back into play.
- Place bowling pins scattered on the other side – some closer and some farther from the opposing team.

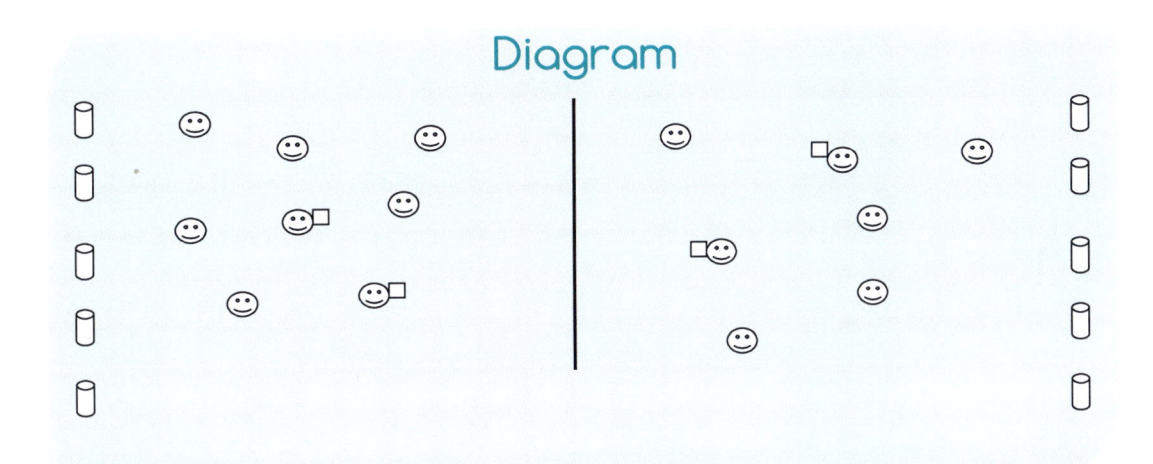

Diagram

185

Fitness Bowling

Recommended Grades:

Grades 3-6

Equipment:

Bowling pins, soft foam ball, exercise printouts, and pencil & score sheets.

Tactical Problems:

Hitting a target.

Rules of Play:

1. Divide students into small groups – one for each "alley".
2. Students should have different roles (i.e. scorekeeper, pin setter, bowler, etc.).
3. Depending on what score the student roles, he/she will look at the exercise printouts corresponding to her score and perform that physical activity.
4. Continue play until a certain time limit is reached or at the end of a set number of rounds.

Safety:

Ensure that there is enough space between groups.

Variations/Progressions:

- Increase or decrease the distance to the pins.
- If a student gets a spare or a strike, he/she could decide the activity for the rest of the group to perform.

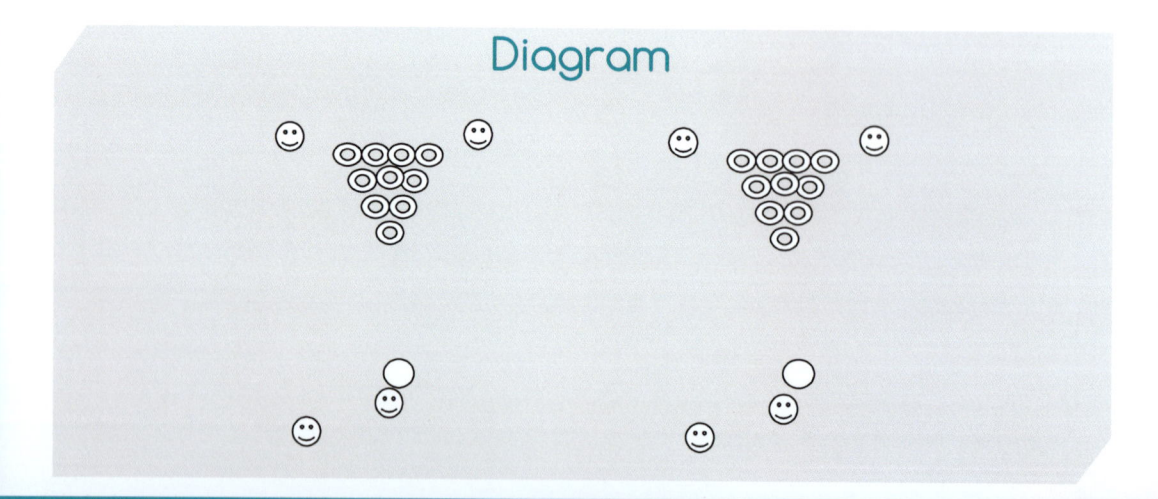

Diagram

Gaga Ball

Recommended Grades:

Grades 3-6

Equipment:

Soft bouncy ball and mats (playing area).

Tactical Problems:

Footwork, throwing, catching, placing the birdie farthest away from player(s), and anticipation.

Rules of Play:

1. Set up mats (waist high) in an octagon format.
2. Students will be spread out within the playing area.
3. Goal of the game is to get the other students out by striking the ball (not throwing it) and hitting the students below the knee.
4. If students get hit above the knee or block the ball with their hands/arms, they are not out.
5. When a student gets hit, he/she will have to walk just outside of the playing area.
6. The student is out until the end of the time limit, end of the game, or until the teachers yells "Jailbreak", which signals for all outside students to re-enter the game.

Safety:

Keep your head up to avoid collisions in such a small playing area and aim the ball below the knees.

Variations/Progressions:

- Increase or reduce playing area.
- Add another ball.
- Disallow blocking.

Diagram

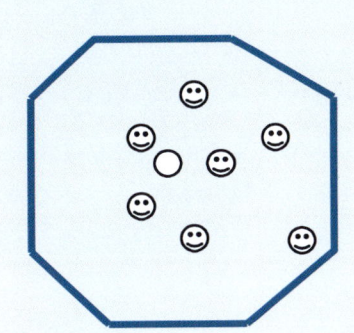

Goalie Dodgeball

Recommended Grades:

Grades 3-6

Equipment:

Hockey or soccer nets and dodgeballs.

Tactical Problems:

Hitting a target, footwork, dodging, change of speed, and change in direction.

Rules of Play:

1. Students will be divided into two teams with each side having a goalie protecting their net.
2. If a student is hit by the ball, he/she is out of the game.
3. If a student is able to "score" into the net, the goalie is out of the game.
4. If a goal is scored, whoever is out for that team comes back into the game.
5. Goalies cannot be eliminated from being hit directly with the ball.
6. Last team standing wins.

Safety:

Aim low and keep your head up to avoid collisions.

Variations/Progressions:

- Introduce a time limit.
- Use either a hockey or soccer net.
- Increase or reduce the playing area

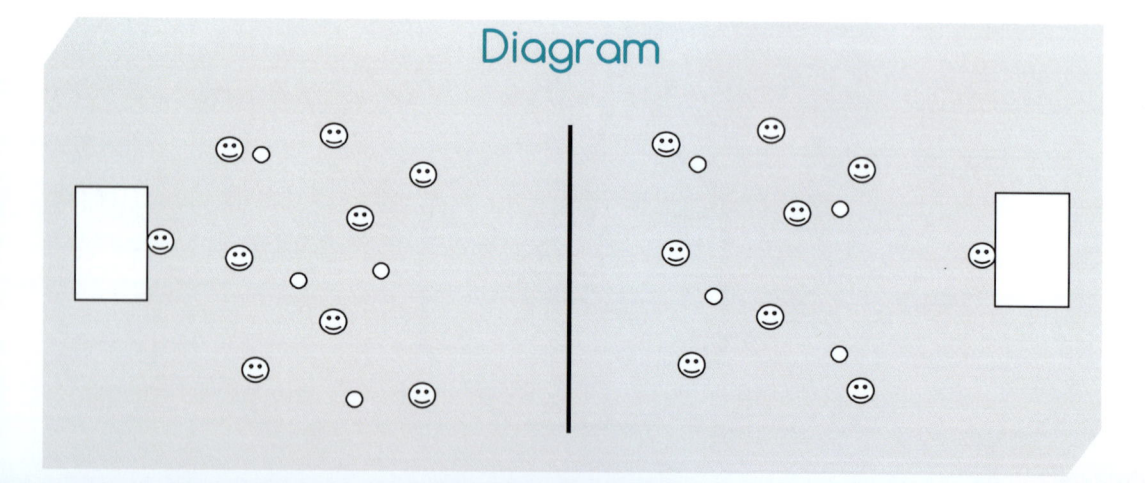

Diagram

Inspector Dodgeball

Recommended Grades:

Grades 3-6

Equipment:

Soft balls.

Tactical Problems:

Hitting a target, sending, receiving, shuffling, change of speed, and change in direction.

Rules of Play:

1. Students are divided into two teams in their respective sides.
2. When a student is hit by a dodgeball, he/she goes out to the side.
3. A student must remember who was the player that got them out.
4. The only way to get back into the game is for that student's team knocks out the player that got him/her out initially.
5. Game continues until a certain time limit is reached or when all the players of the opposing team are eliminated.

Safety:

Keep your head up to avoid collisions, aim below the waist, and be aware of the balls in play.

Variations/Progressions:

- If a student doesn't know who eliminated him/her, he/she must declare that he/she will get in when "x" player is hit.
- Introduce your own dodgeball rules (i.e. player is out if ball is caught, etc.).
- Increase or decrease the playing area

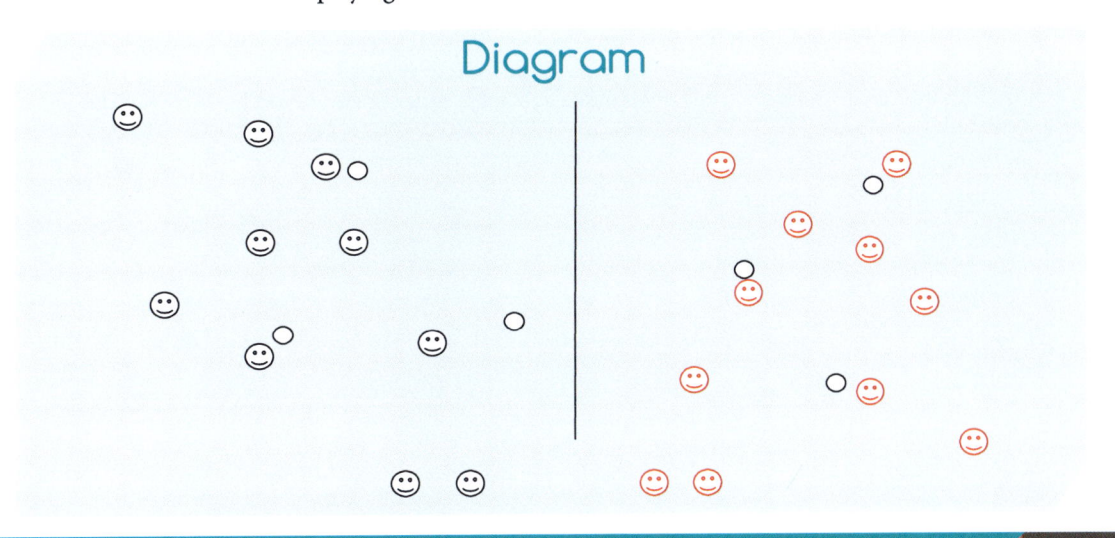

Diagram

Middle or Zero

Recommended Grades:

Grades 3-6

Equipment:

Bowling pins, cones, and beanbags.

Tactical Problems:

Hitting a target.

Rules of Play:

1. Divide students into pairs or small groups.
2. Set up a small circle made up of 6 bowling pins.
3. Use cones to create 3 different distances from this circle, from close to far.
4. The goal of the game is for the player to toss their beanbag into the circle without knocking over the pins.
5. Each player will get 3 consecutive tosses from the 3 different distances – 1 point for the closest, 2 points for the middle, and 3 points for the furthest.
6. First player to 20 wins.

Safety:

Keep your distance from the thrower.

Variations/Progressions:

- Increase or decrease the distances from the pins.
- Increase or decrease the size of the circle made of pins.

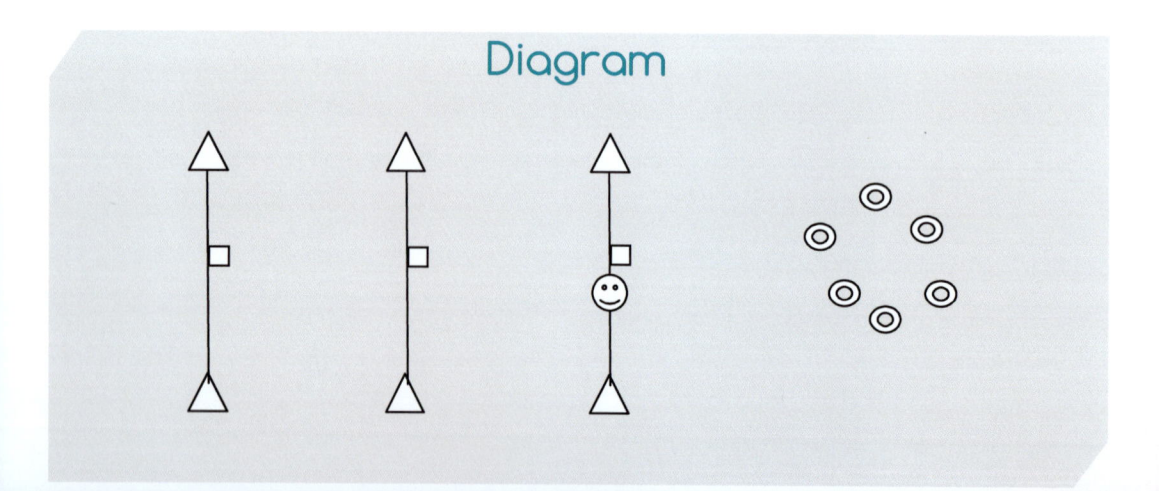

Diagram

Quarter Dodge

Recommended Grades:

Grades 3-6

Equipment:

Soft foam balls and cones.

Tactical Problems:

Hitting a target, sending, receiving, shuffling, change of speed, and change in direction.

Rules of Play:

1. Separated the playing area in four corners and divide the students into four teams, one in each corner.
2. Whenever a student is hit by the ball, he/she must join the team that hit him/her.
3. If there is only one player left in a corner and he/she gets hit by the ball from one of the teams, he/she will join the team that hit them and that team will now remove the cones from that empty corner and own the entire side of the playing area.
4. Play until a time limit is reached or until everyone ends up on the same team.

Safety:

Keep your head up to avoid collisions, aim low, and be aware of the balls at all times

Variations/Progressions:

- Use your own dodgeball rules.
- Increase or decrease the size of the playing area.

Diagram

Split

Recommended Grades:
Grades 3-6

Equipment:
Beanbags, pylons, and soft foam balls.

Tactical Problems:
Hitting a target.

Rules of Play:
1. Divide students into pairs or groups of 3.
2. About 10 – 15 feet away, soft foam balls will be set up in a straight line on top of the pylons.
3. There will be 2 colors for the soft foam balls to represent each of the 2 teams.
4. There will be 10 – 12 throws in total depending if the team has 2 or 3 players.
5. Teams earn point for knocking down the opposition's soft foam balls while points are deducted for a team knocking down their own soft foam balls.
6. Whoever has the most points at the end of a predetermined number of rounds wins the game..

Safety:
Ensure that you keep your distance from your teammates and from the other team.

Variations/Progressions:
- Use different objects to aim for the targets (i.e. frisbee, soccer ball, etc.).
- Increase or decrease the distance to the targets.

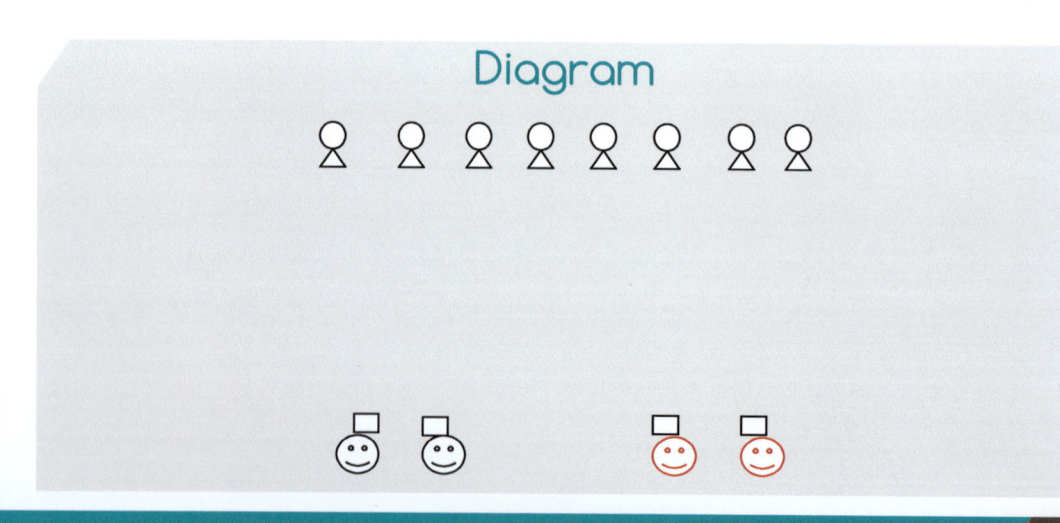

Diagram

Swamp

Recommended Grades:
Grades 3-6

Equipment:
Dodgeballs and mats.

Tactical Problems:
Hitting a target, throwing, catching, evading, and footwork.

Rules of Play:

1. Students will be divided into two teams, one in each half.
2. There will be a mat set up on the floor on each end of the playing area.
3. When a student gets hit by a dodgeball, he/she must go to the opposing team's swamp.
4. When a student catches a dodgeball thrown by another student, the student that threw the ball has to go to the opposing team's swamp.
5. To be freed from the swamp, they must catch a ball while remaining on the swamp area thrown by one of their teammates.
6. A rolling ball or a ball that has bounced does not count.
7. Winning team is the one who has the entire team in their swamp or the team with the least amount of people in the opposing team's swamp.

Safety:
Keep your head up to avoid collisions and aim below the waist.

Variations/Progressions:
- Increase or decrease the playing area.
- Introduce a time limit

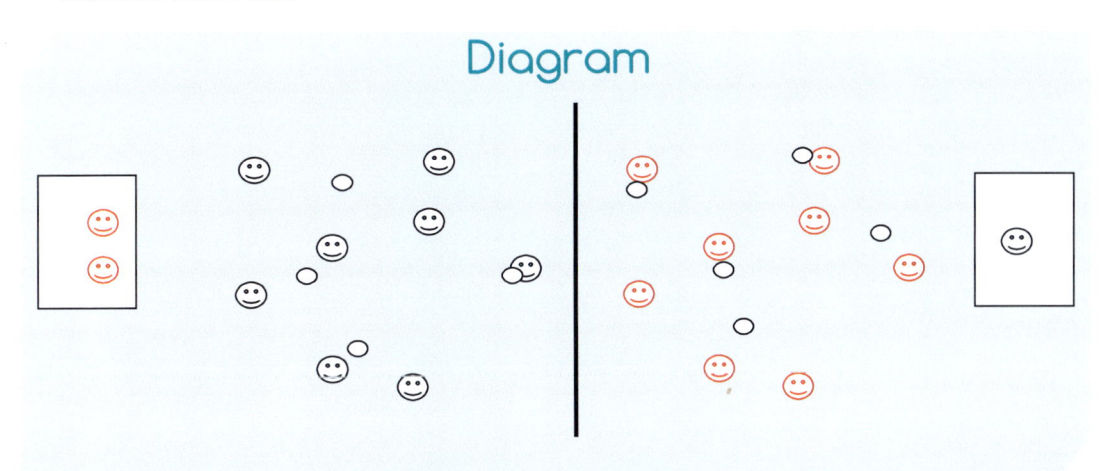

Diagram

Teacher Reversal

Recommended Grades:
Grades 3-6

Equipment:
Soft foam balls.

Tactical Problems:
Hitting a target, throwing, and dodging.

Rules of Play:
1. Dodgeball with a twist – teacher is the only one that can pick up and throw balls.
2. Teacher can carry as many as he/she wants and move in whatever way he/she desires.
3. Students will be spread out around the gymnasium.
4. When a student is hit by the ball, he/she must perform an action (i.e. 10 push-ups, etc.) at the side of the playing area to get back in.
5. Game continues until the teacher is tired!

Safety:
Keep your head up when running around the playing area to avoid collisions with others and the teacher should aim the ball below the waist.

Variations/Progressions:
- Allow students that are struck by the ball to join the teacher's team.

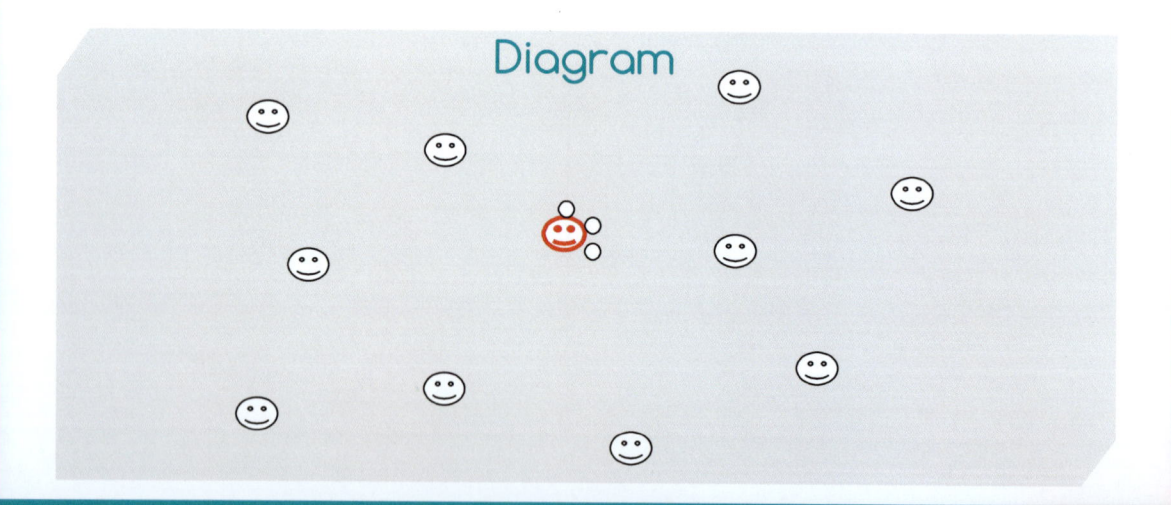

Diagram

This is War!

Recommended Grades:

Grades 3-6

Equipment:

Mats, benches, and soft balls.

Tactical Problems:

Hitting a target, sending, receiving, shuffling, change of speed, and change in direction.

Rules of Play:

1. Students will be divided into two teams on their respective sides of the court.
2. Each side will have mats and benches used as "trenches" to hide behind and take cover.
3. Many dodgeballs will be introduced into the game.
4. When a student gets hit by the ball, he/she will go to the side and remain there until the end of the round (use short time limits).
5. Winner is the team with the most players after the time limit.

Safety:

Keep your head up to avoid collisions amongst students and with the trenches, aim below the waist, and be aware of the balls at all times.

Variations/Progressions:

- Introduce your own dodgeball rules (i.e. catch the ball and you're out, allow students to re-enter the game, etc.).
- Increase or decrease the size of the playing area.

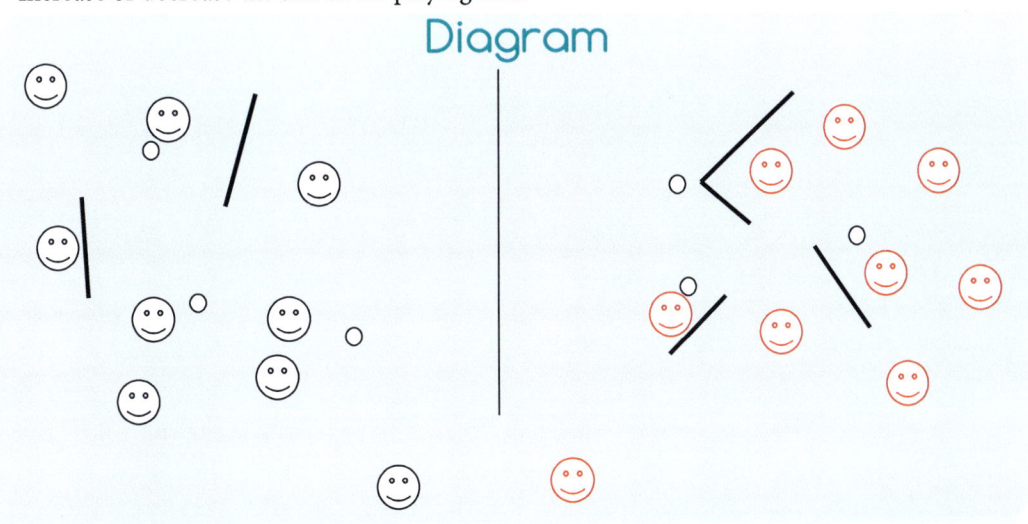

Diagram

Three For Three

Recommended Grades:

Grades 3-6

Equipment:

Tennis balls, hula-hoops, and soft foam balls.

Tactical Problems:

Hitting a target.

Rules of Play:

1. Divide students into pairs.
2. They will join another team to play a 2 V 2 game.
3. Hula-hoops (3) will be set up in a random pattern with 6 soft foam balls placed in each one.
4. There will be 2 different colors in each hoop regarding the soft foam balls – 3 of one color and 3 of the other.
5. Standing approximately 10 feet away, teams will try to knock out as many of the opposing balls out of the hoops as possible.
6. The team with the most balls remaining at the end of the time limit or at the end of their throws wins.

Safety:

Keep your distance from the thrower and ensure that no one starts throwing the tennis balls without any regard for accuracy.

Variations/Progressions:

- Use different balls.
- Increase or decrease the distance to the targets.
- Start with the balls located in the farthest hoops

Diagram

Trainer Dodgeball

Recommended Grades:

Grades 3-6

Equipment:

Pinnies and soft foam balls.

Tactical Problems:

Hitting a target, throwing, and dodging.

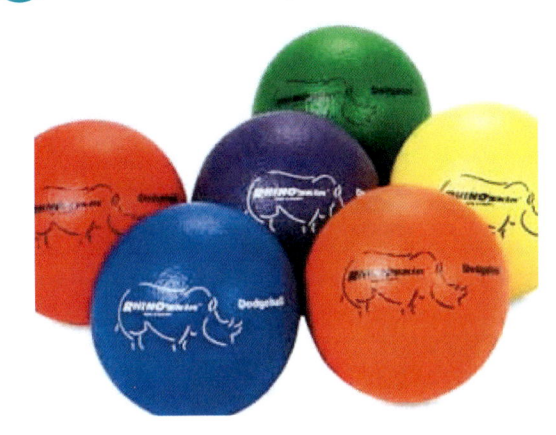

Rules of Play:

1. Two or three students will be chosen to be "trainers" – the rest of the students will be spread out around the playing area.
2. Soft foam balls will be spread out around the gymnasium – only the "trainers" are allowed to grab them.
3. If a student is hit by a ball thrown by a "trainer", he/she will have to go outside of the playing area and perform an action before coming back into the game (push-ups, etc.)
4. Frequently change the "trainers".

Safety:

Keep your head up to avoid collisions and aim the ball below the waistline

Variations/Progressions:

- Students hit by the ball throw on a pinnie and join the "trainers".
- Increase the number of taggers.
- Increase or reduce the playing area.

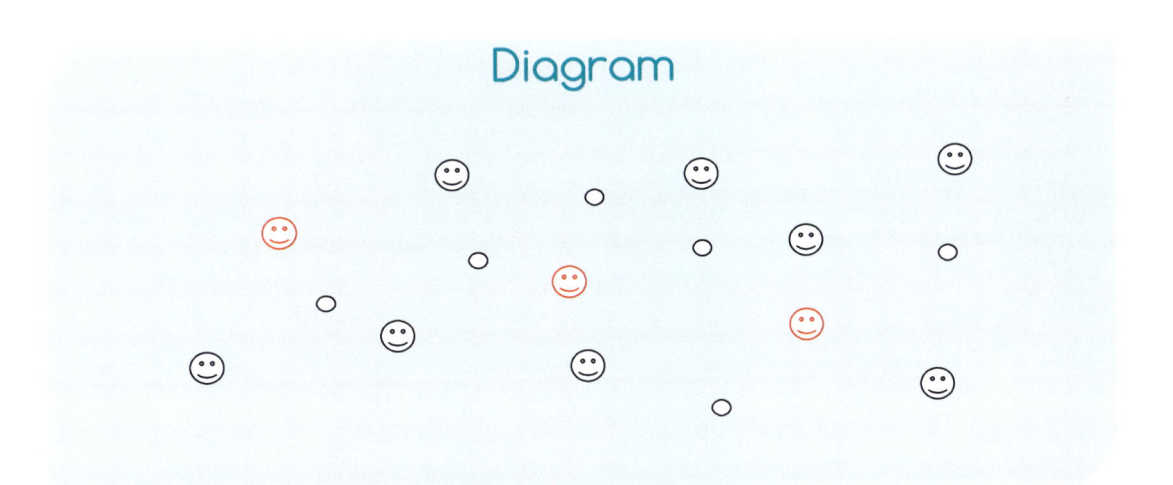

Diagram

Triangle Bowling

Recommended Grades:

Grades 3-6

Equipment:

Scoresheets, beanbags, and a triangular point mat.

Tactical Problems:

Hitting a target.

Rules of Play:

1. Students will be divided into small groups.
2. In each alley, students will "bowl" using a beanbag.
3. Play 10 frames – on each frame, the bowler will have 2 turns.
4. The bowler will slide the beanbag towards the triangular mat, which will contain a grid.
5. Depending on where the beanbag stops, the player will accumulate the number of points written on the mat.
6. If a beanbag stops between two lines, the player will score the value of the highest box.

Safety:

Ensure students slide the beanbag and do not throw it.

Variations/Progressions:

- Increase or decrease the distance to the target.
- Allow only one "bowl" in order to speed up the game.
- Toss the beanbag in the air in an attempt to land it onto the mat.

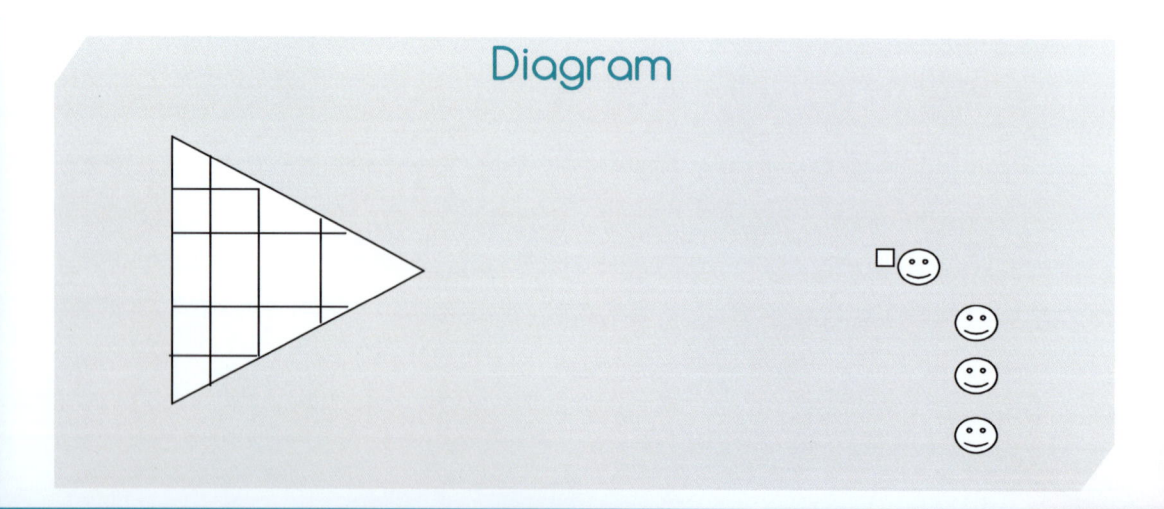

Diagram

Wall It

Recommended Grades:
Grades 3-6

Equipment:
Two soft balls.

Tactical Problems:
Hitting a target, sending, receiving, shuffling, change of speed, and change in direction.

Rules of Play:
1. Two players will be chosen as the throwers.
2. These two players will each have a ball and will line up parallel to one another facing a specific wall about 5 – 10 meters away.
3. Against this wall will be the remainder of the players facing the direction of the tossers.
4. The throwers will begin the game by throwing their balls at the same time ABOVE the players onto the wall.
5. As soon as the balls hit the wall, the remaining players will attempt to run to the other side.
6. The balls will bounce off the walls and the throwers will pick up their rebound, remain in their original position, and try to hit the players.
7. If a player is hit, he/she will sit down and will now be able to tag players that pass by.

Safety:
Keep your head up to avoid collisions and aim below the waist.

Variations/Progressions:
- Allow the throwers to move with the ball.
- Introduce more taggers.
- Reduce or increase the distance of the taggers to the wall.

Diagram

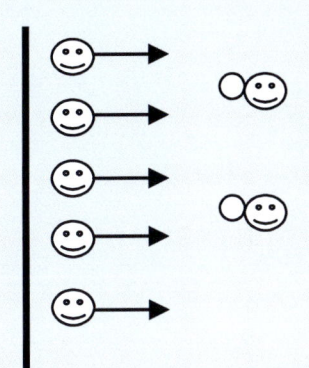

Zone Dodgeball

Recommended Grades:

Grades 3-6

Equipment:

Pinnies, cones, and soft foam balls.

Tactical Problems:

Throwing, catching, and hitting a target.

Rules of Play:

1. The playing area will be divided in four with a "runway" lane running in the middle.
2. There will be four teams – one in each corner.
3. Teams can only move in their corner.
4. When a student gets hit by the ball, he/she will have to enter the middle zone area and will have to try and run from one end to the other without getting hit by a ball.
5. If he/she succeeds, he/she can return to his/her team.
6. If not, he/she must try again.
7. Never-ending dodgeball!

Safety:

Keep your head up to avoid collisions and ensure that you aim below the waist.

Variations/Progressions:

- Instead of a free-for-all, make it a 2 V 2 game.
- Add or reduce the number of dodgeballs in play.

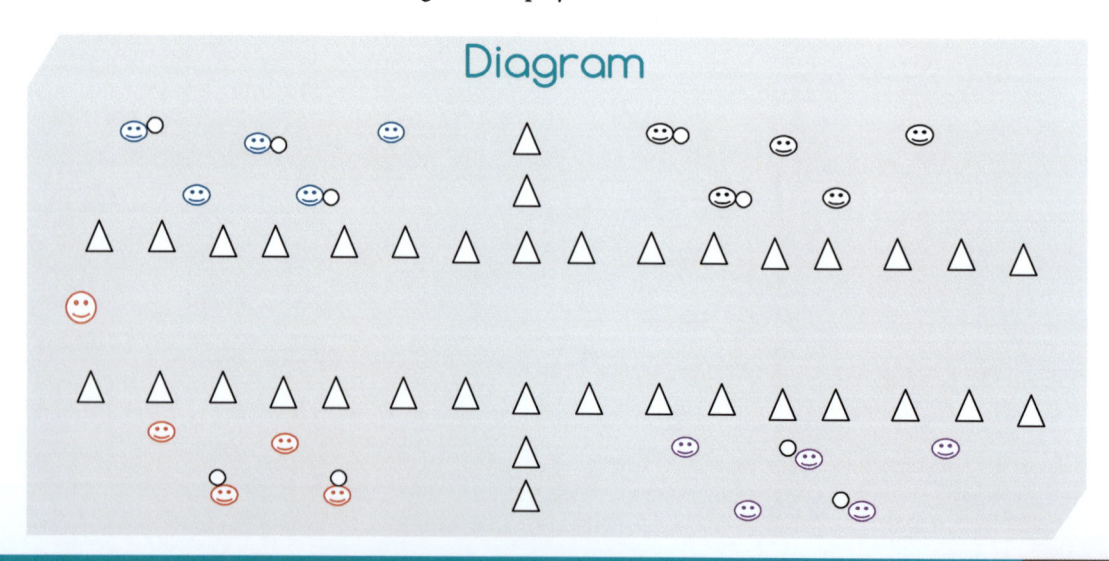

Diagram

4-Way Bowling

Recommended Grades:

Grades 5 – 6

Equipment:

Pinnies, cones, bowling pins, and soft foam balls.

Tactical Problems:

Hitting a target.

Rules of Play:

1. Divide students into four teams – one in each quadrant.
2. Each team will have a predetermined number of bowling pins set up.
3. Goal of the game is to knock down the oppositions' pins while protecting yours.
4. Players may only roll the ball when passing to teammates and when attempting to knock down the pins.
5. Once all of a team's pins are knocked down, the players of that team may still attempt to knock down the pins of the other teams.
6. Blocking is allowed.
7. Play until a certain time limit is reached or until one team remains with at least a pin standing.

Safety:

Ensure students roll the balls and do not throw them.

Variations/Progressions:

- Increase or decrease the number of targets.
- Form coalitions – two teams versus two teams.

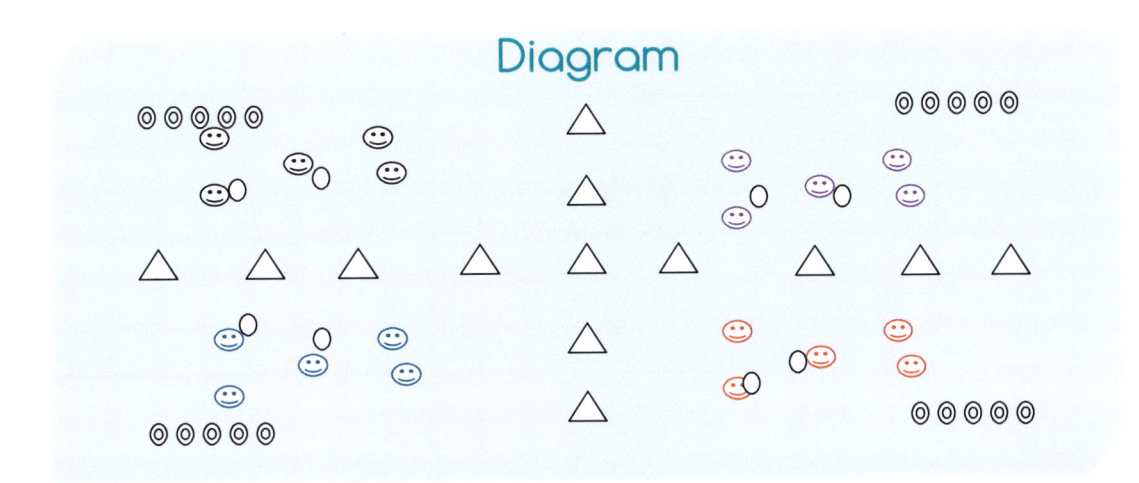

Diagram

Frisbee Attack

Recommended Grades:

Grades 5-6

Equipment:

Cones and frisbees.

Tactical Problems:

Hitting a target.

Rules of Play:

1. Divide students into pairs or small groups – two teams will face off head to head.
2. Cones will be set up about 10 – 15 feet apart.
3. One team member from each team will stand near his/her cone.
4. Each team will have two frisbees – as such, each player will have two attempts to land their frisbee closest to the cone.
5. 1 point for each frisbee that is closer than the opponent's and 3 points for each frisbee leaning against the cone.
6. If a frisbee stays on top of a cone, the entire game is won.
7. Play up until 20 points.

Safety:

Be aware of the frisbee at all times.

Variations/Progressions:

- Increase or decrease the distance between the cones.
- Play while sitting down.
- Throw the frisbee from different angles.

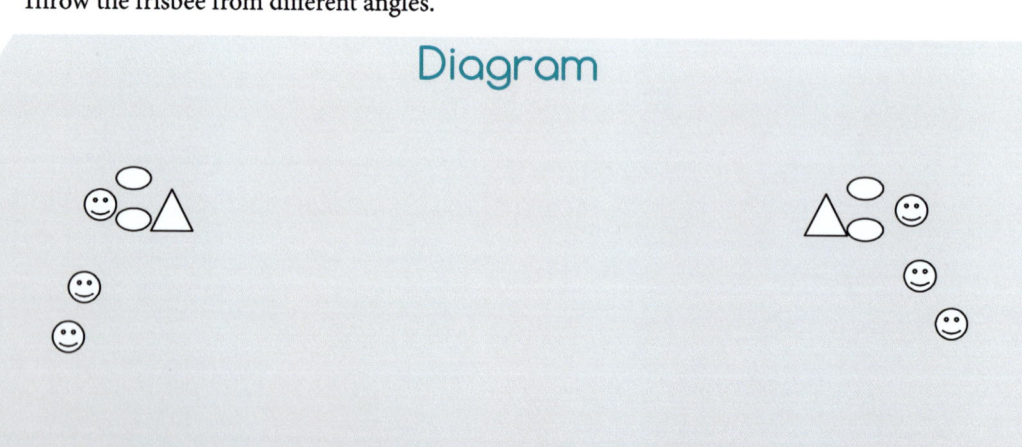

Diagram

Frisbee Golf

Recommended Grades:

Grades 5-6

Equipment:

Frisbees, hula-hoops, and cones.

Tactical Problems:

Hitting a target.

Rules of Play:

1. Recommended to play Frisbee Golf outdoors; however, it can be played indoors.
2. Set up a number of holes using cones – one for the tee-off and the target hole.
3. Students will be divided typically in groups of 2 or 3 – there will be a group at each hole.
4. Goal is to hit the cone with the frisbee in the least amount of attempts.
5. Rotate groups in sync so that there are no unnecessary lineups.
6. Important: create a "par" for each hole.
7. Students will keep track of their score for each hole.

Safety:

Keep your head up for Frisbees in the vicinity.

Variations/Progressions:

- Use different equipment – i.e. soccer ball instead of a frisbee.
- Increase or decrease distance to the hole.

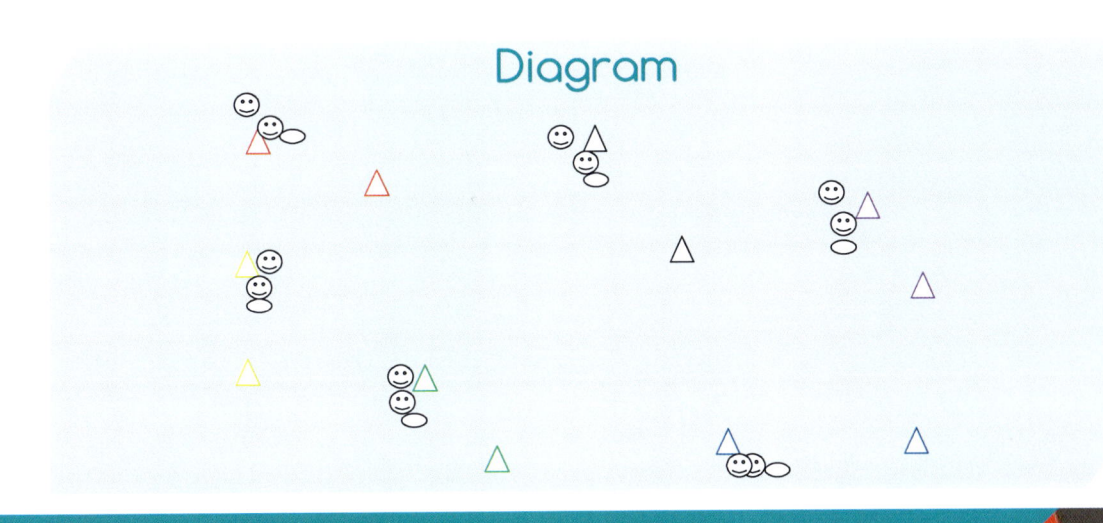

Diagram

300

Recommended Grades:
Grades 5-6

Equipment:
Soccer ball, football, tennis ball, basketball, or a frisbee

Tactical Problems:
Hitting a target, footwork, throwing, and catching.

Rules of Play:
1. At one end of the playing area, there will be one student with the object being thrown.
2. At the other end, the rest of the students will be waiting for the object to be thrown in order to try and catch it.
3. Before each throw, the player with the object will call out a number (i.e. 200) and this represents the number of points that a catch is worth.
4. If a student makes this catch, he/she will be awarded 200 points.
5. If a student attempts to catch the object but drops it, he/she will be deducted 200 points; therefore -200 points.
6. The goal is to be the first to accumulate 300 points.
7. The first to do so becomes the tosser for the next round.

Safety:
Keep your head on the object and keep your head up to avoid collisions with the others.

Variations/Progressions:
- Increase or reduce the playing area.
- Introduce the "Jackpot" – i.e. if the tosser calls out "Jackpot", if the object is caught, the student who caught it is the automatic winner

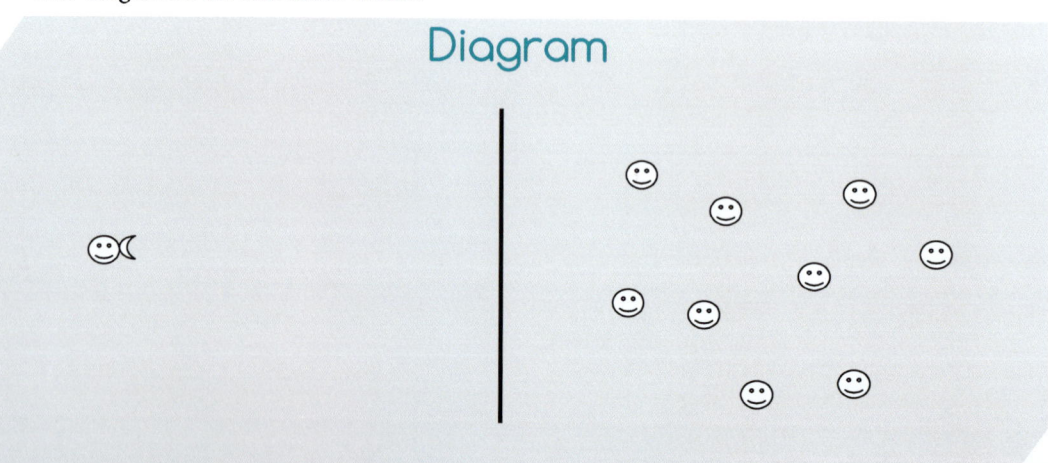

Diagram

Power Strike

Recommended Grades:

Grades 5-6

Equipment:

Exercise balls and dodgeballs.

Tactical Problems:

Hitting a target and sending away the object.

Rules of Play:

1. Two teams – one behind each "zone" (see diagram).
2. Exercise balls will be placed in the middle of both teams (at the center).
3. Dodgeballs are not used to hit the other team, but instead to hit the exercise balls themselves.
4. If an exercise ball crosses the opponent's goal line, the other team earns a point.
5. Students may only cross their goal line in order to grab a loose ball, but he/she must return behind his/her goal line in order to toss a dodgeball at an exercise ball.

Safety:

Keep your head up and leave enough space between you and your teammates.

Variations/Progressions:

- Number of points.
- Assign one or two students from each team who are allowed to recover the balls.
- Increase or decrease the size of the playing area

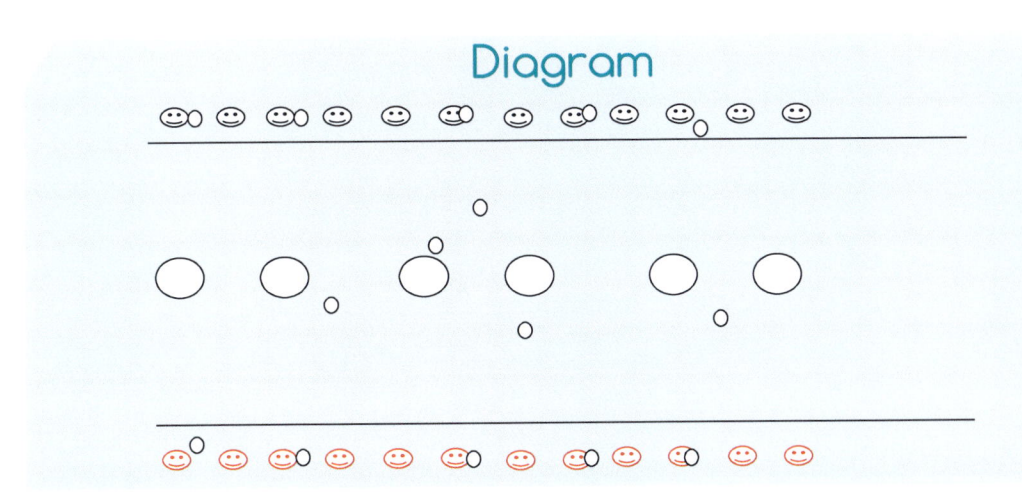

Diagram

Putting Twos

Recommended Grades:
Grades 5-6

Equipment:
Putters, poly spots, and golf balls.

Tactical Problems:
Hitting a target

Rules of Play:
1. Students will be divided into pairs.
2. Players will stand 10 to 20 feet apart with a poly spot in front of each.
3. The goal of the game is to putt the ball near or on the poly spot.
4. Players take turns hitting the ball and the ball must be hit either behind or to either side of the poly spot, but not in front of it.
5. 1 point is awarded if the ball touches/travels over the poly spot and 2 points if the ball remains there.
6. Play until a certain time limit or score limit is reached.

Safety:
Make sure that the ball is not struck hard – this is not hockey.

Variations/Progressions:
- Give players two chances to get the ball on the poly spot (i.e. play the 2nd ball from wherever it stops).
- Increase or decrease the distance to the target

Diagram

Sitting Ducks

Recommended Grades:

Grades 5-6

Equipment:

Dodgeballs.

Tactical Problems:

Hitting a target, throwing, footwork, change of direction, change in speed, and evading.

Rules of Play:

1. Set up a boundary area with sidelines and end-lines (i.e. volleyball or basketball court).
2. One team will line up behind one of the end-lines while the other team will further split behind both sidelines.
3. The players of the team on the sidelines will each receive a dodgeball.
4. The goal of the game is for the team on the end-line to make it to the other line without getting hit by a dodgeball.
5. If a member of the "end-line" team gets hit by the ball, they become sitting ducks and remain seated where they got struck.
6. Now, the players that have been struck can tag from their seated position.
7. Game continues until the entire team has been eliminated.

Safety:

Keep your head up to avoid collisions and aim the ball below the waist.

Variations/Progressions:

- You could set a predetermined number of rounds limiting the chances that the attacking team has to eliminate the runners.
- Make the players that get struck perform an action (i.e. 10 push-ups).

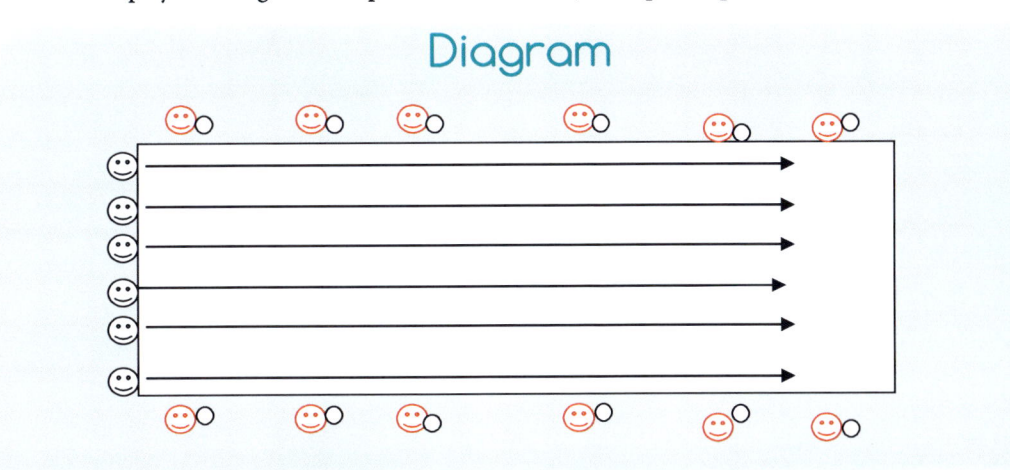

Diagram

About The Author

Nicholas Stratigopoulos is an educator based out of Montreal, Quebec, Canada. He obtained his undergraduate degree from McGill University's physical and health education program and his graduate degree from Concordia University's educational technology program. Through his educational apps & books, Nicholas encourages physical and health education teachers all around the world to enable their students to adopt a more healthy and active lifestyle.

You could connect with Nicholas on:

Twitter - http://www.twitter.com/GraciousWolf_PE
LinkedIn - http://ca.linkedin.com/in/nstratigopz/
WordPress - http://www.educationisphysical.com

& his **apps** here:

http://appstore.com/NicholasStratigopoulos

Printed in Poland
by Amazon Fulfillment
Poland Sp. z o.o., Wrocław